AF608238

THE CATHOLIC UNIVERSITY OF AMERICA
CANON LAW STUDIES
No. 258

THE PROVINCIAL RELIGIOUS SUPERIOR

A Historical Conspectus and a Commentary on the Rights and Duties of the Provincial Religious Superior in Religious Orders of Men

BY

ROMAEUS WILLIAM O'BRIEN, O. Carm.
Priest of the Province of the Most Pure Heart of Mary

A DISSERTATION

SUBMITTED TO THE FACULTY OF THE SCHOOL OF CANON LAW OF THE CATHOLIC UNIVERSITY OF AMERICA IN PARTIAL FULFILLMENT OF THE REQUIREMENTS FOR THE DEGREE OF DOCTOR OF CANON LAW

THE CATHOLIC UNIVERSITY OF AMERICA PRESS
WASHINGTON, D. C.
1947

Revisores Ordinis:

Kilianus J. Healy, O. Carm.
Kennethus B. Moore, O. Carm.

Imprimi Potest:

Matthaeus T. O'Neill, O. Carm.
Prior Provincialis

Nihil Obstat:

Hieronymus D. Hannan, A.M., LL.B., S.T.D., J.C.D.,
Censor Deputatus

Washingtonii, die 6 octobris 1947.

Imprimatur:

Joannes M. McNamara, D. D.
Administrator Baltimorensis-Washingtonensis

Baltimorae, die 6 octobris 1947.

Copyright, 1948, by
The Catholic University of America Press, Inc.

The Abbey Press,
St. Meinrad, Ind.

TABLE OF CONTENTS

PAGE

FOREWORD ix

INTRODUCTION

CHAPTER

I. THE ORIGIN OF THE OFFICE OF PROVINCIAL SUPERIOR 1
1. The Historical Origin of the Office of Provincial 1
2. The Development of Legislation Regarding Provincials 3

CANONICAL COMMENTARY

Part One

PRELIMINARY QUESTIONS

II. THE AUTHORITY OF THE PROVINCIAL SUPERIOR IN THE CODE OF CANON LAW 10
1. The Concept of Jurisdiction 10
2. Dominative Power 14
3. The Existence of the Jurisdiction of the Provincial 15
4. The Extent of the Jurisdiction of the Provincial 17

III. THE CANDIDATE FOR THE OFFICE OF PROVINCIAL SUPERIOR 25
1. Qualities in the Candidate 25
2. The Appointment of the Provincial 28
3. Term of Office 28
4. Obligation to Accept the Office 29
5. The Obligations Arising from the Office ... 31

Part Two

THE LEGISLATIVE AND JUDICIAL POWERS OF THE PROVINCIAL SUPERIOR

IV. THE LEGISLATIVE POWER OF THE PROVINCIAL SUPERIOR 33
1. The Background of the Question 34
2. The Legislative Power of the Provincial ... 35
3. The Power of Precept 37
A. Individual Precepts 39
B. Common Precepts 40

4. The Power of Dispensation 42
   A. Dispensation from the General Laws of the Church 43
      1) Pre-Code legislation 43
      2) Present law 45
   B. Dispensation from Particular Laws of the Institute 49
      1) Pre-Code legislation 49
      2) Present law 50
   C. Dispensation from Vows and Oaths .. 51
      1) Pre-Code legislation 51
      2) Present law 52

V. THE JUDICIAL POWER OF THE PROVINCIAL SUPERIOR 54
      1) Pre-Code legislation 54
      2) Present Law 57

Part Three

THE EXECUTIVE POWER OF THE PROVINCIAL SUPERIOR

VI. THE PROVINCIAL SUPERIOR AS EXECUTIVE HEAD OF THE PROVINCE 61
1. Residence 62
2. Enforcement of the Decrees of the Holy See 64
3. Other Personal Obligations 65
   A. Personal Example in Act and Word .. 65
   B. Canonical Visitation 66
      1) Pre-Code legislation 66
      2) Present law 69
   C. The Obligation to Correct Defects ... 72
   D. The Obligation of Prayer 73
4. The Council 74
5. Jurisdiction over Nuns 78

VII. THE PROVINCIAL SUPERIOR AND THE TRAINING OF HIS SUBJECTS 82
1. The Admission of Candidates 82
   A. The Admission of Postulants 83
   B. The Admission of Novices 87
      1) Pre-Code legislation 87
      2) Present law 88
      3) The Novice Master and the Training of the Novices 91

2. Religious Profession 95
3. Other Jurisdiction Regarding Religious Vows 98
4. The Program of Studies 102

VIII. The Provincial Superior and Religious Observance 109
1. The Observance of the Vows 111
A. The Common Life 112
B. The Cloister 114
2. The Observance of the Rule and the Obligation to Strive after Perfection 122
3. The Observance of Special Obligations 124
A. Pious Practices Incumbent on Religious 125
B. Wearing of the Religious Habit 127
C. Choral Recitation of the Divine Office 128
D. Assistance at the Conventual Mass .. 131
4. The Censorship and the Prohibition of Books and Articles 135
A. The Publication of Books and Articles 135
B. The Prohibition of Books 135
5. The Care of Souls 136
A. Assistance to the Diocesan Clergy ... 137
B. Religious Parishes 140

IX. The Provincial Superior and Members Leaving The Order 146
1. Transfer of Religious Within the Province and Order 146
2. Transfer of Religious to Another Order ... 148
3. Departure of Religious 151
A. Lawful Departure 152
B. Unlawful Departure 155
4. Dismissal of Religious 157
A. *Ipso Facto* Effective Dismissal Enacted in Canon 646, § 1. 157
B. Dismissal Effected according to the Norms of the Law 159
1) Dismissal by decree of the Superior 159
2) Ordinary dismissal of Religious in temporary vows 160
3) Ordinary dismissal of Religious in solemn vows 161

X. THE PROVINCIAL SUPERIOR AS ADMINISTRATOR OF TEMPORAL GOODS 163
1. The Acquisition of Goods 163
2. The Administration of Goods 167
A. Temporal Goods of Individual Houses 169
B. Temporal Goods of the Province 172
C. Investments 175
D. Debts and Obligations 177
E. Sanctions Invoked by Law Against Violations 180

XI. THE PROVINCIAL SUPERIOR AND THE SACRAMENTS 182
1. Baptism and Confirmation 182
2. Matrimony 183
3. The Holy Eucharist and Extreme Unction . 183
4. Penance 187
A. Appointment and Approval of Confessors 187
1) Pre-Code legislation 187
2) Present law 193
B. Absolution from Reserved Sins and Censures 198
1) Pre-Code legislation 198
2) Present law 202
C. Power to Reserve Sins 204
1) Pre-Code legislation 204
2) Present law 206
D. Power to Dispense from Irregularities 206
1) Pre-Code legislation 206
2) Present law 210
5. Holy Orders 212
A. Pre-Code legislation 212
B. Present Law 216
6. Sacred Places and Worship 221
7. The Approval of Preachers 226
A. Pre-Code legislation 227
B. Present law 229

XII. THE COERCIVE POWER OF THE PROVINCIAL SUPERIOR 232
1. The Existence of the Provincial's Coercive Power 232
A. Pre-Code legislation 232
B. Present law 235
1) Judicial coercive powers 236
2) Extra-judicial coercive powers . 238
2. The Extent of the Provincial's Coercive Power 242
A. Judicial Coercive Powers 243
B. Extra-judicial Coercive Powers 245
1) Penal remedies 245
2) Canonical penances 250
3) Penalties within the Provincial's extra-judicial competence 251
CONCLUSIONS 257
BIBLIOGRAPHY 261
ABBREVIATIONS 269
BIOGRAPHICAL NOTE 281

FOREWORD

The Provincial Superior of clerical exempt Orders is called a Major Superior in the Code of Canon Law which gives all Major Superiors the rank of an Ordinary. In view, therefore, of his preeminent position in the religious province and in the hierarchy of religious Superiors, a study of his office and of the extent of his jurisdiction is desirable. Even under the law of the Code, which has so greatly clarified the jurisdictional position of the Provincial, questions of competence arise. At times the Code speaks generically of *Superiors* when the nature of the case indicates that the Provincial alone is usually given the competence involved. Again, the Code speaks of *Ordinaries* when only the local Ordinary can be intended. The purpose of this study, therefore, is to examine the office of the Provincial Superior and to determine specifically the extent of his jurisdiction according to the common law of the Church through a study of and a commentary on the canons pertaining to that office.

A brief historical introduction precedes the commentary. The subject matter of the commentary lends itself to a division into three parts. Part One is concerned with an examination of the authority invested in the office of Provincial and with the qualifications of the candidate for that office. Parts Two and Three comprise the principal elements of the commentary, the primary aim of which is to determine the extent of the Provincial's jurisdiction according to the common law. These Parts, therefore, will be devoted to an analysis of the legislative, judicial, and executive functions of his power. Part Two is concerned with his legislative and judicial rights and duties. Part Three, the most extensive portion of the work, examines his executive rights and duties in accordance with their classification into those of an administrative and of a coercive nature. The order of treatment of the administrative rights is practically that of the tract which in the Code deals with Religious. The treatise however considers, in addition to those rights which are treated by the Code under the tract on Religious, the rights pertaining to the Sacraments and Sacred Places.

Historical notes have been combined throughout this work with the canonical commentary. In view of the rather broad field involved, it was thought that the combination of history, law, and commentary would facilitate a comprehensive, if compressed, understanding of the many rights and duties which are derived from the jurisdictional office of the Provincial.

The writer wishes to express his gratitude to his Provincial, the Very Reverend Matthew T. O'Neill, O. Carm., for the opportunity of advanced study in Canon Law; to the Faculty of the School of Canon Law of the Catholic University of America for instruction and generous assistance; to his fellow Carmelites of Whitefriars Hall, Washington, D. C., for their willing help in preparing the manuscript; and, finally, to those who have assisted him in any way in the course of this work.

INTRODUCTION

CHAPTER I

THE ORIGIN OF THE OFFICE OF PROVINCIAL SUPERIOR

1. *The Historical Origin of the Office of Provincial.*

The office of the Provincial is a distinctly non-monastic function, which had its origin in the Mendicant Orders of the thirteenth century. Asceticism in the midst of the faithful was practised up to that time mainly by the "secular" clergy who lived in the world, caring for the spiritual wants of the people at the crossroads and in the market places of cities and towns. On the other hand, the monks, who were not always priests, lived apart from the world in their monasteries, devoting themselves through religious exercises to the perfection of their souls.

There came a time, however, when this time-honored arrangement no longer suited the needs of the Church. The wealth and power accumulated over the centuries by the religious and the clergy resulted in a relaxation of religious discipline and a waning of zeal for the ministry to souls. The result was the scandal of the faithful, the loss of their respect, and rebellious movements of heresy and schism. Two men arose to meet the challenge of the times: Saint Dominic (1170-1221) and Saint Francis (1181-1226). The former organized a band of learned and able preachers to combat the heresies of the Cathari, Albigensians, and Waldensians; the latter restored to religious life the ideal of absolute evangelical poverty. These characteristics of the Dominican and Franciscan Orders were not exclusively possessed by each, but were blended to form a type of religious life known as mendicancy. The Mendicant Orders were characterized by two essential elements: (1) absolute poverty, and (2) the exercise of the active ministry among the faithful.

The austere lives and the devoted zeal of the mendicant friars earned for them the devotion of the masses, and they spread rapidly, founding many houses throughout western Europe. It soon became impossible for the founders and their successors to keep in contact with their far-flung organization, and a detailed system of organization was soon devised. The first general chapter of the Dominicans, held at Bologna in 1220, added to the earlier "*consuetudines*" of St. Dominic a number of constitutions regulating the organization of the Order, and the ensemble of these laws was further codified and arranged in 1239 by the distinguished canonist, St. Raymond of Pennafort (1175-1275).[1] Among the Franciscans, the mature product of the early legislative development is found in the "*Constitutiones Narbonnenses,*" arranged in 1260 by St. Bonaventure (1221-1274).[2]

These documents reveal a highly centralized form of government. Under it, individual houses, though governed by a local Superior, do not constitute autonomous units, as was the case with monasticism, but are all dependent upon one head, the "General." As the houses grew more numerous, a further division of administration occurred. The houses of a certain country or locality were subjected to an authority midway between the local Superior and the Supreme Moderator of the Order. This authority was called among the Dominicans and Franciscans a "Provincial," and the sphere of his domain was called the "Province."

Already in the thirteenth century, two previously existing Orders, the Carmelites and the Augustinians, adopted the Mendicant form of administration. Together with the Do-

[1] Denifle, "Die Constitutionen des Predigerordens in der Redaction Raimonds von Peñafort," *Archiv für Literatur und Kirchengeschichte des Mittelalters*, V (1889), 530-564.

[2] *Doctoris Seraphici S. Bonaventurae Opera Omnia* (11 vols., prope Florentiam, Ad Claras Aquas (Quarrachi), 1882-1902; Vol. VIII, ed. Aloysius Lauer, 1898), VIII, 449-467.

minicans and the Franciscans, these two Orders came to constitute the well-known "Four Mendicant Orders." Subsequent religious Orders, from that day to this, have, with variations according to particular laws and constitutions, patterned their institutions on the Mendicant scheme of centralization of authority. Finally, the new form of religious life was canonized in the Code, which devotes many canons to the regulation of its functions. The history of the legislation affecting it is a distinct question, however, and calls for further consideration.

2. *The Development of Legislation Regarding Provincials.*

One who enjoys ordinary jurisdiction in the external forum is called a prelate.[3] According to present day legislation, Provincial Superiors of exempt clerical communities are truly prelates, since they possess ordinary jurisdiction in the external forum.[4]

Formerly the common law recognized the Superiors of exempt religious Orders as Regular prelates, but no distinction was made in the latitude of the jurisdiction exercised by individual Superiors.

The concept of a Regular prelate was fundamentally connected with the privilege of exemption granted almost from the beginning to the four Mendicant Orders. Through this privilege the members, called Regulars, were removed from

[3] Can. 110: "Quamvis Praelati titulo, honoris causa, a Sede Apostolica etiam nonnulli clerici donentur sine ulla iurisdictione, proprio tamen nomine Praelati in iure dicuntur clerici sive saeculares sive religiosi qui iurisdictionem ordinariam in foro externo obtinent."—*Codex Iuris Canonici Pii X Pontificis Maximi iussu digestus Benedicti Papae XV auctoritate promulgatus* (Romae: Typis Polyglottis Vaticanis, 1917). Hereafter reference to this work is made merely by means of the abbreviation "can." for canon, followed by the appropriate number.

[4] Can. 198, § 1. "*Ordinarii* vocantur ii tantum qui potestatem ordinariam in foro *externo* obtinent, exceptis tamen Superioribus minoribus localibus religionis clericalis exemptae."—Vermeersch-Creusen, *Epitome Iuris Canonici cum Commentariis ad Scholas et ad Usum Privatum* (5. ed., 3 vols., Mechliniae, Romae: Dessain, 1933-1936), I, n. 317. (Hereafter this work will be cited as *Epitome.*)

the jurisdiction of local Ordinaries. However, lest the privilege of exemption result in a discrimination against religious through this non-subjection to proper pastors in the Church, their own proper Superiors were endowed as prelates with the jurisdiction which no longer remained within the competence of the local Ordinaries.[5]

The Decretals recognized the jurisdiction of religious prelates, but did not offer details in regard to the nature of the prelates' jurisdiction.[6] Alexander IV (1254-1261) alone seemed to touch on the question when he restricted an abbot to conferring his blessing only upon those over whom he exercised *quasi-episcopal power.*[7] The glossators apparently accepted the term *quasi-episcopal power* as used by him in the sense logically indicated, namely, jurisdiction like that of a bishop.[8] Those who were thus endowed with jurisdiction received the title of "prelate." Their jurisdiction was considered as attached to their office, and hence it was *ordinary* in the sense of the present day usage in the Code.[9] The

[5] C. 30, X, *de privilegiis et excessibus privilegiatorum,* V, 33; c. 17, X, *de excessibus praelatorum et subditorum,* V, 31; c. 3, *de privilegiis,* V, 7, in VI°; Wernz, *Ius Decretalium ad usum Praelectionum in Scholis Textus Canonici sive Iuris Decretalium* (6 vols. in 7, Romae—Prati, 1899-1913), III, p. 763, n. 683. (Hereafter this work will be cited as *Ius Decretalium.*) Cf. also Bouix, *Tractatus de Jure Regularium* (3 ed., 2 vols., Parisiis: 1883), II, 378. (Hereafter this work will be cited *De Jure Regularium.*)

[6] C. 24, *de electione et electi potestate,* 1, 6, in VI°.

[7] C. 3, *de privilegiis,* V, 7, in VI°.

[8] *Glossa ordinaria* ad c. 1, *de rebus ecclesiae non alienandis,* II, 4, in Clem., s.v. *proprii.*

[9] C. 3, 7, X, *de officio iudicis ordinarii,* I, 31; Jaffé, *Regesta Pontificum Romanorum ab condita Ecclesia ad annum post Christum natum MCXCVIII* (2. ed., correctam et auctam auspiciis Gulielmi Wattenbach curaverunt S. Loewenfeld, F. Kaltenbrunner, P. Ewald, 2 vols. in 1, Lipsiae, 1885-1888), n. 9001 (hereafter this work will be cited *Regesta*); Potthast, *Regesta Pontificum Romanorum, inde ab A. post Christum natum MCXCVIII ad A. MCCCIV* (2 vols., Berolini: 1874-1875), n. 57 (hereafter this work will be cited *Regesta*), Cf. can. 197, § 1.

Council of Trent did not revoke this jurisdiction,[10] and post-Tridentine authors emphasized the dignity of the position held by the Regular prelate, pointing out that it was an office to which only the more worthy should be appointed.[11] The Decretal reference to the quasi-episcopal power of Regular prelates continued, after the Council of Trent, to serve as the norm of their jurisdiction, guided of course by particular law.

Various popes likewise recognized the jurisdictional position of prelates in Regular Orders. Clement IV (1265-1268) spoke of their "care of souls";[12] Sixtus IV (1471-1484) declared their power in spiritual and temporal affairs ordinary;[13] Paul III (1534-1539) attributed unrestricted power to them;[14] and Pius V (1566-1572) spoke of their supreme

[10] Sess. XXV, *de regularibus*, c. 6—*Canones et Decreta Sacrosancti Oecumenici Concilii Tridentini* (editio novissima ad fidem optimorum exemplarium castigate impressa, XIX Reimpressio Stereotypa, Taurini: 1913). (Hereafter this work will be referred to merely by citation of the session and canon after the abbreviation Conc. Trident.)

[11] Clemens VIII, const. *Nullus omnino*, 25 iul., 1599—Codicis *Iuris Canonici Fontes*, cura Emi Petri Card. Gasparii editi (9 vols., Romae [postea Civitate Vaticana]: Typis Polyglottis Vaticanis, 1923-1939. [Vols. VII-IX, cura et studia Emi Iustiniani Card. Serédi], [hereafter cited *Fontes*]), n. 187; Donatus, *Rerum Regularium Quadripartita Praxis Resolutoria* (4 vols., Neapoli, 1652-1661), Tom. II, pars I, tr. I, qu. XXVII, n. 3 (hereafter cited as *Rerum Regularium Praxis*); Reiffenstuel, *Jus Canonicum Universum* (5 vols. in 7, Parisiis: 1864-1870), Lib. I, tr. I, VI, n. 241; Passerinus, *Tractatus de Electione Canonica* (ed. post Romanam prima in Germania, Coloniae Agrippinae, 1694), cap. VII, n. 418.

[12] Const. *Virtute conspicuos*, 21 iul. 1265, § 1—*Bullarum Diplomatum et Privilegiorum Sanctorum Romanorum Pontificum Taurinensis Editio* (25 vols., Augustae Taurinorum: 1857-1872), III, 735. (Hereafter cited *Bull. Rom. Taur.*)

[13] Const. *Regimini universalis*, 31 aug. 1474—*Bull. Rom. Taur.*, V, 217-223.

[14] Const. *Exponi nobis*, 25 aug. 1535, § 5—apud Molitor, *Religiosi Iuris Capita Selecta* (Ratisbonae, Romae, Neo-Eboraci et Cincinnati: Pustet, 1909), p. 249.

jurisdiction in spiritual and temporal matters.[15]

Innocent III (1198-1216) recognized the dominative power of religious prelates over their subjects, and the Council of Trent reaffirmed (1545-1563) this power.[16]

With the rise of the Mendicant Orders, a threefold hierarchy of prelates arose. Pre-Tridentine as well as pre-Code writings abound in references to the *praelatus medius, supremus,* and *inferior,* which terms correspond to our Provincial, General and Local Superior.

The Constitutions of the individual Orders supplied the lack of Decretal references to the specific details of the office of the Provincial Superior, which was included with that of the other Mendicant Superiors under the general title of *prelate.*[17] He was the *Praelatus Medius* in the constitutional hierarchy of the Orders, and held a power that was broader than that of the local prior, since he was the proper pastor over all the members of a province and the representative of the General in that particular province. Matters pertaining to the general welfare of the province, such as the approval of confessors and preachers, the reception of novices, the approval of novices for profession and the transfer of religious were reserved to him. Even before the Council of Trent his position in the hierarchy of Superiors as a Major Superior was foreshadowed.

The Council of Trent recognized his rôle as the Major

[15] Const. *Ad immarcescibilem,* 13 febr. 1567, § 3, § 5—*Bull. Rom. Taur.,* VII, 26.

[16] C. 6, X, *de statu monachorum et canonicorum regularium,* III, 35; Conc. Trident., sess. XXV, *de regularibus,* c. 1—Schroeder, *Canons and Decrees* of the *Council of Trent* (St. Louis: Herder, 1941), pp. 217, 485 (hereafter cited *Canons and Decrees*); Clancy, *The Local Religious Superior,* The Catholic University of America Canon Law Studies, n. 175 (Washington, D. C.: The Catholic University of America Press, 1943), p. 26 (hereafter cited *The Local Superior*).

[17] *Glossa ordinaria* ad c. 1, *de rebus ecclesiae non alienandis,* III, 4, in Clem., s. v. *proprii;* c. 2, *de rebus ecclesiae non alienandis,* III, 9, in VI°

Prelate of the Province.[18] Because of its major position, authors after the Council of Trent considered the Provincial Superiorship a dignity to which only the more worthy religious should be appointed.[19] Moreover his quasi-episcopal position was clearly asserted.[20] In fact, the only difference between the jurisdiction of the bishop and that of the Provincial Superior was traced by some authors to the episcopal consecration of the bishop.[21]

Pre-Code authors began to distinguish more clearly between Major and Minor Superiors, and some even considered as prelates only the Major Superiors.[22] They granted a higher rank as a prelate to the Provincial than to the Local Superior. His jurisdiction, they taught, was broader in regard to both subject matter and the number of religious affected by it. Accordingly, Donatus (1663) and Reiffenstuel (1642-1703) even bestowed upon him the title of *Major Superior.*

Canon 488, 8°, now incorporates this idea into the Code,

[18] Sess. XXIV, *de ref.*, c. 3; sess. XXV, *de regularibus*, c. 25.

[19] Clemens VIII (1592-1605), const. *Nullus omnino*, 25 iul. 1599—*Fontes*, n. 187; Donatus, *Rerum Regularium Praxis*, Tom. II, pars II, cap. XIII, n. 26; Reiffenstuel, *Jus Canonicum Universum*, Lib. I. tit. VI, n. 240.

[20] *"PP. Generales et Provinciales possunt in suos subditos totum illud quod possunt Episcopi in clericos sibi subjectos."*—Donatus, *Rerum Regularium Praxis*, Tom. II, pars I, tr. X, qu. III, n. 3.

[21] *"Praelati maiores uti sunt Generales et Provinciales in sua dioecesi* quae comprehendit eorum monasteria, et ab illis [Episcopis] sola consecratione differunt, ut docent communiter Doctores."—*Ibid.*, n. 7.

[22] Reiffenstuel, *Jus Canonicum Universum*, Lib. V, tit. VII, n. 417; Donatus, *Rerum Regularium Praxis*, Tom. I, pars II, tr. IX, qu. 12, nn. 2-3. It is to be noted, however, that the position held by these two authors was contrary to that held by many other pre-code authors. Cf. Suarez, *Opera Omnia* (ed. nova, 28 vols., Parisiis, 1856-1878), *De Religione*, tr. VIII, Lib. II, Cap. II, n. 10 (hereafter cited as *De Religione*); Passerinus, *Tractatus de Electione Canonica*, cap. XXVI, n. 14; Bouix, *De Jure Regularium*, II, 382; Bachofen, *Compendium Juris Regularium* (New York, 1903), p. 222; Clancy, *The Local Superior*, p. 31.

for it includes the Provincial Superior in its classification of the Major Superiors of religious Orders. When compared with the office of the local Superior in a province of an exempt clerical community, the office of the Provincial assumes a position of greater importance which the Code properly recognizes. Furthermore, the Provincial's jurisdictional position is clarified to a greater degree by canon 198, § 1, which includes the Major Superiors of clerical exempt religious communities in the class of Ordinaries. As head of a particular province of a religious Order the Provincial Superior is therefore the religious Ordinary of the subjects in that province.

When the Code employs the term "Ordinary" without qualification, it can include not only the Sovereign Pontiff, but residential bishops for their own territory, Abbots *nullius*, Prelates *nullius*, and their Vicars-General, Apostolic Administrators, Vicars Apostolic and Prefects Apostolic together with their lawful substitutes, and, finally, the Provincial as well as the other Major Superiors of exempt clerical communities. On the other hand, restrictive phrases, such as "of the place" added to the word "Ordinary" exclude the Provincial and Major Superiors of religious. Of the three hundred and fifty-three instances of the unqualified use of the term "Ordinary" in the Code,[23] the text and context make it obvious that Major Superiors are excluded in instances where it is evident that the diocesan bishop is intended. In other instances the use of this term confers a cumulative right on the Provincial and General. Particular law of the individual Orders will clarify certain of these issues. In a study of the office of the Provincial Superior one of the problems will be the determination of which specific instances of the use of the word "Ordinary" refer to the Provincial Superior. The proper allocation of powers can be seen to better advantage by the analytical method

[23] Keene, *Religious Ordinaries and Canon 198*, The Catholic University of America Canon Law Studies, n. 135 (Washington, D. C.: The Catholic University of America Press, 1942), p. x.

of handling individually the various phases of the office of Provincial. In this way the limits within which the Provincial exercises authority according to canon 502 will be clarified.[24]

[24] Canon 502: "Supremus religionis Moderator potestatem obtinet in omnes provincias, domos, sodales religionis, exercendam secundum constitutiones; alii Superiores ea gaudent intra fines sui muneris."

CANONICAL COMMENTARY

PART ONE

PRELIMINARY QUESTIONS

CHAPTER II

THE AUTHORITY OF THE PROVINCIAL SUPERIOR IN THE CODE OF CANON LAW

1. *The Concept of Jurisdiction.*

The definition of a society as the union of several individuals striving through common means toward the same end postulates the existence of some social authority.[1] As the head rules the physical body, so does a central authority regulate the activity of the social organism. It is thus that families and organizations of a civic or of a religious nature can work reasonably towards their particular goals. Otherwise the end of the society would be attained by only a few and in a haphazard fashion, for direction is necessary to attain an end.[2]

The Church is a juridically perfect society instituted by Christ. As such it possesses its own organization, activity and goal toward which the faithful are directed. Therefore its sphere exceeds the activities of private individuals who are directed of necessity to an end subordinate to that of a perfect society. As a consequence of its nature as a perfect society the Church assumes the character of a public or social being.[3]

[1] Ottaviani, *Compendium Iuris Publici Ecclesiastici ad Usum Auditorum S. Theologiae* (Romae: Typis Polyglottis Vaticanis, 1936), pp. 11-26.

[2] *Sancti Thomae Aquinatis Doctoris Angelici Opera Omnia iussu impensaque Leonis XIII, P.M. edita* (Romae: 1882-); *Summa Theologica* (Romae: *1888-1906*), IIa-IIae, qu. 186, art. 5 (hereafter cited as *Summa Theologica*).

[3] Ottaviani, *Institutiones Iuris Publici Ecclesiastici* (2 vols., Romae:

Since authoritative leadership is necessary in any society, there must be such an authority in the Church. The character of its ecclesiastical authority, however, is derived from its nature as a society. Therefore the authority it wields over its subjects must be, like itself, public and perfect.[4] The accepted name given to this ecclesiastical power of government is *jurisdiction.* It may be defined as the public power of government communicated by Christ to His Church. It confers on the hierarchy the right and the duty to regulate, restrain, supervise, and control the faithful in matters pertaining to the Church's end.[5]

The Code repeats the definition of the Vatican Council that the Roman Pontiff as the Successor of St. Peter in the primacy has not only a primacy of honor, but also supreme and universal jurisdiction over the entire Church.[6] In view of this dogmatic truth, the Holy Father may truly be called, in the words of the Code, "the Pastor of all the faithful, of all the churches, and of all bishops."[7] The hierarchy participates in this plenitude of jurisdiction only to a subordinate degree.[8]

The historic development of the definition of jurisdiction as the public power of government can be traced from its original usage in Roman Law. There the term was originally taken in its literal meaning of *declaring or administering what was right.* It implied a certain relationship between a superior and a subject, and its connotations were confined to the judicial forum.[9] Justinian (527-565) later

---

apud Aedes Facultatis Iuridicae ad S. Apollinaris, 1925), I, n. 96 (hereafter reference will be made to this work as *Institutiones*).

[4] *"Inde fuit imperandi ius seu auctoritas, unde orta est societas."*—Ottaviani, *Institutiones*, I, n. 29. Michiels, *Normae Generales Iuris Canonici* (2 vols., Lublin, Polonia: Universitas Catholica, 1929), I, p. 135 (hereafter cited as *Normae Generales*).

[5] O'Brien, *The Exemption of Religious in Canon Law* (Milwaukee: Bruce Publishing Co., 1943), p. 23.

[6] Can. 218, § 1. [7] Can. 218, § 2. [8] Can. 329, § 1.

[9] Van de Kerckhove, *"De Notione Jurisdictionis in Jure Romano,"*—*Jus Pontificium*, XVI (1936), 49 (hereafter referred to as *JP*).

enlarged upon its meaning so as to make it contain a more general notion of authority.[10] By the beginning of the seventh century the Church employed the term in this broader sense, so as to comprise in its concept the power of both spiritual and temporal administration.[11] In succeeding centuries, however, canonists restricted the meaning of the term. Toward the end of the twelfth century it signified for them only a spiritual administration, and as early as 1215 it was even distinguished from the power of Orders. Thus, thirteenth-century canonists defined it as the *"public power of ruling a perfect community."*[12]

A proper concept of ecclesiastical jurisdiction includes the notion of power to be exercised in the internal as well as the external forum. Current usage of the term to signify power in the internal forum was first employed by Joannes Teutonicus (†1245) in his *Summa ad Decretum;* and the use of the term to refer to the power of the keys is found in the writings of St. Raymond of Pennafort (1175-1275).[13] The accepted definition in pre-Code writings was *"a public power for the government of souls."*[14]

In canon 196 the Code notes this power as comprehending the internal forum as it speaks there of both the internal and the external forum. This twofold species of jurisdiction in the Church is necessary, since the sanctification of its members involves the internal as well as the external

[10] *Ibid.*, p. 62.

[11] Hilling, "Über den Gebrauch des Ausdrucks *iurisdictio* im kanonischen Recht während der ersten Hälfte des Mittelalters"—*Archiv für katholisches Kirchenrecht,* CXVIII (1938), 165-170; Clancy, *The Local Superior,* p. 3.

[12] "Potestas publica regendi communitatem perfectam"—Kerckhove, "De Notione Jurisdictionis apud Decretistas et Priores Decretalistas," —*JP,* XVIII (1938), 13; Clancy, *The Local Superior,* p. 4.

[13] *Summa* (ed. nova, Veronae, 1744), Lib. III, tit. XXIV, § 5, 451-452; Clancy, *loc. cit.*

[14] "Potestas publica circa regimen animarum"—Larraona, "De Potestate Dominativa Publica in Iure Canonico"—*Acta Congressus Iuridici Internationalis* (5 vols., Romae: apud Custodiam Librariam Pont. Instituti Utriusque Iuris, 1935-1937), IV, 147; Clancy, *loc. cit.*

forum. Power over the internal forum seeks primarily the private good of the individual in relation to his salvation through the government of his moral relations with God. Authority of this type can be exercised through the ministry of the Sacraments, as in Penance, or independently of the Sacraments, as in the dispensation of private vows or matrimonial impediments.[15] Jurisdiction over the external forum, however, seeks primarily the common good of the community. Nevertheless, both species are forms of a public or social power. The Church as a perfect society possesses such power and imparts it to its ministers who participate in the ecclesiastical government of the faithful.[16]

Canon 197 notes a final division of jurisdiction which bears reference to the office of the Provincial Superior. Jurisdiction attached by law to an office is called *ordinary*, and can be either *proper* or *vicarious*. *Proper ordinary* jurisdiction is that of a lawfully appointed minister and exercised by him in his own name in virtue of the office which he possesses. *Vicarious ordinary* jurisdiction, on the other hand, is also attached to an office, but is exercised by the minister possessing it, not in his own name but in the name of another.[17] Opposed to these two species of ordinary jurisdiction is that which is *delegated*, or conferred on a subject to be used independently of any office.

One may illustrate these divisions as follows: the Holy Father has complete and perfect jurisdiction communicated by Christ to his office as Head of the Church. By its very nature, therefore, it is proper and ordinary. A diocesan bishop in virtue of his office also possesses proper ordinary power. The vicar general of a diocesan bishop has, in virtue of his office, ordinary but vicarious jurisdiction. Not only the Holy Father but also the diocesan bishop as well

[15] Cf. can. 258, § 1. In either case it pertains to the salvation of the individual.

[16] Ottaviani, *Institutiones*, I, n. 120.

[17] Can. 197, § 1.

as his vicar general can delegate his power to his subjects.

Further analysis of the concept of jurisdiction reveals its three distinct functions: legislative, judicial, and executive. The legislative function confers the power of proposing in an obligatory manner necessary and useful means for the common good. The judicial power defines authoritatively controverted rights in particular cases, and applies penalties. The executive function comprises the rights of an administrative nature for the proper government of subjects, as well as the rights of a coercive nature. The latter provide for the proper fulfillment of the legislative, judicial, and administrative decrees and measures.[18]

2. *Dominative Power.*

Superiors and chapters of religious Orders possess also dominative power over their subjects, which power is to be exercised according to the norms of their particular constitutions and the Code.[19] Dominative power is the authority possessed by the heads of imperfect societies. It is frequently called a private power, as distinct from the public power of jurisdiction.[20] It may be defined as the power of ruling an individual person or imperfect society which tends primarily to the private good of individuals, as opposed to the public good of a perfect society. Dominative power flows from the natural law, e.g., the power exercised by a father over his family; from a vow, or from an agreement whereby one subjects himself to another, as in a religious community; or, from some positive disposition of law which recognizes, erects, or orders an imperfect society.[21] As a means of government, it is possessed by the head of an im-

[18] Ottaviani, *Institutiones*, I, nn. 38, 163.

[19] Can. 501, § 1.

[20] Vermeersch-Creusen, *Epitome*, I, n. 619.

[21] Beste, *Introductio in Codicem* (editio altera, Collegeville, Minn.: St. John's Abbey Press, 1944), p. 213 (hereafter referred to as *Introductio*); Michiels, *Normae Generales*, I, 134; Toso, "De Conceptu Legis", *JP*, IV (1924), 34.

perfect society in a degree necessary to safeguard the domestic and social order of the institute and to insure the attainment of its particular end.

Religious, by their vow of obedience, subject themselves to the dominative power of their proper Superiors in accordance with the constitutions of the institute and the prescriptions of the Code. In view of this relationship between Superior and subject, the former has the duty of safeguarding the order of the house or institute as well as the fulfillment of the constitutions. Necessarily, at times, this will entail injunctions and precepts. Dominion also includes the right of administration of the temporalities of the institute. Finally, in accordance with the constitutions, the Superior, in virtue of dominative power, can employ certain coercive measures and make certain relaxations of the constitutions.[22]

The acts of government spoken of above are all directed to the achievement of the particular good of the imperfect society itself. They are of a private nature as compared with those acts of jurisdiction which permit exempt religious Superiors to share in a more intimate manner in the direct government of the Church. Thus religious Superiors of exempt clerical communities possess jurisdiction and can direct their activities towards every objective within the scope of dominative power, and yet maintain a public position in the Church because of their ecclesiastical jurisdiction. Consequently the powers of such religious Superiors are of greater extension and nobility than those proper to dominative power alone. The Code recognizes this nobility by attributing the title "prelate" to these Superiors of exempt clerical communities.[23]

3. *The Existence of the Jurisdiction of the Provincial.*

Authors believe that the first positive statement of the

[22] Schaefer, *De Religiosis ad Normam Codicis Iuris Canonici* (3. ed., Romae: S. A. L. E. R., 1940), n. 107, p. 229 (hereafter cited *De Religiosis*).

[23] Can. 110.

possession of dominative and jurisdictional power by Regular prelates is had in canon 501, § 1. Here the Code explicitly states that jurisdictional and dominative powers are possessed by Superiors and chapters of clerical exempt communities.[24] These powers are to be exercised according to the norm of the constitutions of the particular Order and of the common law.

The interpretation of the clause pertaining to dominative power in canon 501, § 1, offers no difficulty, since it is explicitly stated that the dominative power of Superiors is to be exercised in accordance with the constitutions and the common law.[25] It is obvious from the position of the phrase "according to the norm of the constitutions and the common law" that it is intended to specify the extent to which dominative power may be exercised. Question might arise, however, with regard to the latter half of this paragraph of the canon, which deals with the jurisdiction to be exercised by clerical exempt Superiors. There it is stated that Superiors of clerical exempt communities possess jurisdiction over both the internal forum and the external forum.[26]

Does the phrase "according to the constitutions and the common law," which is contained in the first part of the paragraph, apply as well to the second half of the paragraph, so that the jurisdiction of clerical exempt Superiors can also be restricted by the constitutions of the institute or by the common law? It will be indicated in the following pages that the teaching and practise before the Code accepted the view that both the common law and the constitutions did,

[24] Can. 501, § 1. Cf. Chelodi, *Ius de Personis iuxta Codicem Iuris Canonici* (ed. altera a Sac. Ernesto Bertagnolli recognita et aucta, Tridenti: Libr. Edit. Tridentum, 1927), n. 252 (hereafter cited as *Ius de Personis*); Schaefer, *De Religiosis*, n. 105, p. 221; Clancy, *The Local Superior*, p. 26.

[25] "Superiores et Capitula, *ad normam constitutionum et iuris communis*, potestatem habent dominativam in subditos; ..." (The italics are those of the writer.)

[26] "... in religione autem clericali exempta, habent iurisdictionem ecclesiasticam tam pro foro interno, quam pro externo."

in certain instances, limit the exercise of jurisdiction by different Superiors. It will likewise be indicated that the canons governing the rights and duties of Superiors make frequent allowances for the constitutions to determine the competence of specific Superiors for the exercise of a right conferred by the common law. Thus the question can be answered by stating, with Schaefer, that the constitutions can moderate and define the jurisdiction conferred by law upon Superiors, but that they cannot take it away entirely.[27] A restriction, by the common law, of the jurisdictional power of Superiors is noted in the second portion of this canon in the light of which all cases pertaining to the Holy Office are removed entirely from the competence of Religious Superiors.[28] To cite an instance of limitation by the particular law, it is necessary to turn to privileges, customs or specific constitutions. Thus, by reason of privilege that is unrevoked by the common law, the Provincial Superior of Regulars can dispense from the impediment of illegitimacy in a postulant about to enter the novitiate.[29] The Carmelite Constitutions, however, reserve such a case to the General.[30]

4. *The Extent of the Jurisdiction of the Provincial.*

The problem of a study of jurisdiction in Regular Orders is to determine the extent of the power of each of the Superiors. The assistance offered by canon 502 of the Code

[27] "Constitutiones iurisdictionem a iure Superioribus concessam, moderari et definire valent, non autem auferre."—*De Religiosis*, n. 105, p. 222. Cf. also Berutti, *Institutiones Iuris Canonici* (6 vols. in 7, Vol. III, *De Religiosis*, Taurini-Romae: Marietti, 1936), III, n. 23 (hereafter cited as *Institutiones*); Larraona, "Commentarium Codicis" —*Commentarium pro Religiosis*, III (1922), 135, nota 203 (hereafter cited as *CpR*.)

[28] Can. 501, § 2. [29] *Cf. infra*, pp. 209-211.

[30] *Constitutiones Ordinis Fratrum Beatissimae Virginis Mariae de Monte Carmelo iussu Revmi. P. Eliae Magennis Prioris Generalis in Lucem Editae praemisso Regula S. Alberti* (Romae: Typis Polyglottis Vaticanis, MCMXXX), Pars. I, caput II, art. III (hereafter cited as *Constitutiones O. Carm.*).

is not available in the law of the pre-Code period. Canon 502 states that the Supreme Moderator holds over all provinces, houses, and members of the Order power which is to be exercised according to the individual constitutions; other Superiors enjoy their power within the limits of their offices.[31] Even under the law of the Code the interpretation of the phrase "within the limits of their offices" presents a difficulty.

In the formative years of the Mendicant Orders, all Superiors were prelates and enjoyed quasi-episcopal powers in virtue of their privilege of exemption and their consequent rôle of pastor over their subjects.[32] Though the *Praelatus Medius, Supremus* and *Inferior,* of the pre-Tridentine and pre-Code eras enjoyed quasi-episcopal jurisdiction, the Provincial Superior's office was analogous to that of the bishop of a diocese rather than to that of a Local Superior. His jurisdiction was broader as to subjects, and matters pertaining to the welfare of the province were reserved to his judgment. The superiority of his rank as a Prelate over the Local Superior was recognized by the Council of Trent, which prescribed for him a provincial visitation like that of the diocesan visitation of the bishop.[33]

In the period after the Council of Trent, Donatus and Reiffenstuel maintained that the Provincial and General held the same jurisdiction in relation to their religious subjects as bishops in relation to their diocesan subjects.[34] For them the jurisdiction of the Provincial Superior was certainly greater than that of the Local Superior, whose powers

[31] Can. 502. "Supremus religionis Moderator potestatem obtinet in omnes provincias, domos, sodales religionis, exercendam secundum constitutiones; alii Superiores ea gaudent intra fines sui muneris."

[32] Cf. *supra,* p. 4.

[33] Sess. XXIV, *de ref.,* c. 3; sess. XXV, *de regularibus,* c. 25.

[34] Cf. *supra,* p. 10. "Praelati Regulares, uti sunt Generales et Provinciales, ac hujusmodi Superiores Majores exempti, habent jurisdictionem quasi-episcopalem in suos subditos, prout loquuntur omnes auctores."—*Jus Canonicum Universum,* Lib. V, tit. VII, n. 417.

were restricted to his house and the subjects living therein. Consequently, he merited the title of Major Superior.

The question now arises as to the extent of this quasi-episcopal power of the Major Prelates. Besides the obvious exception of those matters which require episcopal consecration, the jurisdiction of the Provincial was further limited. This latter limitation resulted from his position as *Praelatus Medius*. His jurisdiction was not confined, indeed, to a particular house or to a limited number of subjects within his province. Extending over the entire province, it embraced all the subjects and houses of that province. Outside of that province, however, the Provincial possessed no jurisdiction except that which he exercised over his own subjects. Therefore, the extension of the Provincial's jurisdiction was limited in relation to the General's, which extended over the entire Order, yet it was broader than that of the Local Superior. In relation to the Local Superior his was indeed a major position, and exhibited to a greater degree a quasi-episcopal character.[35]

The same limitations of power for the Provincial exist in the Code. Obviously enough, he does not enjoy jurisdiction resulting from a true episcopal character. Canon 502 declares that the power of the General is universal in relation to the Order, while the Provincial and the other Superiors exercise jurisdiction within the limits of their offices. Yet, all the Superiors of Regulars retain their rank as prelates in the Code since they exercise ordinary jurisdiction in the external forum.[36] The Provincial and General, however, are *Ordinaries* for the reason that they are Major Superiors.[37]

It has been seen above that the jurisdiction enjoyed by religious Superiors in virtue of canon 501, § 1, can be

[35] Cf. *supra*, p. 7.

[36] Can. 110. "Quamvis Praelati titulo, honoris causa, a Sede Apostolica etiam nonnulli clerici donentur sine ulla iurisdictione, proprio tamen nomine Praelati in iure dicuntur clerici sive saeculares sive religiosi qui iurisdictionem ordinariam in foro externo obtinent."

[37] Can. 198, § 1; can. 488, 8°; *supra* p. 7.

limited by the particular law or by the Code itself.[38] However, some instances of rights and obligations of Superiors in the Code will not therein be determined as belonging to a specific Superior. The law may speak generically of Superiors, as in canon 501, § 1, or more specifically of *Major Superiors*, as in canon 503. When the particular constitutions do not determine these spheres of competence as belonging to a particular prelate, the application of fundamental principles will be of assistance for establishing the extension of jurisdiction of one or the other Superior.

In regard to the general faculties granted by law to Superiors, one must bear in mind the axiom that, when the law does not distinguish, no distinction is to be invoked. Thus canon 503 states that Major Superiors can constitute notaries for the work of their Order. Consequently, if the particular law of an Order does not restrict the power of the Provincial, he can establish notaries in virtue of his position as a Major Superior. When the particular law can determine the exercise of jurisdiction, it should not always do so in favor of the higher Superior, lest such a practice, in effect, reduce to nugatory proportions the jurisdiction of the inferior prelate.[39] The lawfulness of such a practice could hardly be upheld. True, canon 501, § 1, grants jurisdiction to Superiors to be exercised according to the norm of the constitutions, but it is assumed that the constitutions are not to render the office of a Superior merely honorary. Indeed, some canons definitely indicate that the authoritative disposition regarding the particular needs and circumstances of a community should fall within the competence of inferior prelates. A universal restriction of the power of inferior prelates would make the exemption of religious burdensome. Deprived of their proper diocesan pastors, the religious would be subordinated entirely to a Major Superior who would not be as easily accessible as an inferior one.

[38] Cf. *supra*, p. 17.

[39] Larraona, "Commentarium Codicis"—*CpR*, III (1922), 135, nota 203; Schaefer, *De Religiosis*, n. 107, p. 225.

The question may well be asked how, in accordance with the common and particular law, the determination of the competent Superior is to be made in a given case. Matters which, in the common law, are attributed expressly and exclusively to the Provincial Superior are to be understood as his proper rights. Therefore he is not to be hindered by the higher Superior in their exercise. The General Superior has no universal authority over the common law of the Church, and it is only in certain specific instances that he is empowered to dispense from the obligations of the common law.[40] Accordingly the enumeration by the common law of the exclusive rights belonging to the Provincial Superior is to be considered a denial of the General's power to interfere, even when a cause for so doing seems present. Examples of such powers of the Provincial Superior are: that of acting as judge of first instance in controversies between members of his province;[41] in certain cases that of dismissing a subject immediately;[42] and that of giving a canonical warning with a view to canonical dismissal.[43]

On the other hand, the common law may confer a power to be exercised by Major Superiors as determined, not by the common law, but by the particular norms of the constitutions.[44] In this case the general statement of the limitation of the powers of the Superiors by the constitutions as made in canon 501, § 1, is given particular emphasis, and a specification of competence by the constitutions is practically solicited. However, the rights may be conferred by the canons on Major Superiors with no indication that a specification should be made by the constitutions. In that case, if the constitutions do not determine the respective spheres

[40] Can. 81. [41] Can. 1579, § 1. [42] Can. 653.

[43] Can. 611. Regarding this whole question of jurisdictional competence among the respective religious Superiors, the writer calls attention to the following two articles which have come to his notice: Goyeneche, "Consultationes"—*CpR,* III (1922), 217-218; Jombart, "Subordination dans l'Exercice de l'Autorité"—*Révue des Communautés Réligieuses,* XI (1935), 69-74.

[44] Cans. 543; 539, § 2; 572, § 1, 6°.

of competence, the Provincial and the General are equally competent. For the General to deny these rights to the Provincial would be tantamount to a new particular law, which however can be derived only from the General Chapter.

Because of the fact that canon 502 attributes supreme jurisdiction over all members of an Order to the General, and because of his duty to seek the common good of the Order, it may be that in a particular case he would have a just and lawful reason to deny a Provincial the power to exercise some right which is his by nature of his office of Provincial. Such a denial of the exercise of a right would be within the competence of the General and his duties toward the Order.[45] Indeed, the General is always empowered to act in cases of Provincial competence when disciplinary purposes in view of extant abuses make such a demand. He is not only empowered to act, but he is authorized temporarily to restrict, in these matters, the right of the Provincial to act jurisdictionally, or even to suspend that right entirely.[46]

In normal cases, then, i.e., those wherein there is no reason for interference on the part of the General, the Provincial is equally competent when the Code attributes power to Major Superiors without any further specification, and the particular law is silent as to such specification. Ordinarily custom or the nature of the case will indicate the sphere of activity proper to the respective Superior. If the issue over which both are equally competent involves the general welfare of the Order, the General's right and duty to intervene is undisputed. Thus, for instance, the Ordinary, and hence the Provincial as well as the General, has extensive faculties in virtue of canon 2237 over penalties incurred by his subjects. If particular law has not determined the point, major issues involving grave canonical penalties can certainly affect the general welfare of the Order. The proper solution of such an issue may demand

[45] Goyeneche, "Consultationes"—*CpR*, III (1922), 218.

[46] Cf. can. 2389; Goyeneche, *loc. cit.*

the transfer of a subject to another province with a view to preventing the divulgation of his delict, or to promoting his amendment. In such grave cases the Provincial's right, by the very nature of the case, in restricted, and the General alone becomes competent.

Finally, in many issues that do not involve the welfare of the Order the competence of the respective Superiors may be determined through the auxiliary reference to general principles of jurisdiction. A judicial norm, for instance, is given in the Fourth Book of the Code: when two or more judges are equally competent, his is the right to hear the case who first takes judicial action in the case. This norm may be applied analogously, not only to the judicial phase of the jurisdiction of religious Superiors, but also to its voluntary phase.[47] Thus, when several Superiors are equally competent, the matter is to be judged within the jurisdictional sphere of him who first acts according to law in the case. Then the jurisdiction of him who is not acting remains intact, but becomes inoperative.[48] Consequently, when one of two Superiors has been called upon to act in such a matter and has actually begun to do so, the other, even though he be of a higher rank, should refrain from action unless a grave and just cause warrants his interference.

Questions of competence between the Provincial and Local Superior can more readily arise than between the Provincial and the General. The same principles, however, should guide the determination of their respective spheres. It is obvious that when the Major Superior is specified by the common or particular law as competent, the Local Superior cannot interfere. The same is to be said of the case in which the constitutions make such a specification.[49]

If no particular Superior is specified as competent by the Code or the constitutions, but the matter is of more than local interest and concern, then the Provincial Superior, to the exclusion of the Local Superior, is competent. Even as

[47] Can. 1568. [48] Can. 204, § 2. [49] Cf. *supra*, pp. 21-22.

the General can supervise the acts of the Provincial, so, too, the Provincial can supervise the acts of the Local Superior. Disciplinary reasons may require the Provincial at times to moderate temporarily the exercise of the jurisdiction of the Local Superior. On the other hand, undue restrictions jeopardize the rights of office bestowed by the common law. Over these, ordinary jurisdiction is not granted to the Provincial. In cases of mutual competence, the jurisdictional power is his who first acts in the case; the power of the other remains inoperative. Precisely what the limits of the office of Provincial Superior are will now be examined specifically.

CHAPTER III

THE CANDIDATE FOR THE OFFICE OF PROVINCIAL SUPERIOR

Through the presentation of the history of the office of Provincial and of the legislation regarding his duties and the general norms for assessing the extent of the jurisdiction conferred on the Provincial Superior in the Code of Canon Law, the way has been prepared for a detailed study of the rights and duties of the Provincial Superior according to the norms enacted in the Code of Canon Law. The first consideration is accordingly directed toward the prerequisites stated in the law as affecting the prospective Provincial before he takes office.

1. *Qualities in the Candidate.*

The qualifications required by canon 504 in the candidate for the office of Provincial Superior are very ancient. Express solemn religious profession in the respective Order has been required from the time of Boniface VIII (1294-1303).[1] The Decretal law did not require any specific period of profession,[2] but it did demand the completion of the twenty-fourth year, the possession of the clerical state, the status of legitimacy, and the absence of censures or other disqualifications for office.[3]

The prescriptions of the Decretal law are retained by the Code, which requires in canon 504 that the candidate must be a member of the same Order, professed for a period of ten complete years from the time of the first profession, born of lawful wedlock, and fully thirty years of age. The

[1] C. 28, *de electione et electi potestate*, I, 6, in VI°; c. 1, *de electione et electi potestate*, I, 3, in Clem.

[2] Appeltern, *Compendium Praelectionum Juris Regularis* (editio altera aucta et emendata, Parisiis: 1913), p. 345, qu. 390 (hereafter cited as *Compendium*).

[3] Wernz, *Ius Decretalium*, III, p. 766, n. 686.

necessity of the clerical state is obvious from canon 118, which allows the power of jurisdiction to clerics alone.[4]

A religious transferring from one Order to another would, however, enjoy no seniority in virtue of his former profession, nor would he be eligible for election till ten years had elapsed from the time of profession in the new Order.[5] A religious who after secularization rejoins the community must compute the time for eligibility from the date of his new profession.[6] Years spent in military service, however, are computed, since the religious remains a subject of his Superiors. Similarly, the years or months passed while the religious lived outside the cloister with a special indult of exclaustration are not lost to this computation.[7]

Regarding the condition of birth in lawful wedlock, the position taken by the Code is less strict in the case of the Provincial than in that of a bishop. Status of legitimacy, even when acquired through the subsequent marriage of the parents, suffices for the eligibility of the Provincial, since the Code states that children legitimated through marriage are equal in every respect to those conceived in lawful wedlock, unless the law specifies contrariwise.[8] The Code does specify that legitimation by subsequent marriage is not

[4] Can. 118: "Soli clerici possunt potestatem sive ordinis sive iurisdictionis ecclesiasticae et beneficia ac pensiones ecclesiasticas obtinere." Cf. also can. 154.

[5] The time is to be computed according to the rule contained in can. 34, § 3, 1°, 3°. Coronata, *Institutiones Iuris Canonici ad Usum Utriusque Cleri et Scholarum* (5 vols., Vols. I-IV, 2. ed., Taurini: Marietti, 1936-1945: Vol. I, 1939), I, p. 653, n. 538 (hereafter cited as *Institutiones*).

[6] Vermeersch-Creusen, *Epitome*, I, n. 622; Goyeneche, *Iuris Canonici Summa Principia de Religiosis* (Roma: Tip. Pol. "Cuore di Maria", 1938), 36 (hereafter cited as *De Religiosis*).

[7] S. C. de Religiosis, decr. "*Cum in Codice*", 19 iul. 1919—*Acta Apostolicae Sedis, Commentarium Officiale* (Romae: 1909-), X (1919), 321 (hereafter cited with the abbreviation *AAS*). Cf. Larraona, "Commentarium Codicis"—*CpR*, VII (1926), 247; Coronata, *Institutiones*, I, p. 653, n. 538.

[8] Can. 1117.

sufficient for eligibility in the cases of a cardinal, a bishop, or an abbot and prelate *nullius*.[9]

Legitimation resulting from solemn profession or from a general dispensation, though sufficient for the reception of Orders, does not suffice for eligibility to the Provincial's position.[10] What is to be said of one born of an invalid marriage in regard of which the privilege of radical sanation (*sanatio in radice*) has been granted? A conclusion from canon 1138, § 1,[11] is that such a person is eligible, provided that his birth followed that point of time to which the juridic effects of the sanation have by way of retroactivity been extended.[12]

An important quality also required in the candidate for the post of Provincial is the note of personal worthiness. Basing their views on the Council of Trent (1545-1563),[13] pre-Code authors debated the validity of the election of an unworthy candidate. Though the electors might have involved themselves in sin by selecting a less worthy candidate, the election was considered valid, provided that the candidate was not made unworthy through the presence of an ecclesiastical censure.[14] The necessity of personal worthiness is seen in the restatement by the Code of a Constitution of Clement VIII (1592-1605) requiring the electors in Orders of men to bind themselves under oath to elect worthy

[9] Cans. 232, § 2, 1°; 320, § 2; 331, § 1, 1°.

[10] Schaefer, *De Religiosis*, p. 483, n. 221, 5; Goyeneche, *De Religiosis*, p. 36, nota 25; Vermeersch-Creusen, *Epitome*, II, n. 261; Coronata, *Institutiones*, I, p. 653, nota 11; Larraona "Commentarium Codicis"—*CpR*, VII (1926), 296-7.

[11] "Matrimonii in radice sanatio est eiusdem convalidatio, secumferens, praeter dispensationem vel cessationem impedimenti, dispensationem a lege de renovando consensu, et retrotractionem, per fictionem iuris, circa effectus canonicos, ad praeteritum."

[12] Vermeersch-Creusen, *Epitome*, I, n. 622.

[13] Sess. VI, *de ref.*, c. 1; sess. XXIV, *de ref.*, c. 1.

[14] Appeltern, *Compendium*, p. 373, qu. 419; Schmalzgrueber, *Ius Ecclesiasticum Universum* (5 vols. in 12, Romae, 1843-1845), Lib. I, tit. VI, nn. 19, 3.

Major Superiors.[15] The difficulty naturally presenting itself is the question of determining this fitness. Here the problem must be solved by the electors themselves. Ordinarily the latter are men of sound judgment who enjoy the esteem of the community. Therefore it pertains to them, after considering all the circumstances and qualities of the times, places and individuals, prudently to decide which candidate possesses the best qualities.

Personal worthiness demands that the candidate be free not only from canonical incapacity for office, but also from censures, from infamy whether of fact or of law, and from other vindicative penalties.[16]

2. *The Appointment of the Provincial.*

It is not within the scope of this work to concern itself at length with the appointment of the Provincial. The constitutions will determine whether he is to be appointed or elected to office, and in the latter event will make specifications regarding the election. Accordingly the particular law must necessarily be the guide in this matter. In the absence of specifications of the particular law regarding elections, however, canons 160-182, which deal with election and postulation, will serve as the norm.

3. *Term of Office.*

There next arises the question of the term of the Provincial's office. In general it may be said that the Code favors a temporary tenure of office on the part of all religious Superiors.[17]

No limitation, however, to a three-year term or to a six-year term is imposed upon the Provincial's term of office, as in the case of Local Superiors. Furthermore, the Code

[15] Can. 506, § 1.

[16] Cappello, *Summa Iuris Canonici in Usum Scholarum Concinnata* (3 vols., Romae: apud Aedes Universitatis Gregorianae; Vols. I et II, 3. ed., 1938-1939), I, p. 337, n. 276 (hereafter cited *Summa Iuris Canonici*).

[17] Can. 505.

makes no restrictions regarding the re-election of Major Superiors. True, the mind of the Sacred Congregation of Religious seems to favor temporary terms of office for Major Superiors in that restrictions by the constitutions of the number of terms of office have been declared by it to produce an incapacity, in consequence of which a postulation of the candidate becomes indicated as the proper procedure if he is to hold an additional term of office.[18]

Nevertheless a case could be visualized in which the rapid expansion, or also the decimation of a province, e.g., through an insufficient number of vocations over a period of years, might demand that a Major Superior be retained in office until other eligible candidates are available. The electors share with the Supreme Moderator or General the responsibility of making the choice. It is for them to decide whether an additional term of office is to be accorded in place of entrusting the responsibility of the office to youthful, inexperienced or incompetent hands. Obviously enough, however, such a condition can only be a temporary one which exists apart from any perpetual sanction of the law. In cases of positive doubt, it seems the choice should be given to a new candidate in view of the *stylus curiae,* which favors temporary terms of office.

4. *Obligation to Accept the Office.*

The question may be asked whether the Provincial-elect is obliged to accept the office. Particular law, in some cases, grants the right to refuse. Pre-Code authors held various opinions on the right of the appointee to reject the office of prelate. Some held that a candidate could reject his appointment before confirmation in the office, but not afterwards.[19] Others claimed that the candidate could state his

[18] S.C. de Rel., 3 iun., 1910—*AAS,* II (1910), 483; Goyeneche, "Consultationes", *CpR,* VII (1926), 249; Goyeneche, *De Religiosis,* p. 37.

[19] Reiffenstuel, *Jus Canonicum Universum,* Lib. I, tit. VI, nn. 34, 313; Donatus, *Rerum Regularium Praxis,* Tom. II, pars. I, tr. VI, qu. IV, n. 1; Appeltern, *Compendium,* p. 370, qu. 415.

reasons for wishing to reject the office, but had to accept if the Superior insisted.[20] Such an obligation can hardly be said to exist, however, since no Superior, other than the Pope, can command a subject to change his status.[21]

Under the law of the Code the difficulty is obviated. When particular law, approved since the Code or established by privilege, does not determine a point regarding elections, the general prescriptions of the Code are to be followed.[22] The common law, however, grants an option to every appointee, including the candidate for the office of Provincial.[23] Thus, unless the constitutions forbid the act of renunciation, a candidate is free to accept or renounce the election.[24]

If the office is conferred by nomination or appointment by a higher Superior, acceptance is not a matter of choice but rather one of obedience. It is certainly within the candidate's rights to explain his reasons for declining the office, but if this is of no avail he must obey. The Holy Father, however, is the Superior over all religious, and therefore recourse may lawfully be had to him in the event of such an unusual case.[25]

Formerly the authors held that one knowing himself to be unfit was obliged to decline. The better view, however, seems to be that the one elected need not refuse, even if he foresees possible occasions of sins. In such a case the good to be drawn from religious obedience excels the probable private good, and measures can be taken to make the occasion of sin remote. Moreover, no one is bound to defame himself.[26] Therefore the candidate is free to accept the

[20] Appeltern, *loc. cit.*

[21] Donatus, *Rerum Regularium Praxis*, Tom. II, pars I, tr. X, qu. XIX, n. 1.

[22] Can. 507, § 1. [23] Can. 175.

[24] Can. 184. Cf. Vermeersch-Creusen, *Epitome*, I, n. 293. Goyeneche, however, maintains that a religious can be obliged to accept an office. "Consultationes"—*CpR*, VI (1925), 207-208).

[25] Larraona, "Consultationes"—*CpR*, II (1921), 341.

[26] Goyeneche, "Consultationes"—*CpR*, VI (1925), 207; Schaefer, *De Religiosis*, n. 136, p. 284.

office or to give his reasons for declining it. Religious perfection, being based on the renunciation of the individual's will, seems to be more fully realized when the individual accepts what comes his way after an honest and obedient statement of his own misgivings. Following the will of his Superiors, the religious need not be fearful of the consequences.

5. *The Obligations Arising from the Office.*

The office of Provincial imposes on its incumbent the personal obligation of striving for the conservation and preservation of the institute. To this end the Provincial should implore the help of God when he is confirmed in office, and make the Profession of Faith as required of Superiors by the Code.[27] Moreover, he ought to strive to attain the qualities required of a bishop, since he is the Ordinary for his subjects. The closer he approaches the perfections required of a bishop, the closer will he be to faithfully fulfilling the Church's desire for worthy religious Ordinaries. Thus, he should aim at improving his character, so that he may be prudent and zealous. Moreover, he should labor to increase his knowledge of Sacred Theology and Canon Law.[28] Personal example in word and deed should be his strongest weapon in promoting the common good. Fear and human respect must never deter him from prudently using coercion when necessary. Within the limits of his duties he should set the example in observing the constitutions, the Rule and the statutes of the General Chapters.[29]

Before the Code, Wernz (1842-1914) taught that a Regular Prelate should offer Mass occasionally for his subjects, not in virtue of a strict obligation of justice, but rather as motivated by the virtue of charity.[30] That the obligation is derived from the virtue of charity and not from that of

[27] Can. 1406, § 1, 9°.

[28] Can. 331, § 1, 4°.

[29] Appeltern, *Compendium,* p. 406, qu. 460, 3.

[30] *Ius Decretalium,* III, p. 775, n. 694.

justice seems indicated in the fact that the Sacred Congregation of the Council never did reply to the question whether the Local Superiors of the Augustinian Order were obliged to offer Mass for their subjects.[31] The obligation of charity was based upon the fact that Superiors were to pray for the subjects committed to their care.[32] In view, then, of the obligation imposed upon bishops by the Code,[33] and of the obligation resting on Superiors to pray for those committed to their care in accordance with the law of the Council of Trent, Wernz-Vidal (1867-1938) maintain that the Provincial and other Regular Superiors should offer Mass for their subjects in virtue of the divine precept of charity.[34] A strict obligation in justice to offer Mass for his subjects cannot indeed be urged as binding the Provincial, but it does seem that he *should* do so at least occasionally, lest his exempt subjects actually be deprived of spiritual benefits in consequence of their privilege of exemption from the jurisdiction of the local Ordinary and the local pastors, who frequently are obliged to apply the Mass for their subjects.

[31] Verhoeven, *De Praxi a Parochis Observanda in Celebratione Missae pro Populo* (Hasseleti, 1849), pp. 90-93.

[32] Conc. Trident., sess. XXIII, *de ref.*, c. 1. "Since by divine precept it is enjoined on all to whom is entrusted the *cura animorum* to know their sheep, to offer sacrifice for them, . . . the holy council admonishes and exhorts them that, mindful of the divine precepts . . . they in judgment and in truth be shepherds and leaders."—Schroeder, *Canons and Decrees*, p. 164.

[33] Can. 339.

[34] Wernz-Vidal, *Ius Canonicum ad Codicis Normam Exactum* (7 toms. in 8 vols., Romae: apud Aedes Universitatis Gregorianae, 1923-1938; Tom. II, *De Personis*, 2. ed., 1928; Tom. III, *De Religiosis*, 1933; Tom. IV, Pars I-II, *De Rebus*, 1934-1935, IV, p. 86, n. 76. (Hereafter reference will be made to these tomes through their respective titles.)

PART TWO

THE LEGISLATIVE AND JUDICIAL POWERS OF THE PROVINCIAL SUPERIOR

CHAPTER IV

THE LEGISLATIVE POWER OF THE PROVINCIAL SUPERIOR

Legislative competence is one of the chief attributes of the power of jurisdiction in the Church. Through its use a Prelate directs his subjects in an obligatory manner toward the end for which the Church was instituted. Since, as has been pointed out,[1] the Provincial Superior enjoys quasi-episcopal power, there now arises the question whether he possesses the legislative power in the manner in which it is explicitly granted to the residential bishop in canon 335, § 1. The present chapter, then, seeks to explore the extent, if any, of his legislative power. Subsequent chapters will examine his judicial and executive powers.

The authority to enact true ecclesiastical laws is a manifestation of the perfect participation in the ecclesiastical power of government. This arises from the fact that the principal function of ecclesiastical jurisdiction is the enactment of law for the direction of subjects to their ultimate good.[2] Law, in its classical definition, is "an ordination of reason directed to the common good and promulgated by him who exercises authority over the community."[3] Ecclesiastical laws are ordinations of reason directed toward the common good of the Church. By nature these are permanent in character and obligatory upon all. Legislative authority would accordingly attribute to the office of Pro-

[1] Cf., *supra*, pp. 4-9.

[2] Michiels, *Normae Generales*, I, 135.

[3] St. Thomas, *Summa Theologica*, Ia-IIae, qu. 90, a. 4 (Translation by the writer.)

vincial Superior the power to enact true ecclesiastical laws. As inherent in that office, it could be defined as the right of the Provincial, in virtue of his rôle as a member of the ecclesiastical hierarchy, to impose general and lasting obligations upon the members of his province in keeping with their common good as members of the Church.

1. *The Background of the Question.*

From the beginning the Mendicant Orders reposed the plenitude of their jurisdictional power in the General Chapter, which alone was acknowledged as having the power to legislate.[4] St. Thomas denied legislative power to the Provincial, teaching that only the head of a society can legislate.[5]

Pre-Code authors also held that the Provincial had no power to enact true laws in consequence of his subordinate position in the constitutional structure of the Order.[6] Though the particular law of some Orders, e.g., the Carmelites, granted legislative power to their Generals,[7] the writer has found no indication anywhere of a similar grant for a Provincial Superior. Although the majority of the pre-Code authors, with the exception of Suarez (1548-1617), did not

[4] Lezana, *Summa Quaestionum Regularium seu de Casibus Conscientiae ad Personas Religiosas utriusque Sexus valde Spectantibus* (2 vols. in 4 parts, Venetiis: MDCLIV), Vol. I, pars I, cap. XVIII, n. 90 (hereafter cited as *Summa Quaestionum Regularium*); Vermeersch, *De Religiosis Institutis et Personis Tractatus Canonico-Moralis ad Recentissimas Leges Exactus* (2 vols., Romae et Ratisbonae: 1902), I, n. 423.

[5] "Non cujuslibet ratio facere potest legem, sed multitudinis, vel principis vicem multitudinis gerentis."—*Summa Theologica,* Ia-IIae, qu. 90, a. 3.

[6] "Ad facienda autem statuta perpetua, quae vim habeant et rationem legis nec inferiores Praelati, nec Provinciales ordinariam potestatem habent."—Suarez, *De Religione,* Lib. II, cap. VIII, n. 4, Lezana, *Summa Quaestionum Regularium,* Vol. I, pars I, cap. XVIII, n. 90; Wernz, *Ius Decretalium,* III, p. 769, n. 690.

[7] Lezana, *loc. cit.* Cf. Vermeersch-Creusen, *Epitome,* I, n. 620, for a similar privilege of the Jesuit Superior General.

deny the absolute right of the Provincial Superior to enact laws, yet[8] these same authors agreed that the individual constitution could lawfully, and actually did, restrict the Provincial in this matter.

2. *The Legislative Power of the Provincial.*

The Code has affected no change in the former teaching concerning the legislative power of the Provincial. His jurisdiction is to be determined in accordance with the constitutions of his Order. Legislative authority is not incompatible with his office. Since the Provincial fills an official and public office in relation to his exempt subjects, there are reasonable arguments why he should possess this power. His relationship is that of an Ordinary to his subjects.[9]

Inasmuch as canon 335, § 1, specifically grants legislative power to the diocesan Ordinary for his territory, it may be argued in view of the analogy between the Provincial Superior and the local Ordinary, that under the law of the Code the Provincial also enjoys legislative power. Like the diocesan bishop, the Provincial is an Ordinary and possesses jurisdiction. Now, legislative authority is a primary function of jurisdiction and is explicitly granted to the local Ordinary. Hence, if the Code has not explicitly granted legislative authority to the Provincial, it seems that nevertheless the denial of this authority is unwarranted, for the Code has not denied this authority to him.

The possibility for the existence of this authority in the Provincial could be questioned only on the score of the capability of his community to receive a law. A religious community can be considered capable of receiving a law if three elements in its composition are verified: namely, the possession of some kind of autonomous subsistence; the union of its members through some common bond; and, finally, its direction by a Superior with public authority

[8] Appeltern, *Compendium*, p. 379, qu. 429.
[9] Can. 198, § 1.

toward the end of the perfect society, which is the Church, to which the community is subordinated.[10]

The Province of an exempt clerical community satisfies these requirements for the capacity to receive a law. Moreover, the Code does not deny the analogy between a religious province and a diocese, as proposed by the pre-Code commentators.[11] Since there is no justification in the Code for ignoring this analogy, to do so would be unwarranted.[12] This is particularly true since the Provincial is an Ordinary,[13] a Major Superior,[14] and an official possessing public authority over a community which possesses the elements which make it capable of receiving a law. The Code seems to be in harmony, then, with the former jurisprudence, in so far as it does not deny the absolute capacity of the Provincial to enjoy the right to enact laws.

Against these reasons for the assertion of legislative authority in the Provincial, it is to be noted that the analogy drawn between the Provincial and the diocesan bishop, as also the assertion of legislative authority for the Provincial in virtue of a similar authority granted explicitly to the bishop by canon 335, § 1, cannot be upheld in its entirety. In the first place, the question of the jurisdictional powers of Superiors has not been overlooked in the Code, for it receives attention in one of the first canons to deal with religious Superiors. The actual existence of legislative authority in the office of the Provincial Superior is to be verified, not from the Code, but, according to canon 501, § 1, from the constitutions of the individual Orders.[15] The

[10] Michiels, *Normae Generales*, I, 141-142; 190; Chelodi, *Ius de Personis*, pp. 418-419.

[11] Cf. *supra*, p. 7.

[12] Can. 20.

[13] Can. 198, § 1.

[14] Can. 488, 8°.

[15] "Superiores et Capitula, ad normam constitutionum et iuris communis, potestatem habent dominativam in subditos; in religione autem clericali exempta, habent jurisdictionem ecclesiasticam tam pro foro interno, quam pro externo."

Code, therefore, leaves the question entirely to the particular law of the Order for settlement.

It has been seen above, however,[16] that the fullness of jurisdiction communicated by the Church to exempt Orders, inclusive of the legislative authority, was possessed by the General Chapters of the Orders alone.[17] Thus, in view of this former jurisprudence, an assertion of legislative authority for the Provincial would seem unwarranted if it were made without reference to the constitutions of the Order. This conclusion is particularly true since the present law is in perfect harmony with the former teachings, so that any justified departure from the former teachings cannot be alleged as a basis for the assertion of legislative authority, when canon 501, § 1, states so clearly that the jurisdiction of Superiors is to be determined according to the constitutions.

In consequence of the foregoing one may conclude that there is absolutely no incompatibility between the office of the Provincial Superior and the authority on his part to enact true laws. Rather, his position as Ordinary and Major Superior seems to favor a right analogous to that explicitly granted to the local Ordinary in canon 335, § 1. The actual existence of such authority, however, must be verified, in accordance with canon 501, § 1, in the particular constitutions of the Order.

3. *The Power of Precept.*

A precept may be defined as a command given to subjects by a competent authority. Preceptive power flows as a corollary from the principle that all societies require authoritative leadership.[18] Hence, even Superiors of non-exempt religious communities possess preceptive power as a result of the dominative power conceded to them in canon

[16] Cf. *supra*, p. 34.

[17] Cf. *supra*, pp. 34-35, for the exceptional privilege enjoyed by the Carmelite and Jesuit Generals.

[18] Cf. *supra*, p. 10.

501. Superiors of clerical exempt communities possess, in addition, jurisdiction in virtue of which they can impose jurisdictional precepts. Accordingly, precepts can be distinguished into two classes, namely, jurisdictional and dominative, according to the type of authority from which they flow.[19] The Provincial Superior of Regulars can issue precepts of either a dominative or a jurisdictional nature according as he makes use of his corresponding power of government.

Various differences between precepts and laws can be noted. A precept is directed towards individuals, while a law is imposed upon a community. The good to be attained through a precept is directly of a private and individual nature, while that sought through a law is the common good. A precept is imposed upon individuals and begets in the subject a personal obligation which binds everywhere, whereas the obligation of a law usually exists within territorial restrictions. Precepts may proceed from dominative or jurisdictional power, but laws are derived only from jurisdictional power possessed in a full and perfect degree.[20] Finally, the character of a precept is generally regarded as temporary, while that of a law is perpetual.[21]

Statutes or ordinances, such as those issued by the Provincial for the government of his province, cannot be considered laws when he lacks legislative authority.[22] They are, moreover, temporary in character and proceed from his pre-

[19] Michiels, *Normae Generales*, I, Appendix, 509; Vermeersch-Creusen, *Epitome*, I, n. 134.

[20] Cf. Chelodi, *Ius de Personis*, n. 70; Michiels, *Normae Generales*, I, 507; Maroto, *Institutiones Iuris Canonici ad Normam Novi Codicis* (2 vols., Romae-Barcinone-Matriti, 1919; Vol. I, 3. ed., 1921), I, n. 261 ff., (hereafter cited as *Institutiones*); Vermeersch-Creusen, *Epitome*, I, n. 31 ss; Pejška, *Ius Canonicum Religiosorum* (3. ed., Friburgi Brigoviae: Herder, 1927), p. 231.

[21] Cappello, *Summa Iuris Canonici*, I, p. 106, n. 102; Coronata, *Institutiones*, I, p. 47, n. 31.

[22] Cf. *supra*, pp. 35-37.

ceptive power, which thus works for the achievement of some particular good of the community.[23]

It is not clear whether canon 24 is applicable to the dominative precepts of a Superior.[24] It is the opinion of the writer that canon 24 refers only to jurisdictional precepts imposed upon individuals.[25]

The following two reasons are offered for this view: canon 24, though dealing with precepts, is placed at the end of the Title on Ecclesiastical Laws, and it expressly refers to the judicial enforcement of precepts when they are imposed by a document or before witnesses. Precepts of a dominative nature cannot be enforced judicially, though the fulfillment of them may be urged extra-judicially. Adherence to this view seems to conform to the treatment of the subject by the Code.

It is clear, then, that the Provincial Superior can impose jurisdictional precepts in virtue of his possession of public authority over his subjects. It remains now to analyze this power with regard to precepts imposed upon individual subjects and precepts imposed upon an entire community or the whole of a province.

A. Individual Precepts.

A precept imposed by the Provincial Superior upon a subject binds the individual everywhere with the effect of a personal law. The obligation ceases, however, with the

[23] Appeltern, *Compendium*, p. 379, qu. 429; Van Hove, *Commentarium Lovaniense in Codicem Iuris Canonici*, Vol. I, tom. I, *Prolegomena* (Mechliniae-Romae: H. Dessain, 1928), n. 66 (hereafter referred to as *Prolegomena*).

[24] "Praecepta, singulis data, eos quibus dantur, ubique urgent, sed iudicialiter urgeri nequent et cessant resoluto iure praecipientis, nisi per legitimum documentum aut duobus testibus imposita fuerint."

[25] Van Hove, *Commentarium Lovaniense in Codicem Iuris Canonici*, Vol. I, tom. II, *De Legibus* (Mechliniae-Romae; H. Dessain, 1930), p. 362, n. 356, (hereafter referred to as *De Legibus*); Cappello, *Summa Iuris Canonici*, I, p. 107, n. 104; Coronata, *Institutiones*, I, p. 49, n. 32; Clancy, *The Local Superior*, p. 45.

cessation of the authority of the Provincial Superior who imposed the precept, unless it be imposed canonically before witnesses or by means of a document. Thus, if the Provincial Superior wishes a particular precept to enjoin a lasting obligation, he must impose it in a document, the authenticity of which is unquestionable. In lieu of a document the Provincial may impose it, with the same effect, in the presence of two qualified witnesses.[26]

Relative to the manner in which it is imposed, the precept of the Provincial ceases with the loss of his authority unless the norms of canon 24 are followed. This is true despite the fact that the Provincial Superior who imposed the precept is re-elected after the cessation of the term during which he imposed the precept. As in the case of a law, the binding force depends upon the verification of the following conditions: the matter must be within the competence of the Provincial; it must be lawful and possible; and it must be made known to the subject.[27]

Through the medium of jurisdictional precepts compensation is made for the lack of legislative authority in the office of the Provincial, for through them he may impose personal and juridically binding obligations upon his subjects. By the constitutional law of the Mendicants, these are normally required to be temporary, since the Provincial's term of office is temporary. Permanent obligations can be imposed, however, in the manner prescribed by canon 24, although, even then, they remain within the competence of a successor to review, mitigate or abrogate. Similarly, recourse to the General is open as a means of relief.[28]

B. Common Precepts.

Common precepts, as the name indicates, are precepts imposed, not upon individuals considered singly, but upon

[26] Cf. can. 1757.

[27] Coronata, *Institutiones*, I, p. 49, n. 33.

[28] The relationship of the individual precept to penal legislation will be considered in Chapter XII.

groups or communities considered as collective units. Without attempting to settle the differences among the authors concerning the nature of the common precept and its distinction from a law,[29] one may state that a command which is imposed upon a community which is incapable of receiving a law, or by a Superior who does not enjoy legislative authority, lacks the character of a true law, since an essential requisite for the presence of a law is thus wanting either in the Superior, or in the community. If such a command, however, is imposed upon the community considered as a collective unit, the notion of a common precept is verified, since the command lacks the character of a law but, nevertheless, pertains to the necessary government of the community and is imposed by one endowed with public authority over the community.[30] Such a command with regard to the government of religious was frequently referred to as an *ordinance* by the pre-Code authors, who vindicated the right of the Provincial to issue it to his subjects collectively.[31]

Canon 24 seems to indicate a consideration of precepts imposed upon individuals through its use of the words "*praecepta, singulis data.*" Since there is nothing in this or the other canons of the Code, however, to deny the existence of common precepts, it can reasonably be said, in accordance with former jurisprudence, that the Provincial can impose commands or precepts upon groups considered collectively. Since he lacks legislative authority, unless it is explicitly granted by the constitutions, his collective commands which are necessary for the government of the province and are derived from his public authority will be endowed, not with

[29] Cf. Vermeersch-Creusen, *Epitome,* I, n. 135; Michiels, *Normae Generales,* I, 519-521; Coronata, *Institutiones,* I, p. 50, n. 33; Van Hove, *De Legibus,* nn. 93-100.

[30] Van Hove, *De Legibus,* n. 95.

[31] Lezana, *Summa Quaestionum Regularium,* Vol. I, pars. I, cap. XVIII, n. 90; Bouix, *De Jure Regularium,* 380-399; Bachofen, *Compendium Juris Regularis,* 228.

the character of law, but with the character of common precepts.

What is to be said of the temporary character of such precepts? Since they pertain to the necessary government of the community and are derived from a public authority, they will, of themselves, be temporary or permanent according to the will of the Superior, the text of the precept, or the nature of the command.[32] However, it will be necessary, in individual cases, to consult the particular constitutions to determine whether or not the authority to issue permanent ordinances is granted to the Provincial.

A general summary of the Provincial's power to issue precepts should note the following conclusions. His power in this respect is not only dominative but jurisdictional as well. His precepts to individuals are temporary, unless they are imposed in the proper juridic form which fortifies them with a perpetual obligation. Since the conditions for perpetuity must be verified in the imposition of collective precepts or ordinances that are intended to be perpetual, one must consult the constitutions to determine the conditions for their temporal or perpetual character whenever the mind of the Superior or the nature of the command does not plainly indicate a merely temporary obligation.

4. *The Power of Dispensation.*

Dispensation is defined as the relaxation of a law by a proper authority in a particular case and it can be granted by the lawmaker, his successor, his superior, or their delegates.[33] Thus the dispensatory power is primarily a function of legislative jurisdiction.

[32] Van Hove, *De Legibus*, n. 97; Vermeersch-Creusen, *Epitome*, I, n. 135.

[33] Can. 80: "Dispensatio, seu legis in casu speciali relaxatio, concedi potest a conditore legis, ab eius successore vel Superiore, nec non ab illo cui iidem facultatem dispensandi concesserint." Cf. also, c. 20, X, *de temporibus ordinationum et qualitate ordinandorum*, I, 11; c. 1, 2, *de filiis presbyterorum et aliis illegitime natis*, I, 11, in VI°; Benedictus XIV, ep. *Aestas*, 11 oct. 1757, § XI—*Fontes*, n. 556.

A. Dispensation from the General Laws of the Church

1) PRE-CODE LEGISLATION

Although in Decretal law inferior prelates possessed dispensatory powers, their authority over the general laws of the Church was allowed to operate solely in the cases tacitly or expressly admitted by the law.[34]

The Mendicants claimed certain powers of dispensation for their Prelates from their foundation as juridical institutes. The extent of the Provincial's power of dispensation as contained in the Decretals was sometimes defined by particular law. Thus, according to the Decretal law, Regular Prelates could permit the intellectually backward to be ordained,[35] but particular law reserved to the Provincial the granting of dispensations for ordinations.

Innocent III (1198-1216) established the guiding principle that only laws pertaining to the essence of the religious state were not susceptible to dispensation by Regular Prelates.[36] The Council of Trent confirmed the teaching that the essential laws of the religious life were beyond the quasi-episcopal jurisdiction of Regular Prelates.[37]

In the period after the Council of Trent, the Constitution "*Romani Pontificis*" of St. Pius V (1566-1572) offered the clearest enunciation of the power of Regular Prelates over the general laws of the Church, and formed the basis upon which pre-Code authors maintained as a general principle that the powers of Regular Prelates in the matter of dispensation were co-extensive with those of the bishop for their respective subjects. This Constitution explicitly stated that it gave the male religious Superiors of the Dominican Order, including the Local Superiors, all the faculties en-

[34] *Glossa ordinaria* ad c. 15, X, *de temporibus ordinationum et qualitate ordinandorum*, I, 11, s.v. *permissa*.

[35] C. 4, *de temporibus ordinationum et qualitate ordinandorum*, I, 9, in VI°.

[36] C. 6, *de statu monachorum*, III, 35.

[37] Sess. XXV, *de regularibus*, c. 1; Lezana, *Summa Quaestionum Regularium*, Vol. I, pars I, cap. XVIII, n. 54.

joyed by a bishop in relation to his subjects, whether the question was one of absolution or of dispensation.[38]

In view of the extant rule of the concurrent participation of all Regulars in whatever privilege was granted to one specific Order, all Regular Prelates obtained the same dispensatory powers.[39] Matters of frequent occurrence, such as the observance of fasts on feasts, and assistance at Mass, were within the dispensing competence of religious Prelates. The faculties to dispense, however, were to be exercised only in individual cases.[40] The religious Prelates themselves were not to be deprived of the benefits of such a use of jurisdiction, although it was generally held that they should dispense themselves indirectly through their confessors, even granting them faculties, if necessary, to give the dispensation desired.[41]

In extraordinary cases of grave and urgent need, Regular Prelates could dispense the entire community from an ecclesiastical law. Benedict XIV (1740-1758) emphasized, however, in his encyclical letter *"Non ambigimus"* of May 30, 1741, that a grave and urgent reason was necessary for such a general dispensation.[42]

It was also held by pre-Code authors that, like bishops,

[38] 21 iul. 1571: "Ipsi per se ipso idem omnino possint . . . in subditos, quod possunt Episcopi in clericos sibi subjectos, tam quoad absolvendi et dispensandi hujusmodi, quam alias quascumque facultates . . . etiam perpetuo concedimus, et indulgemus ac etiam declaramus."—*Bull Rom. Taur.*, VIII, 931; Piatus, *Praelectiones Iuris Regularis* (3. ed., 2 vols., Tornaci: 1906), I, qu. 752 (hereafter cited as *Praelectiones*).

[39] Lezana, *Summa Quaestionum Regularium*, Vol. I, pars I, cap. XVIII, n. 54; Donatus, *Rerum Regularium Praxis*, Tom. II, pars I, tr. X, qu. VI, 1; Suarez, *De Religione*, Lib. II, Cap. XII, n. 3; Van Etten, *Compendium Privilegiorum Regularium Praecipue Ordinis Eremitarum S. Augustini* (Romae; 1900), p. 128.

[40] S.C.C., 15 dec. 1725—*Fontes*, n. 3306.

[41] Lezana, *Summa Quaestionum Regularium*, Vol. I, pars I, cap. XVIII, n. 54; Donatus, *Rerum Regularium Praxis*, Tom. II, pars I, tr. XI, qu. VI, n. 1; Schmalzgrueber, *Ius Canonicum Ecclesiasticum*, Lib. I, Tit. II, n. 6, 1.

[42] Paragraph 3—*Fontes*, n. 308.

Regular Prelates could dispense in cases of doubt as to the need of a dispensation, since, according to Reiffenstuel, the reservation of the right to grant a dispensation implied a restriction of one's power, which restriction applied in only such cases wherein certainty existed that a dispensation was not needed.[43]

2) PRESENT LAW

For the first time in the common law the Provincial's position is declared to be that of an *Ordinary* and a *Major Superior.*[44] In this way the Code vindicates the earlier analogy drawn between the jurisdictional office of the diocesan bishop and the Provincial Superior. In general, therefore, the pre-Code principle holds today that the Provincial has the same jurisdiction for the dispensation of his subjects as that possessed by the diocesan Ordinary for his subjects, with the exception of those limitations which are placed by the Code.[45] Moreover, as Coronata notes,[46] the Provincial possesses additional privileges which in many Institutes have remained unrevoked by the general law. Thus, in relation to the general laws of the Church, the Provincial has whatever power of dispensation has been attached by the Code explicitly or implicitly to his office or that of a residential bishop, unless, in the latter case, an express limitation is placed by the Code or in consequence of the nature of the matter concerned.

Pre-Code legislation recognized the right of Ordinaries to dispense in urgent cases. This right now belongs to the Provincial in virtue of canon 81, which gives it to all Ordinaries, when the following conditions are verified: 1) the

[43] *Jus Canonicum Universum*, Lib. I, Tit. II, n. 474; Schmalzgrueber, *Ius Canonicum Ecclesiasticum*, Lib. I, Tit. II, n. 59, 4; Piat, *Praelectiones*, I, qu. 752.

[44] Cc. 198, § 1; 488, 8°.

[45] Cf. *supra*, pp. 43-44; can. 198, § 1, Schaefer, *De Religiosis*, p. 235. n. 110; Coronata, *Institutiones*, I, p. 124, n. 112; Vermeersch-Creusen, *Epitome*, I, n. 193.

[46] *Loc. cit.*

case is one in which the Holy See is accustomed to dispense; 2) recourse to the Holy See is difficult; 3) failure to dispense will probably be the source of grave injury to the subject.[47]

Other powers of dispensation recognized in the earlier jurisprudence as belonging to the Provincial have been adopted by the Code. The Provincial shares with the Local Superior the power to dispense from the observance, in individual cases, of feasts, fasts, abstinence, or both fast and abstinence.[48] Although canon 1245, § 1, limits the dispensation to individuals, or to individual families or groups, the Provincial can certainly dispense one or more entire communities in his province, when the proper cause exists, since each house can be considered as a family within the province.[49]

The Provincial likewise possesses, in common with the Local Superiors, rights to dispense or suspend the non-reserved vows of his subjects in virtue of canons 1313, 2°, and 1314, and also a similar power to dispense a subject from the obligations of a promissory oath, or to annul or commute them in accordance with canon 1320.[50]

Powers of dispensation peculiar to the Office of the Pro-

[47] Can. 81: "A generalibus Ecclesiae legibus Ordinarii infra Romanum Pontificem dispensare nequent, ne in casu quidem peculiari, nisi haec potestas eisdem fuerit explicite vel implicite concessa, aut nisi difficilis sit recursus ad Sanctam Sedem et simul in mora sit periculum gravis damni, et de dispensatione agatur quae a Sede Apostolica concedi solet."

[48] Can. 1245, § 1. In this paragraph the right is conferred upon the Provincial as an Ordinary, whereas paragraph 3 of the canon states that exempt clerical Superiors possess the same rights in these matters as pastors. Since pastors are also included in the possession of the rights listed in paragraph 1, it follows that local Superiors also possess these rights together with the Provincial, but only for the subjects of their house.

[49] Vermeersch-Creusen, *Epitome*, II, n. 556.

[50] Both these questions will be discussed later in this Chapter, pp. 51-53.

vincial, exclusive of the Local Superior, may be summarized as follows:

1) He can dispense from invalidating or incapacitating laws in cases which involve a doubt of fact, provided the Holy See is accustomed to grant a dispensation in the same matter. Thus, in a case of positive doubt as to the legitimacy of a subject's birth, the Provincial Superior could grant a dispensation for his admission to the novitiate, unless particular law reserves this right to a higher Superior.[51]

2) He can dispense from the observance of days of fast, abstinence and Sunday or holy day obligations, not only for individual subjects, but also for individual houses within the province, for, in the opinion of the writer, these are to be considered as individual families.[52]. Furthermore, he can dispense the entire province from the laws of fast or of abstinence, or of both, in consequence of a large gathering of his subjects, or for reasons of public health.[53]

One does not find this right universally alleged by the authors as one enjoyed by the Provincial in virtue of canon 1245, § 2. The express mention of the word *diocese* in canon 1245, § 2, could seem to exclude the Provincial. However, the present writer favors the affirmative view for the following reasons which can be alleged in its support. These are: a) the word *Ordinary* is used in canon 1245, § 2, without qualification in its designation of the authority to which this power is entrusted; b) the first and third paragraphs of this canon are clear in their designations of the respective competence of the local Ordinary and the religious Superior; the second paragraph, which presents the difficulty, should therefore designate the local Ordinary specifically if the lawgiver intended to exclude the religious Ordinary; c) the

[51] Can. 15.

[52] Can. 1245, § 1. Cf. also Vermeersch-Creusen, *Epitome*, II, n. 556.

[53] Can. 1245, § 2.

dispensatory rights granted to the religious Ordinary for his subjects were co-extensive with those of the diocesan Ordinary in the Constitution *"Romani Pontificis"* of St. Pius V, and therefore the application of the term Ordinary in canon 1245, § 2, to the Provincial does not seem to be necessarily excluded; for this view can be urged by pointing to the fact that pre-Code authors pointed to an analogy between the religious province and the diocese.[54]

Against this view, the strongest argument rests in the fact that the sources listed for canon 1245, § 2, are all taken from documents addressed to local Ordinaries.[55] According to the proponents of this view then, doubt as to the reservation of this right to the local Ordinary would thus seem to be excluded.[56]

3) The Provincial or his delegate may dispense his subjects from all irregularities incurred through an occult delict, except those resulting from voluntary homicide, abortion, or those which have been brought to the judicial forum.[57]

[54] Cf. *supra.*, p. 43; Fanfani, *De Iure Religiosorum ad Normam Codicis Iuris Canonici* (2. ed., Taurini-Romae: Marietti, 1925), p. 69 (hereafter cited *De Iure Religiosorum*); Biederlack-Führich, *De Religiosis* (Oeniponte: Rauch, 1919), pp. 59-60; Wernz-Vidal, *De Religiosis*, pp. 111-112, n. 133; Keene, *Religious Ordinaries and Canon 198*, p. 86.

[55] Benedictus XIV, ep. encycl. *Non ambigimus*, 30 maii, 1741, § 3 —*Fontes*, n. 308; ep. encycl. *In suprema*, 22 aug. 1741, § 2—*Fontes*, n. 314; S.C.S. Off., decr. 5 dec. 1894—*Fontes*, n. 1172; 18 mart. 1896—*Fontes*, n. 1176; S.C.C., litt. 3 maii 1912, n. 2°—*Fontes*, n. 4362. Cf. also, Keene, *Religious Ordinaries and Canon 198*, p. 86.

[56] Coronata, *Institutiones*, II, p. 821, n. 139; Claeys-Bouuaert—Simenon, *Manuale Juris Canonici ad Usum Seminariorum* (Vol. I, 3. ed., 1930; Vol. II, 1931; Vol. III, 3. ed. 1930, Gandae et Leodii: apud auctores in Seminariis Gandavensi et Leodiensi), I, 135 (hereafter cited as *Manuale Juris Canonici*); Woywod, "Law of the Code on Sacred Seasons,"—*The Homiletic and Pastoral Review*, XXVI (1926), 81, 946-954, 1050.

[57] Can. 990, § 1. For further discussion of his faculties in this regard, cf. *infra*, Chapter XI, pp. 210-212.

4) In occult cases the Provincial or his delegate can remit all *latae sententiae* penalties established by the common law and incurred by subjects, except those censures which are reserved in a special or most special manner to the Holy See. In public cases he can remit all such penalties except: (1) the cases already brought to the judicial forum; (2) censures reserved to the Holy See; (3) penalties declaring one ineligible for benefices, offices or dignities in the Church, or depriving one of active and passive electoral rights, or inflicting a perpetual suspension, infamy of law, or the privation of the right of patronage, or of a favor granted by the Holy See.[58]
5) In urgent cases the Provincial may dispense from the prohibition of individual books for individual subjects.[59]

Besides these faculties over the general laws of the Church, the Provincial may also use those which have been acquired by privilege or indult as long as they have not been revoked.[60]

In summary, then, the Provincial Superior's position in relation to his subjects in the matter of dispensation is truly quasi-episcopal, in virtue of which the faculties granted by the Code make him truly the proper pastor of the province.

B. Dispensation from Particular Laws of the Institute

1) Pre-Code Legislation

Innocent III (1198-1216) established the principle that laws pertaining to the essence of the religious life were beyond the dispensing power of the Provincial or other Regular Prelates.[61] This principle was confirmed by later legislation.[62]

At no time did the Provincial possess power to change the constitutions or the Rule of the Order. As *Praelatus Medius*

[58] Can. 2237, § § 1, 2.

[59] Can. 1402, § 1.

[60] Can. 4.

[61] Cf. *supra*, p. 43.

[62] Conc. Trident., Sess. XXV, *de regularibus*, c. 1; Lezana, *Summa Quaestionum Regularium*, Vol. I, pars I, cap. XVIII, n. 54.

he was inferior to the General who also lacked this power.[63] His power to dispense a community collectively from the observance of some point of the Rule or of the constitutions was also denied, since such a dispensation was alleged to be the equivalent of a change in the constitutions or the Rule.[64] Moreover, when the Rule or the constitutions forbade the granting of a dispensation, the power of the Provincial was restricted.[65] Otherwise, the Provincial could dispense individual subjects according to their needs, if particular law did not reserve this power in a specific point to the General.[66]

2) Present Law

Certain specific cases allowing for a dispensation from the particular law of the institute are mentioned by the Code as being within the competence of the Provincial Superior. Thus canon 589, § 2, gives him, as well as the Local Superior, the right to exempt subjects in particular cases from certain community acts as often as it is necessary for the fostering of studies. Canon 596 leaves to Major Superiors, and therefore to the Provincial as well as to the General, the judgment of the gravity of the reason for excusing a subject from wearing the habit. For a just and grave cause, in virtue of canon 606, § 2, he, as well as the Local Superior, can dispense one from living the common life for a period of six months or less, or also for a longer period, if absence from the monastery be required in the pursuit of studies.

The mention of these instances serves as an illustration of the powers granted by the Code to the Provincial in the matter of dispensation. Moreover, it may be that the constitutions of the institute will reserve other specific items to the power of the Provincial for dispensation.

[63] Lezana, *ibid.*, n. 22.

[64] Lezana, *ibid.*, n. 23; Donatus, *Rerum Regularium Praxis*, Tom. II, pars I, tr. XI, qu. III, 2.

[65] Donatus, *loc. cit.*

[66] Suarez, *De Religione*, Lib. II, Cap. XII, n. 25 ss.

If the constitutions and the Rule are approved *in forma specifica* by the Holy See, they become true pontifical laws. In such a case there is room for the application of canon 81 as with relation to the general laws of the Church.

In general, the Provincial and other Superiors can also dispense individuals in minor points of observance which do not pertain to the essential status of the particular Order, since, as Goyeneche asserts, authors commonly held and should hold today, that Regular Prelates enjoy a certain tacit authority to dispense in these minor matters, unless they have been expressly forbidden to do so.[67]

The present legislation regarding the dispensatory powers of the Provincial is in harmony with the former legislation and jurisprudence in the matter of the Rule and the constitutions. His office is primarily intended to promote their observance. Certain specific cases are enumerated for his dispensatory powers. If the Rule and the constitutions have been approved *in forma specifica,* he can use the extraordinary faculties of canon 81. Besides these the common teaching of canonists grants him power to dispense individuals in minor points of observance. Particular law may further specify his individual rights over that law. In all other instances, he is subject to the Rule and the constitutions and accordingly cannot dispense from their observance.

C. Dispensation from Vows and Oaths

1) Pre-Code Legislation

In virtue of the law of Innocent III (1198-1216), which in the period before the Council of Trent prohibited all Prelates inferior to the Pope from granting a dispensation relative to the essential laws of religious life,[68] Regular Superiors were unable to dispense their subjects from the essential vows of the religious life. Non-reserved vows,

[67] Goyeneche, "Consultationes"—*CpR,* III (1922), 55; Schaefer, *De Religiosis,* p. 240, n. 113; Vermeersch-Creusen, *Epitome,* I, n. 193.
[68] Cf. *supra,* p. 43.

however, which did not pertain to the essence of the religious state, could be relaxed by dispensation or commutation on the part of all Regular Superiors.[69]

Similarly in the period before the Council of Trent Regular prelates could dispense or commute their subjects' obligations resulting from promissory oaths.[70]

The Council of Trent confirmed the earlier teaching that dispensation from the vows of the religious state was reserved to the Holy Father or his delegate.[71] Subsequent to this Council non-reserved vows which did not pertain to the essence of the religious state could be relaxed by dispensation or commutation on the part of all Regular Prelates, as in the period before the Council of Trent.[72] The former teaching with regard to the obligations resulting from promissory oaths was maintained, so that Regular Prelates could relax or commute them, provided only that the rights of a third party were not violated.[73]

2) Present Law

The Code follows the jurisprudence of the pre-Code days in the fact that it does not restrict the rights of any particular Superior, but grants dispensatory power over oaths and vows to Regular Superiors in general. Hence, such rights are possessed cumulatively by Major and Minor Superiors, although particular law may reserve them to the Provincial or the General.

In virtue of canon 1313, 2°, Regular Superiors can dis-

[69] C. 1, X, *de voto et voti redemptione,* III, 34; C. 5, *de regularibus et transeuntibus ad religionem,* III, 14, in VI°.

[70] C. 19, X, *de iureiurando,* II, 24.

[71] Sess. XXV, *de regularibus,* c. 1.

[72] Suarez, *De Religione,* Lib. II, Cap. XII, n. 10; Lezana, *Summa Quaestionum Regularium,* Vol. I, pars I, cap. XVIII, n. 54; S.C.S. Off. (Novae Aureliae), 2 aug. 1876—*Fontes,* n. 1048; S.C. de Prop. Fide (C.G.), 24 aug. 1885—*Fontes,* n. 4912; Bouix, *De Jure Regularium,* II, 475.

[73] Lezana, *Summa Quaestionum Regularium,* Vol. I, pars I, cap. XVIII, n. 53.

pense all who fall under their jurisdiction[74] from non-reserved vows whenever a just cause is had, and provided the rights of a third party are not injured. The pre-Code limitation of this power with regard to the essential vows of religion still exists, since these vows, by their very nature, are public, and are thus reserved to the Holy See in virtue of their public acceptance by the Superior in the name of the Church.[75] Reserved also are the private vows of perfect and perpetual chastity and the vow to enter an institute of solemn vows, if pronounced absolutely by one who has completed the eighteenth year of age.[76]

Regular Superiors who can dispense from non-reserved vows can also modify or even lighten their obligation by commutation if a cause exists for such a commutation, even when the cause is not sufficient to justify the granting of a dispensation.[77]

Canon 1320 renews the pre-Code legislation with regard to the power of Regular Superiors to dispense from oaths. Superiors who can relax non-reserved vows of subjects by dispensation or commutation can do the same with regard to the promissory oaths of subjects. However, if the obligation of the oath involves the right of a third party, only the Holy See can dispense from it or commute it when the third party refuses to cede his right.

In the matter of the power of relaxing vows and oaths by dispensation or commutation, the Provincial possesses, by the common law, the identical competence of other Regular Prelates. Ordinarily the jurisdiction involved in dispensing subjects from their vows or oaths, or in commuting them, is exercised by the immediate Local Superior rather than by the Provincial. The right, however, is a cumulative right, which either the latter or the Local Superior may exercise.

[74] Cf. can. 514, § 1: "... professis, novitiis, aliisve in religiosa domo diu noctuque degentibus causa famulatus, aut hospitii aut infirmae valetudinis ..."

[75] Beste, *Introductio*, p. 642. [76] Can. 1309. [77] Can. 1314.

CHAPTER V

THE JUDICIAL POWER OF THE PROVINCIAL SUPERIOR

Judicial power is a function of jurisdiction in virtue of which a Superior declares authentically whether the actions of his subjects conform to law, and defines the legal effects following from this conformity or lack of it.[1] As the Ordinary and Major Superior of the province, the Provincial Superior possesses judicial power, the origins of which may be traced to the historical foundation of his office.

1. *Pre-Code Legislation*

Decretal references show that Regular Prelates possessed judicial power whereby they could inflict canonical censures upon their subjects.[2] A reply of Alexander III (1159-1181) to a certain abbot is worthy of note. It not only helps establish the fact of the possession of the power to inflict canonical penalties, but also concerns itself with the effect of appeal against sentences inflicting them. Alexander III advised the abbot to punish subjects according to the rules and institutes of his Order, and thereupon also to take judicial cognizance of the suspensive effect of an appeal only if the rules and institutes justified it, since an appeal was not to be recognized as a means of showing favor to delinquents.[3] From this it appears that the seeking of redress through the lodging of an appeal was accompanied with a

[1] "Ius authentice declarandi quaenam subditorum actiones sunt juri conformes et quaenam difformes, simulque statuendi effectus legitimos huius conformitatis vel difformitatis."—Cappello, *Summa Iuris Publici Ecclesiastici* (ed. altera, Romae: 1928), p. 74, n. 65.

[2] C. 26, X, *de accusationibus, inquisitionibus et denuntiationibus*, V, 1; c. 2, *de verborum significatione*, V, 11, in Clem.; c. 24, X, *de regularibus et transeuntibus ad religionem*, III, 31.

[3] *Glossa ordinaria* ad c. 3, X, *de appellationibus, recusationibus, et relationibus*, II, 28, s.v. *nostram.*

suspensive effect only when the particular law permitted it, or when the penalty was manifestly unjust.

In virtue of a privilege granted by Boniface VIII (1294-1303) to the Order of Preachers, and subsequently shared in by the other Orders, Regular Prelates were not obliged, when punishing their subjects, to follow a strict judicial procedure in all its fullness; it sufficed that its substantial elements were observed.[4] In cases of a specially serious nature, such as involved suspension or excommunication, a previous canonical warning was necessary unless the nature of the crime itself demanded a given penalty.[5] If Prelates abused their judicial power by threatening penalties for revealing their negligences, they, in turn, were to be punished.[6]

Particular law in the Dominican Order vindicated for the Local Superior as well as for the Provincial the power of inflicting censures.[7] The Carmelite Constitutions granted the power specifically to the Provincial, and even to Local Superiors with the consent of the majority of the community under his rule, provided that the majority represented the older members of his house.[8]

As noted, then, in the period before the Council of Trent Regular Prelates, including Local Superiors, possessed judicial power, although particular law in some cases reserved

[4] C. 24, X, *de accusationibus, inquisitionibus, et denuntiationibus*, V, 1; Bonifatius VIII, const. *Ad augmentum*, 10 maii, 1296—*Bull. Rom. Taur.*, I, 134; Reiffenstuel, *Jus Canonicum Universum*, Lib. V, Tit. I, n. 319.

[5] C. 26, X, *de appellationibus, recusationibus, et relationibus*, II, 28; Schroeder, *Disciplinary Decrees*, p. 252.

[6] C. 4, *de officio iudicis ordinarii*, I, 16, in VI°; Potthast, *Regesta*, n. 24310.

[7] Bonifatius VIII, const. *Ad augmentum*, 10 maii, 1296—*Bull. Rom. Taur.*, I, 134.

[8] *Monumenta Historica Carmelitana* (Vol.I, Continens Antiquas Ordinis Constitutiones, ed. Benedictus Zimmerman, Lirinae, 1907), I, 64-65. Hereafter reference to the ancient Constitutions in this work will be made by referring to the title of the work, namely, *Monumenta Carmelitana*.

it to the Provincial or the General. Authors after the Council of Trent held that judicial power belonged to Regular Prelates to be exercised as a necessary adjunct of their office lest their institute be without penal sanction.[9] Judicial power, however, was not regarded by them as an exclusive function of the Provincial's office. Rather, it was held that all Regular Prelates were endowed with the right to proceed as inquisitors against their subjects, to hear their causes, to correct and to punish their delicts and to inflict penalties. The use of such judicial power was not limited to a particular territory, and hence it could be exercised throughout the world, if necessary.[10] Particular law established the scope of the judicial power of the various prelates. Thus each had the right and duty to judge his own subjects in accordance with the particular law of his institute. For example, the Provincial of the Carmelites incurred an excommunication if he failed to depose a negligent Local Superior.[11] However, unless the particular law stated the contrary, the Provincial as well as the Local and General Superiors could function as ordinary judges.[12]

The common law restricted the judicial power of Regular Prelates in certain cases. Thus the religious residing in smaller houses were subject to the judicial power of bishops in disciplinary matters whenever the number of members

[9] Lezana, *Summa Quaestionum Regularium,* Vol. I, pars I, cap. XVIII, n. 17; Lega, *Praelectiones in Textum Iuris Canonici, de Iudiciis Ecclesiasticis* (4 vols., Romae: 1896-1901), IV, n. 500; Piat, *Praelectiones,* I, qu. 772, nota 6.

[10] Schmalzgrueber, *Ius Ecclesiasticum Universum,* Lib. I, Tit. XXXI, nn. 23, 26; Reiffenstuel, *Jus Canonicum Universum,* Lib. V, Tit. I, n. 313 ss; Bouix, *De Jure Regularium,* II, 439; Lezana, *Summa Quaestionum Regularium,* Vol. I, pars I, cap. XXVII.

[11] Clemens VII, const. *Pro statu religiosorum,* 15 mart. 1526—*Bullarium Carmelitanum* (4 vols., Romae: Vols. I-II, ed. E. Monsignano, 1715—1718; Vols. III-IV, ed. I. A. Ximenez, 1768), II, 24 (hereafter cited *Bull. Carm.*); *Monumenta Carmelitana,* p. 64.

[12] Lezana, *Summa Quaestionum Regularium,* Vol. I, pars I, cap. XVIII, 16 ss.

assigned to the house was less than twelve.[13] The Council of Trent,[14] and later also Gregory XV (1621-1623),[15] subjected Regulars to bishops in matters pertaining to the care of souls. Likewise, the jurisdiction of Regular Prelates was completely withdrawn in matters pertaining to heresy and the inquisition regarding it.[16]

Despite privileges[17] the post-Tridentine jurisprudence held that Regular Prelates were to preserve the substantial elements of judicial procedure.[18]

A restriction established by particular law which affected the exercise of judicial power by Regular Superiors was exemplified in the Carmelite Constitutions. These indicated that to the Provincial Superior, as the designated official Visitator of the province, was reserved the right of proceeding judicially at the time of visitation.[19]

2. *Present Law*

Canon 1579, § 1, clarifies the teaching of the pre-Code period regarding the judge of first instance. In controversies between exempt religious, unless the constitutions rule otherwise, the competent judge is the Provincial Superior.[20] Thus the possibility of the Local Superior's acting as judge of first instance is not excluded, although in the absence of such a provision by particular law the Provincial

[13] Urbanus VIII, const. *Cum saepe contingat,* 21 iun. 1625—*Bull. Rom. Taur.,* XIII, p. 336; Innocentius XII, const. *Nuper,* 23 dec. 1697—*Fontes,* n. 260; *Bull. Rom. Taur.,* XX, p. 806.

[14] Sess. XXV, *de regularibus,* c. 11.

[15] Const. *Inscrutabili,* 5 febr. 1622—*Fontes,* n. 199; *Bull. Rom. Taur.,* XII, p. 656.

[16] Paulus V, const. *Romanus Pontifex,* 1 sept. 1606—*Fontes,* n. 194; *Bull. Rom. Taur.,* XI, p. 346.

[17] *Supra,* p. 55.

[18] Schmalzgrueber, *Ius Ecclesiasticum Universum,* Lib. II, Tit. IV, n. 3; Donatus, *Rerum Regularium Praxis,* Tom. III, tr. XII, cop. II, 1 ss.

[19] Lezana, *Summa Quaestionum Regularium,* Vol. I, pars I, cap. XXVII, n. 1.

[20] Can. 1579, § 1.

is designated for that office by the general law. In the event that the Provincial performs the office of judge in the first instance in accordance with canon 1579, § 1, the General becomes the judge of second instance by reason of canon 1594, § 4. If particular law departs from the general legislation regarding the judge of the first instance, however, it should, for the sake of consistency, determine the judge of second instance. Thus, for example, if the Local Superior of an institute is the judge of first instance in accordance with the particular law of the institute, the court of second instance should be held before the judge whom the constitutions designate as the one immediately superior to him who acted in the first instance.[21]

The Provincial Superior is competent as ordinary judge in controversies between two houses of the same province, between two religious of the same province, or between a religious and a house of the same province. If a controversy arises between religious of the same Order but of different provinces, the Provincial of the party called into trial is the competent judge, since the plaintiff follows the court of the party convened.[22]

The General Superior, however, is the competent judge to decide a controversy between two provinces, unless the constitutions rule otherwise.[23] Since the Provincial is the ordinary judge, he may delegate this office to another.[24] When he does this, he should designate or constitute a notary, since

[21] Noval, *Commentarium Codicis Iuris Canonici,* Lib. IV, *De Processibus* (2 vols., pars I, *De Iudiciis,* 1920; Pars II, *De Causis Beatificationis Servorum Dei et Canonizationis Beatorum,* 1932; Pars IV, *De Modo Procedendi in Nonnullis Expediendis Negotiis vel Sanctionibus Poenalibus Applicandis,* 1932; Augustae Taurinorum-Romae, Marietti), Pars I, *De Iudiciis,* p. 88, n. 156 (hereafter cited *De Iudiciis*).

[22] Cans. 1559, § 3; 1579, § 2; Beste, *Introductio,* ad can. 1579, p. 768; Vermeersch-Creusen, *Epitome,* III, n. 39; Schaefer, *De Religiosis,* n. 394.

[23] Can. 1579, § 2.

[24] Can. 199, § 1.

only a Major Superior can do this, and the presence of such an official is required at the trial.[25]

Selection from among his subjects of assistant judges,[26] promoters of justice,[27] and auditors,[28] may be made by the Provincial. He is subject to the rules of the Code in conducting the process. Thus, the prescriptions of the Fourth Book on procedure, the Fifth Book on penalties, and the Second Book on the dismissal of religious must be followed. Contrary privileges permitting him to proceed in summary fashion without the formalities of judicial procedure are revoked.[29] Thus the Provincial is bound by the prescriptions of the Code as it affects the appointment and the employment of judges. He must take the oath of office to fulfill his duty faithfully and properly before proceeding as judge. This is to be done in the presence of the notary of the tribunal.[30] Nothing is said in the Code regarding the place of judgment, and therefore the Provincial is free to determine it.

Limitations on his judicial competence are placed by the Code. Thus, despite contrary privileges or customs which are now reprobated by the Code, a tribunal of three judges must be established in criminal causes when it is a question of inflicting or declaring a sentence of excommunication.[31]

For the constitution of collegiate tribunals, particular law will generally require the associate judges to be taken from the Provincial's council. The Provincial may also commit

25 Cans. 503; 1585.

25 Cans. 503; 1585.

27 Cans. 1586; 1589.

28 Can. 1580, § 2.

29 Capobianco, *Privilegia et Facultates Ordinis Fratrum Minorum* (Salerno: 1946), p. 59.

30 Coronata (*Institutiones*, III, p. 58, n. 1149, nota 7) cites Torrubiano as stating that the oath need only be taken the first time, although, as Coronata observes, this contradicts Noval (*De Iudiciis*, p. 126, n. 208), who requires the oath each time the ordinary judge of a religious Order acts.

31 Can. 1576, § 1, 1°.

to a tribunal of five judges the judgment of even other cases of a serious nature.[32] A restriction of the judicial power of the Provincial is also noted in canon 501, § 2, which removes entirely from his jurisdiction cases pertaining to the Holy Office.[33]

Other rights in relation to trials, such as the granting of permission to his subjects to act as plaintiff,[34] procurator or advocate,[35] or arbiter,[36] are possessed by the Provincial either in common with the Local Superior, if the constitutions permit such powers to the latter, or, to the exclusion of the Local Superior, if the constitutions refer these matters to the Provincial. In trials pertaining to the beatification and canonization of Saints, the Provincial, and also the Local Superior, must provide that their subjects testify in the process, if it is their duty to do so.[37] In the beatification cause of a member of his province, the Provincial must cause to be published in his province the edict requesting the transmission of all the writings of the servant of God to the tribunal collecting them, which duty also devolves on the Local Superior with regard to his subjects.[38]

The judicial powers of the Provincial in relation to the dismissal of religious will be discussed in a later chapter.[39]

[32] Can. 1576, § 2.
[33] Cans. 501, § 2; 247.
[34] Can. 1652.
[35] Cans. 1657, § 3; 1658, § 4.
[36] Can. 193.
[37] Can. 2026.
[38] Cans. 2025, § 2; 2043, § 2.
[39] Cf. *infra*, pp. 161-162.

PART III

THE EXECUTIVE POWER OF THE PROVINCIAL SUPERIOR

Executive power is a function of jurisdiction which confers rights of an administrative and coercive nature. Most of the activities of the Provincial Superior can be classified in one of these categories of executive power. The legislative and judicial functions of his office were examined in previous chapters. The remaining rights and duties of the Provincial are derivations of his executive power, and will be examined in this third part of the study. In general, the order of treatment will follow that of the Code.

CHAPTER VI

THE PROVINCIAL SUPERIOR AS EXECUTIVE HEAD OF THE PROVINCE

Though the whole of the common law in the tract *De Religiosis* touches on the executive functions of the Provincial, Chapter I, *"De Superioribus et de Capitulis,"* of Title X establishes a number of regulations which may be regarded as affecting the Provincial more specifically in his position as the executive head of the province. Here, for instance, the Code commands the Provincial Superior to observe residence, whence his influence may go out to the houses under his jurisdiction. As the executive head of the province he must relay to his subjects the decrees of the Holy See. He must be guided by the counsel of an advisory council. He must enforce regular discipline by means of canonical visitation, salutary correction, word, example, and prayer. Each of these matters will now be considered in detail.

1. *Residence*

Canon 508 states that all Superiors should reside in the house assigned for them, and should not absent themselves from it except in accordance with the reasons and time established in the constitutions. In the precedence given to this brief injunction over the other obligations of Superiors, the fundamental importance attached by the Church to the residence of Superiors is abundantly stressed.

It has been shown that a higher Superior should not persistently reserve to himself the jurisdictional powers of his subordinate.[1] Besides derogating from the common law, such procedure would handicap religious subjects, since their easy access to the higher Superior for their needs might not always be available. Analogously, the subject-Superior relationship of religious societies demands that the more closely the exercise of jurisdiction approaches the individual subjects, the more strictly is this canon on residence to be interpreted. For that reason the obligation of residence on the part of Local Superiors has always been strictly imposed by papal legislation,[2] and specifically determined in particular law.

In accordance with canon 508, the Provincial Superior should reside at the provincial house. The purpose of his office is to supervise the direction and management of the province as a subordinate unit in the Order.[3] The nature of his office, accordingly, requires a determined residence within the confines of the province.

Reasons justifying his absence from this house are to be judged according to the specifications of particular law and the needs of the province. The task of promoting the common good of the province, the duty of visitation, the responsibility of an act of extraordinary administrative supervision and the like can repeatedly demand the absence of the

[1] Cf. *supra*, pp. 21 ff.

[2] C. 10, *de statu monachorum vel canonicorum regularium*, III, 10, in Clem.

[3] Can. 488, 6°.

Provincial from the provincial house. Hence the interpretation of the obligation of residence in a particular *house* cannot be a completely rigorous one unless particular law requires it. But a fully rigorous interpretation is to be applied when the absence involves his leaving the province.[4] Unless such absence is required by the good of the province, particular law frequently demands the permission of the General.[5]

No definite time during which the Provincial may absent himself either from the house or from the province is established by the Code, as it is established in the case of the diocesan bishop.[6] Particular law should determine this period. As in the case of the Local Superior, however, the very nature of the Provincial's office demands that he designate a Vicar for the period of his absence, if particular law does not thus provide for the needs of his subjects.

Negligence in the observance of the law of residence by the Provincial can be punished by the General according to the gravity of the delinquency. Accordingly, the General may oblige him to residence under threat of penalty to be administered in the manner of a precept,[7] or, if his negligence in fulfilling this law has been most serious or has furnished the occasion of serious scandal, the General may punish him according to canon 2222, § 1. Larraona states that the privation of office established in canon 2381, 2°, for non-resident secular clerics may be used as a norm in inflicting penalties for such offenses, even to the extent of removal from office, unless the constitutions forbid such a measure. Great care must be taken however in the matter of abiding by the norms enacted in canons 20 and 2219, § 3, so that there will be no transgression of the principle which precludes the application of laws enacted in similar matters when the question of applying penalties is involved.[8]

[4] Cans. 19; 508.

[5] Larraona, "Commentarium Codicis"—*CpR,* VIII (1927), 167.

[6] Can. 338, § 2. [7] Can. 2381, 2°.

[8] Larraona, "Commentarium Codicis"—*CpR,* VIII (1927), 165 ff.

Though neglect of the law of residence is a breach of the *common life,* it is such only in the broad sense of the term, since the observance of the common life relates strictly to the sharing in common of the community of goods.[9] Neglect in the matter of residence cannot, therefore, be construed as a violation of the common life punished in canon 2389, even to the extent of deprivation of vote and office. For in penal matters the terms of the law must be interpreted strictly.[10]

The Provincial Superior, in turn, has an obligation to enforce the residence of Local Superiors. It is not in keeping with his office and the well-being of his province to be negligent in this matter, and the prescriptions of particular law in this respect are to be carefully enforced by him. He may even be obliged to remove subordinate Prelates from office for their failure to comply with the law of residence. This penalty may be inflicted as an *ab homine* derived penalty after the example illustrated in canon 2381, 2°.[11]

2. *Enforcement of the Decrees of the Holy See*

Canon 509 states that every Superior must provide that the decrees of the Holy See pertaining to religious are promulgated and carefully observed by his religious subjects. The canon further obliges Local Superiors to have certain documents read annually in their houses, and also to provide proper catechetical instructions for resident lay-brothers and lay members of the household. The obligations enacted in this canon rest primarily on the Local Superiors. It is the duty of the Provincial to investigate the observance of these injunctions during the annual visitation and his periodic visits to the houses of his province.

[9] Smith, *The Penal Law for Religious,* The Catholic University of America Canon Law Studies, n. 98 (Washington, D. C.; The Catholic University Of America, 1935), p. 124, footnote 4; Clancy, *The Local Superior,* p. 58; Schaefer, *De Religiosis,* n. 337, p. 697.

[10] Cans. 19; 2219, § 1, § 3; Smith, *loc. cit.*; Clancy, *loc. cit.*

[11] Larraona, "Commentarium Codicis"—*CpR,* VIII (1927), 166.

Moreover, under the first paragraph of the canon, the Provincial seems obliged to call the attention of the Local Superior to the decrees or documents and to direct him to inform his subjects of them. As Vermeersch (1858-1936) noted, the enacted obligation is a personal one and requires the absolute fulfillment of the law. On the other hand, the obligation enacted in the second paragraph of canon 509 is not a personal one, and can moreover be satisfied by means of an observance which allows moral interruptions, so that, for example, catechetical instructions and pious exhortations may be omitted on holidays.[12] When the Local Superior is found to be negligent in fulfilling his personal obligation, it devolves as a personal obligation on the Provincial.

Regarding the catechetical instructions and the pious exhortations required of the Local Superiors, the matter of administrating them is strictly a right and an obligation of the Local Superior with which the Provincial cannot interfere, but the observance of which he must enforce in virtue of his office.

3. *Other Personal Obligations*

The principal duty of a Superior is to watch over the regular discipline, and to exert every effort that his subjects may attain the primary and secondary ends to the achievement of which their community must tend.[13] The obligations thus imposed upon the Provincial require him to promote the common good of both his province and his Order. Adequate provision for the fulfillment of this obligation can be made by personal example both in word and deed, by canonical visitation, by the proper and necessary correction of his brethren, and by personal prayers for his subjects.

A. Personal Example in Act and Word

In providing for the election of Major Superiors in communities of men, canon 506, § 1, requires that the electors

[12] Vermeersch-Creusen, *Epitome*, I, n. 630; Larraona, *ibid.*, p. 170.
[13] Pejška, *Ius Canonicum Religiosorum*, p. 232.

bind themselves under oath to elect worthy candidates. It has also been seen above[14] that the more fully the candidate for the office of Provincial Superior possesses the qualifications required in candidates for the episcopate,[15] the more closely will he meet the mind of the Church which has designated him an Ordinary.[16] The Code presupposes, then, that the Provincial Superior is an exemplary religious. Spiritual writers list as the chief means for winning the religious observance of subjects the good example of the Superior.[17] This will be readily admitted by all students of human behavior; it needs no further elaboration.

B. Canonical Visitation

Major Superiors designated by the constitutions of the particular Order are required to conduct canonical visitations personally, or, if they are lawfully impeded, through a delegate.[18] In many constitutions this duty is imposed upon the Provincial as the head of a province. The canonical visitation is one of the principal means for the due promotion of the regular observance. Its scope and purpose are defined by canon 343, § 1, which states as its objective the preservation of sound and orthodox doctrine, the safeguarding of good morals, the correction of abuses, and the promotion of peace, innocence and piety. It involves a careful investigation into the general administration and discipline of each house.[19] Regulars have utilized it to advantage from the earliest days of their foundation as Orders.

1) Pre-Code Legislation

Canon 12 of the IV Lateran Council (1215) prescribed the appointment at triennial chapters of canonical visitators

[14] Cf. *supra*, pp. 25 ff.
[15] Can. 331.
[16] Can. 198, § 1.
[17] Appeltern, *Compendium*, p. 406, qu. 460.
[18] Can. 511.
[19] Wernz-Vidal, *De Religiosis*, p. 122, n. 144.

who would have power to inflict canonical penalties for the perfecting of religious observance and the punishment of abuses.[20] Such visitators were to act with pontifical authority as delegates of the Holy See.[21]

The particular law of the Mendicants, approved after this decree, directed the Provincial to conduct his visitation either personally or through a delegate.[22] His position as proper pastor of the province made him responsible for his subjects, since an account of their souls would be required of him at judgment.[23] Moreover, the Carmelite Constitutions not only made the visitation a special prerogative of the Provincial, but also prohibited the General from sending visitators to a province unless these were sought by the Provincial Superior or the Provincial Chapter. Till the time of the Council of Trent the right of visitation belonged to the Provincial, unless the particular law provided otherwise.

The Council of Trent did not relieve the Provincial of the obligation of conducting visitation. It exhorted Superiors in general to use all care and diligence in providing for the observance of the Rule and constitutions.[24] More specifically it decreed that Superiors who are not subject to bishops,

[20] C. 7, 8, X, *de statu monachorum et regularium*, III, 35; Hefele, *Histoire des Conciles* (translated from the 2nd German edition by H. Leclercq, 10 vols. in 19, Paris: Letouzey et Ané, 1907-1938), V (2) 886 (hereafter cited as Hefele); Mansi, *Sacrorum Conciliorum Nova et Amplissima Collectio* (53 vols. in 60, Parisiis, Arnhem, Lipsiae, 1901-1927), XXII, 999 (hereafter cited as Mansi); Schroeder, *Disciplinary Decrees of the General Councils* Text, Translation, and Commentary (St. Louis: Herder, 1937), p. 253 (hereafter cited as *Disciplinary Decrees*).

[21] *Glossa ordinaria* ad c. 7, X, *de statu monachorum et regularium*, III, 35, s.v., *vice nostra*.

[22] *Monumenta Carmelitana*, p. 64; Holzapfel, *Manuale Historiae Ordinis Fratrum Minorum* (Friburgi Brisgoviae, 1909), pp. 124, 156.

[23] "Ne sanguis eorum de manibus suis requiratur."—c. 13, X, *de officio iudicis ordinarii*, I, 31; Schroeder, *Disciplinary Decrees*, p. 247.

[24] Sess. XXV, *de regularibus*, c. 1; Schroeder, *Canons and Decrees of the Council of Trent*, Original text with English translation (St. Louis: Herder, 1941), p. 218 (hereafter cited as *Canons and Decrees*).

"but have a lawful jurisdiction over other inferior monasteries or priories, shall, each in his own locality and Order, visit *ex officio* those monasteries and priories that are subject to them . . ."[25]

Authors after the Council of Trent agreed with the earlier writers regarding the purpose of the visitation. Their position was neatly summarized in the words of Reiffenstuel. He stated that visitation was instituted so that the prelate, like a pastor, might correct the delinquents of his flock and restore regular observance.[26] Similarly they agreed that it was a duty to be performed by the Provincial, with Reiffenstuel asserting that this was *common* and *certain* doctrine.[27] Reiffenstuel taught that the Provincial should perform this duty twice or at least once a year.[28] Piat (1815-1904), on the other hand, maintained that it could not be determined from the common low how frequently the visitation should be conducted by Regular Prelates, and that any such specification was rather to be sought from the particular law.[29] Neglect in the fulfillment of this obligation was considered a transgression against the virtue of justice, since it was a neglect of the duties of office.[30]

During the time of the visitation the government of the monastery pertained, not to the local prelate, but to the Visitator.[31] Lezana (†1659) stated that this pointed to a

[25] *Ibid.*, c. 20; Schroeder, *Canons and Decrees*, pp. 229-230.

[26] Reiffenstuel: " . . . tamquam pastor vultum pecoris sui cognoscens, delinquentes contra regularem observantiam et disciplinam, aliasque obligationes corrigere, castigare, et emendare; bene ambulantes vero praemiare, ac quemvis juxta qualitates et merita promovere, media convenientia contra defectus, vel excessus praescribere; sicque observantiam et disciplinam regularem restituere, conservare et augere, valeat."—*Jus Canonicum Universum*, Lib. V, tit. I, n. 271.

[27] *Ibid.*, n. 272; Lezana, *Summa Quaestionum Regularium*, Vol. I, pars I, cap. XVIII, n. 92; Piat, *Praelectiones*, I, qu. 789.

[28] *Ibid.*, n. 275.

[29] *Praelectiones*, I, qu. 789.

[30] Lezana, *Summa Quaestionum Regularium*, Vol. I, pars I, cap. XVIII, n. 15.

[31] Lezana, *op. cit.*, Vol. I, pars II, cap. XIII, n. 28.

quite natural arrangement, since otherwise confusion might result from the fact that two authorities would be placed over the subjects at the same time.

If during the course of the ordinary visitation occult faults or crimes of a subject were disclosed, the Visitator could apply only such penal remedies which did not occasion any defamation for the delinquent. There could rarely be justification for him to proceed judicially against a delinquent at the time of the general visitation, for according to the general rule the visitation was to be conducted in a paternal manner. If, on the other hand, the delicts were notorious, or if a general knowledge of them had become current, the Visitator could proceed judicially. A similar course was in order if the delinquent made a judicial confession of his own accord, if the delict stood as a threat to a third party or to the common good, or if the crime was of some extraordinary character.[32]

2) Present Law

The obligation to conduct the canonical visitation is incumbent upon Major Superiors according to their constitutions, and may be fulfilled personally or through a delegate.[33] According to some particular laws the General may designate one of his counsellors as General Visitator,[34] but as Wernz-Vidal observe, the duty of conducting visitation nevertheless rests, even in these institutes, with the Provincial Superior or those designated as Provincial Visitators by particular law, since it is their duty to keep the General informed on the state of the province.[35]

The Visitator has the right and the duty to interrogate any or all the religious of a house as he wishes, and the latter are obliged to answer him truthfully in matters pertinent to the visitation. To prevent the arising of difficulties

[32] Bouix, *De Jure Regularium*, II, 451-452.

[33] Can. 511.

[34] Vermeersch-Creusen, *Epitome*, I, n. 631.

[35] Wernz-Vidal, *De Religiosis*, p. 122, n. 145.

through a lack of cooperation on the part of the Local Superior, or in consequence of a possible collusion between him and his subjects to the detriment of the visitation, the canon admonishes Local Superiors not to impede the scope of the visitation in any way.[36] Furthermore, canon 2413 confers the right on the Visitator to declare incapable of holding office any or all who impede the visitation, and to remove them from office if they are Superiors.

As pointed out earlier by the Council of Trent and the pre-Code writers, the obligation to conduct the canonical visitation is grave in itself by reason of its purpose. The penal sanction which canon 2413 enacts against those who impede the visitation corroborates this view. Consequently the Superior who neglects the visitation, and thereby encourages a relaxed discipline, is himself guilty of grave fault.

Particular law is permitted to determine what matters pertain to the visitation. The following points, however, should be inquired into by the Visitator: 1) the observance of the regular discipline; 2) the fulfillment of the choral obligations; 3) the observance of the common life; 4) the celebration of Mass; 5) the relationship between Superior and subjects; 6) the existence of fraternal harmony among the religious; 7) the obedience and the reverence due to Superiors; 8) the fulfillment of Mass obligations; 9) the public reading of the Apostolic decrees and of the constitutions of the particular Order; 10) the public theological conferences; 11) the fulfillment of the duties of professors towards their students; 12) the regular holding of the chapter of faults if it is a prescribed matter; 13) delicts or grievous faults about which the Visitator should be informed; 14) the administration of the temporal goods; 15) the custody of the Blessed Sacrament and the holy oils; 16) the proper care of the church and the chapels.[37]

[36] Canon 513.

[37] Cf. Appeltern, *Compendium,* p. 448, qu. 524; Wernz-Vidal, *De Religiosis,* pp. 124-125, n. 148; Reilly, *Visitation of Religious,* The

Canon 345 outlines the mode of procedure for canonical visitation. Accordingly, the Provincial should proceed paternally in matters pertaining to the object and the end of his visitation.

Canon 513 implies the right of the Visitator to issue decrees as called for by the results of the visitation. When the Provincial proceeds paternally in issuing these decrees, there is no suspensive effect imposed on them if recourse to a higher Superior is undertaken. On the other hand, a suspensive effect is imposed on them if redress is sought when the Provincial has issued them judicially.[38]

It must be noted that the right of the Provincial to conduct the visitation and to interrogate the brethren begets an obligation in the subjects to denounce other gravely delinquent religious according to the laws of charity, in order that they may be paternally corrected by the Visitator. Ordinarily, however, this obligation presupposes fruitless fraternal correction on the part of the one who denounces, though the obligation of administering a fraternal correction may not bind in a given case in view of the serious inconvenience involved in it, or of greater good that is to be obtained through the paternal correction administered by the Provincial.

The gravity of a case may call for the punishment of the guilty party or for a judicial inquisition. Nevertheless, the Superior cannot institute such proceedings until he has persuaded the informer of his obligation to make a canonical denunciation according to canon 1935, § 2, which imposes this obligation not only when a positive law or precept requires it, but also when the natural law demands it.[39] The natural law demands it when the common good is jeopardized, as, for instance, by the delicts which are made punish-

---

Catholic University of America Canon Law Studies, n. 112 (Washington, D. C.: The Catholic University of America, 1938), *passim*.

[38] Can. 513, § 2: "A decretis Visitatoris recursus datur in devolutivo tantum, nisi Visitator ordine judiciario processerit."

[39] Wernz-Vidal, *De Religiosis*, pp. 125-126, nn. 149-150.

able in canons 2336, § 2, and 2368, § 2, or when injury impends for the Faith, or also for the Order.

This denunciation is to be made to the Provincial,[40] who must remind the subject of the law of charity which obligates him not to violate the good name of the guilty party if the denunciation is not morally justified. After the judicial denunciation has been made, the Provincial is to invoke the procedure of inquisition as governed by canons 1939 and the following. The Provincial must recall, however, that in no circumstances may he interfere with matters reserved to the Holy Office.[41]

Ordinarily the employment of a judicial procedure will not be necessary, particularly if the Provincial is faithful and diligent in fulfilling his obligations with regard to the regular visitation. Besides, the visitation should never degenerate into a universal penal inquisition. Rather, the paternal character by which it should ordinarily be marked[42] can be judged from the Constitutions of the Carmelite Order, which indicate that the Visitator may remain indefinitely in a convent for the instruction and consolation of the brethren after conducting the visitation.[43]

C. The Obligation to Correct Defects

The Provincial Superior is required by the very nature of his office to correct the defects of his subjects and to punish their delinquencies. This obligation, moreover, flows as a corollary from the obligation to conduct the visitation, the purpose of which is to correct relaxations and to promote the due observance of religious discipline. Furthermore, the Code obliges all religious, whether Superiors or subjects, to be faithful in the observance of their vows and to conform their lives according to their Rule and constitutions, in order to fulfill their purpose of striving after perfection.[44]

[40] Vermeersch-Creusen, *Epitome,* III, n. 262.

[41] Can. 501, § 2.

[42] Can. 345.

[43] *Constitutiones O. Carm.* p. 169, art. 493.

[44] Can. 593.

The particular law of each Order prescribes the obligations of the Provincial concerning the specific defects of his subjects which are to be guarded against and the means of prevention to be taken.

When it is a matter of invoking penal sanctions, the norms of canon 2223 and of particular law must be followed. In accordance with the prescriptions of that canon, the Provincial will proceed in the following manner, always guided by prudence when *latae sententiae* penalties can, or as required by law, must be declared. When the special enormity of the offense requires it, he may indeed increase a determined penalty. On the other hand, if either the common or particular law in threatening a penalty merely grants him the right to invoke it, he may be guided by prudence and his conscience in his decision to invoke it or to mitigate it. Even if the common or particular law obliges him to inflict a penalty, he may still, in his discretion, postpone the punishment; abstain altogether from inflicting it, if the guilty one has amended his fault and repaired the scandal, or is already sufficiently punished; or, finally, mitigate the punishment, when imputability is notably lessened.

D. The Obligation of Prayer

Canon 339 imposes the obligation on bishops to apply the Mass on certain days for their subjects. Similarly the Code states that it is fitting for titular bishops, at least out of charity, to celebrate Mass occasionally for the people of their dioceses.[45] No corresponding obligation of justice or charity is stated in the common law with regard to the Provincial Superior. However, it appears that he should offer Mass for his subjects out of charity occasionally at least. The analogy between the office of bishop and that of Provincial Superior appears to justify a limited application of canon 339.[46]

[45] Can. 348.

[46] Cf. *supra*, p. 32.

4. *The Council*

The Provincial Superior must have his counsellors, or definitors, whose advice or consent is to be sought in certain measures according to the norms of the Code and of the constitutions.[47] These advisers are prescribed by canon 516 for two reasons. The fact that they are prescribed helps the Superior to achieve a better government and at the same time it serves to circumscribe his individual powers in matters of grave importance.[48] Particulars regarding definitors, such as their appointment and term of office, their requisite qualities, and their number, are left by the Code to be determined by the particular law. For canon 516, § 1, the Code cites only one source, namely, an *Instruction* from the Sacred Congregation of Religious issued in 1909.[49] Similar references to an advisory council are seen, however, in the *Normae* of 1901.[50] Historically then, the existence of such a council, whether with relation to Major or to Minor Superiors, can be traced to the earliest constitutions of each Order.[51]

The definitors or counsellors have no authority in virtue of their office, but are appointed simply to aid the Superior in his task of government. Their function is an advisory one, although the Superior is obliged at times not only to hear them, but also to follow their advice when he acts. Unlike the chapter, therefore, they possess no jurisdiction.[52]

As just indicated, the vote of the definitors may be either binding on the Provincial (*deliberative*) or not binding on him (*consultative*). The Code and the constitutions determine when their vote is deliberative. If a deliberative

[47] Can. 516, § 1.

[48] Wernz-Vidal, *De Religiosis*, p. 128, n. 153.

[49] 30 iul. 1909—*Fontes*, n. 4394.

[50] *Normae secundum quas S. Congr. Episcoporum et Regularium procedere solet in Approbandis Novis Institutis Votorum Simplicium* (Romae: Typis S.C. de Propaganda Fidei, 1901), nn. 194, 203, 221, 239 (hereafter cited as *Normae*).

[51] Cf. *Monumenta Carmelitana*, p. 90.

[52] Can. 509, § 1.

vote is granted the definitors, the Provincial's act in opposition to it would be invalid.[53] If the vote of the definitors is merely consultative, the Provincial need not follow it with a view to acting validly.[54] Though the validity of the Provincial's action in such cases is not dependent upon his following their consultative vote, he should nevertheless give heed to canon 105, § 1, which urges him to follow their unanimous opinion, unless grave reasons demand that he act otherwise. Since the requirement of a deliberative vote of the definitors implies a restriction of the Provincial's powers, the character of the council's vote is to be presumed as consultative if the Code or the constitutions fail to specify the contrary. The authority of the Superior is entitled to the favor of the law, so that his powers are not to be restricted without its express provision to that effect.[55] Thus, if the law requires that the Provincial act "with his council" he must consult it, but his acceptance of their vote is not requisite for the validity of his action. As noted above, however, an unwarranted departure from their view could eventuate as altogether illicit.

Whenever the consent of the definitors is required for the validity of the Provincial's action, the definitors are to be called together for deliberation undertaken in common. This character of the deliberation seems to be required for the validity of the act in question.[56] All are to be summoned to the meeting. If some are not called, but are actually present, the defect in the convocation does not affect the validity of the action taken.[57] Because of the necessity of a common action, therefore, any individual and separate consultation of the counsellors cannot be sustained when their delibera-

[53] Cf. can. 105, § 1.

[54] *Loc. cit.*

[55] Can. 59.

[56] Can. 105, § 2; Vermeersch-Creusen, *Epitome*, I, n. 229; Wernz-Vidal, *De Personis*, pp. 34-36, n. 33; Ojetti, *Commentarium in Codicem Iuris Canonici* (4 vols., Romae: apud Aedes Universitatis Gregorianae, 1927-31), II, 183 (hereafter cited as *Commentarium*).

[57] Can. 162, § 4.

tive vote is required. But, since the council is merely an advisory body, it will not be governed of necessity by the rules of action for collegiate moral persons. The rules governing the latter bodies are to be taken as a norm for action when the particular law is silent concerning the actions of the council. On this basis, therefore, Maroto (1875-1937) admitted the possible application of a particular law which abstracts from the general norms for collegiate moral persons, so that a collective vote need not be required necessarily.[58]

Unless the particular law prescribes otherwise, the Provincial acts as the presiding officer at these deliberations, and the law of canon 101, § 1, 1°, governing the action of moral persons controls the acts of the council. Thus, either an absolute majority on the first or second ballot, or a relative majority on the third ballot, determines the mind of the council. In the event of a tie on the third ballot, the Provincial may decide the issue.

In regard to the convocation of the definitors when their consultative vote is required, the same norms should be applied as those which govern the cases involving the necessity of a deliberative vote. Here again the particular law of the Order may permit individual consultation in certain circumstances, but, in the event that particular law is silent, the general norms for collegiate moral persons are to be applied, so that a collective consultation is necessary. Although canon 105, 1° appears to establish the need of seeking this consultative vote as a necessity for validity,[59] Vermeersch cited several authorities in support of the view that the canon does not actually invalidate the action of a Superior who fails to hear his advisors at all.[60] This contention is

[58] *Institutiones*, I, n. 472.

[59] "Si consensus exigatur, Superior contra earundem votum invalide agit; si consilium tantum, per verba, ex gr.: *de consilio consultorum*, vel *audito Capitulo, parocho*, etc., satis est ad valide agendum ut Superior illas personas audiat, . . ."

[60] *Epitome*, I, n. 229.

based on the fact that the Code is here concerned merely with the validity of an act placed in opposition to the view of the counsellors, and not with the validity of an act placed without the consultation of the council.

This canon, so he argued, merely means to state that, when only a consultation is demanded, the Superior does not act invalidly if he acts in opposition to the council's advice. It does not state, so he maintained, that the Superior acts invalidly in the case in which he does not consult the council. He did not deny, however, that the neglect without reason to secure their vote is illicit. In view of Vermeersch's argument and doctrinal authority the writer admits that a doubt of law seems present in this question, and with Beste, who actually favors the view requiring consultation for the validity of the Superior's actions,[61] believes that either view may be followed, at least *post factum,* till the issue is decided by the Holy See.

The acceptance of this view certainly does not justify its arbitrary mode of action on the part of the Superior. A Superior who acts in this fashion undoubtedly acts illicitly. On the other hand, extraordinary circumstances may sometimes justify his departure from the required manner of action, when the deliberative vote of his council is not prescribed.[62] The definitors, in turn, are obliged to state their view in accordance wth the nature of their office and the norm enacted in canon 105, 3°. In the event, however, that only their consultative vote is required and they refuse to give it, the Provincial may licitly act himself, since they have failed in their advisory capacity.[63]

[61] *Introductio,* p. 162.

[62] For the authors and the arguments supporting either side of this question, cf. Michiels, *Principia Generalia de Personis in Ecclesia* (Lublin, Polonia: Universitas Catholica, 1932), p. 418 (hereafter cited as *De Personis*).

[63] Ojetti, *Commentarium,* II, 184-185; Michiels, *De Personis,* p. 420; Clancy, *The Local Superior,* p. 65.

5. *Jurisdiction over Nuns*

Pre-Code legislation and pre-Code authors frequently discussed the jurisdiction of Regular Prelates over nuns subject to them in questions involving jurisdiction for the Sacrament of Penance.[64] The writer has not, however, found any conclusive reference to prove that nuns were subject at any time to a Local Superior. It seems that they were always subject to the Provincial, since all the houses of the province were comprehended under his jurisdiction. On the contrary, the jurisdiction of the Local Superior was confined, as his designation indicates, to the subjects actually residing within his house or to persons remaining there by reason of some capacity in the household. There is no reason to suppose that an exception was made to this restriction in the case of nuns subject to Regulars.[65] Particular law, however, must be consulted if one is to determine the Superior to whom nuns were subordinated in pre-Code times. This is true also even under the Code. Canon 500, § 2, states that nuns who are subject to Regular Superiors by reason of their constitutions are subject to the Ordinary of the place only in cases expressly indicated in the law. Clearly, reference must even now be made to particular law to determine whether this subjection is to a Superior other than the Provincial; but it would seem proper that the nuns should be subject to the Provincial, rather than to the Local Superior, since his jurisdiction is not restricted to a particular house. Berutti states that nuns are ordinarily subject to the jurisdiction of Major Superiors, and implies that subjection to a Local Superior is the exception.[66]

Nuns who are actually exempt from the local Ordinary in view of their subjection to the jurisdiction of the Provincial are the subjects of his jurisdiction even as male

[64] The question of the confessions of nuns subject to the Provincial will be treated in Chapter XI, p. 196.

[65] Cf., however, Clancy, *The Local Superior*, p. 39.

[66] *Institutiones*, III, 54.

religious of his Order, with certain exceptions expressly mentioned in the Code. At the same time the Code subjects them in a measure to the local Ordinary in spite of their exemption. Thus, the Superioress of a monastery of exempt nuns must render an account of her administration once a year, or more frequently if particular law requires it, both to the local Ordinary and to the Provincial. If the account proves to be unsatisfactory, the Ordinary can request the Provincial to apply the necessary remedies, even to the extent of removing the administrators from office. In the event that the Provincial fails to act in such a case, the Ordinary is authorized to act himself and then proceed to inform the Holy See.[67] Although the report is to be exacted *gratis,* and no remuneration can be sought by the Provincial, he can lawfully require the necessary expenses from the community, when he has journeyed to the convent for the purpose of receiving this financial account.[68]

Further rights in the matter of the supervision of the temporal goods of nuns subject to Regulars are accorded to the Provincial as well as to the local Ordinary. The permission of both is required before a nun still in simple vows can change the dispositions of her property made according to canon 569, § § 1, 2, unless the constitutions ordain otherwise.[69] The permission of both is also required with reference to the investment of the dowry of a nun after her first profession.[70]

The Provincial, if another is not designated by the par-

[67] Can. 535, § 1, 2°. This canon repeats almost verbatim the injunction of Gregory XV (1621-1623) in the Constitution *Inscrutabili* of February 5, 1622, § 5: "Episcopo loci, adhibitis etiam Superioribus Regularibus, singulis annis rationes administrationis, gratis tamen exigendas, reddere teneantur, ad idque juris remediis cogi et compelli queant."—*Fontes,* n. 199.

[68] Cf. can. 346; Berutti, *Institutiones,* II, 124.

[69] Can. 580, § 3.

[70] Can. 549. In accordance with canon 2412, 1°, the local Ordinary can punish a Superioress, even to the extent of deposition, when she has presumed to alienate the dowries of her subjects.

ticular law, has the right to appoint the chaplain for exempt nuns subject to him.[71]

In virtue of canons 876, § 1, and 525, jurisdiction for the hearing of the confessions even of exempt nuns must be received from the local Ordinary. Similarly the jurisdiction to preach to them must come from the local Ordinary, although its lawful exercise depends upon the permission of the Provincial, or of the Superior designated by particular law.[72] Although the chaplain is not a rector of the Church, unless so designated by the bishop,[73] the Provincial has the power to delegate him to bless for use in their chapel the sacred utensils and other articles which require a blessing before being used for divine services.[74]

According to canon 603, § 2, the Provincial, unless particular law specifies another Superior, has the obligation to see to the custody of the cloister of nuns subject to him, and to punish with penalties either the nuns or others who are subject to him when they offend in this regard. The Sacred Congregation of Religious repeated this law in its *Instruction* of February 6, 1924, concerning the cloister of monastic nuns of solemn vows, and established precautions to be observed by the Provincial, or the Visitator, in conducting the visitation mentioned by canon 512, § 2, 1°, with regard to the cloister.[75]

The Provincial is ordinarily the lawful Superior who admits subjects to religious profession.[76] Since canon 572, § 1, 4°, requires the absence of force, fear, or deceit, in the

[71] Can. 529. If he is negligent in doing so, the Ordinary of the place will provide.

[72] Can. 1338, § 2. [73] Can. 479. [74] Can. 1304, 5°.

[75] *AAS*, XVI (1924), 96. The authority of the Provincial is limited both by canon 603, § 1, and the *Instruction* (VI) in so far as the primary duty of watchfulness in the custody of the cloister is entrusted to the local Ordinary, who is also to perform the visitation of the cloister of nuns subject to Regulars when the visitation has not been conducted by the Provincial for five years (can. 512, § 2, 1°).

[76] Cf. canon 572, § 1, 2°, and *infra*, pp. 95-97, where religious profession will be discussed.

act of religious profession as a condition for its validity, the Provincial must see to it that no nun subject to him will make her profession under the influence of any of these factors.[77]

Canon 506, § 2, places a limitation upon the jurisdiction of the Provincial with regard to the elections of superioresses in monasteries of nuns subject to him. The local Ordinary is to be informed in advance of these elections, and has the right to preside at them, even in the event that the Provincial, or any other Superior designated by particular law, is present. Moreover, the precedence which he takes over the Provincial is not merely that of honor, but also one of jurisdiction, as is evident from the declaration of the Pontifical Commission for the Interpretation of the Code.[78] However, when the local Ordinary is informed opportunely and thereupon manifests no reason for the postponement of the election, then the election is valid and licit if conducted as scheduled under the presidency of the Provincial in the absence of the bishop.[79]

[77] Canon 552, § 1, however, confers the right and the duty upon the Ordinary of the place to explore the mind and will of the candidate in these matters before her admission and profession.

[78] 30 iul. 1934—*AAS*, XXVI (1934), 494.

[79] Berutti, *Institutiones*, III, 59.

CHAPTER VII

THE PROVINCIAL SUPERIOR AND THE TRAINING OF HIS SUBJECTS

Titles XI and XII of the tract *"De Religiosis"* in the Code specify certain regulations with regard to the admission, the profession, and the studies of religious. These titles form a convenient unit under which the relationship of the Provincial to the junior members of the province may be studied.

1. *The Admission of Candidates*

Our Savior's invitation to seek evangelical perfection was extended to all the faithful indiscriminately.[1] Therefore, in the abstract, all the faithful may claim as a right the invitation of Christ; in the concrete, however, many are not able to accept it, or are disqualified. Religious Orders are juridic societies, recognized by the Church, in which the faithful may indeed seek evangelical perfection through the observance of the vows of poverty, chastity, and obedience. But only the faithful who are able to meet the required conditions for membership in them, as established by the Code and particular law, have a right to accept the invitation to seek evangelical perfection therein. Only that Catholic candidate accordingly has this right who, inspired by a worthy motive, is capable of bearing the obligations of the religious life, and is lawfully received by the Provincial, or other Superior designated by particular law.[2] Moreover, the candidate must satisfy the requirements of canon 542 for the valid and licit entrance into the novitiate. Candidates found suitable according to the prescriptions of particular law as well as the law of the Code may be accepted by the Provincial, or by other Major Superiors specified by par-

[1] Matt., XIX, 21.

[2] Can. 538. This canon and many others in the tract speak generically of Superiors, and leave the specification to particular law.

ticular law, with the suffrage of his council or chapter according to the norms of the constitutions of the Order.[3]

Because of the obligations resulting from the transformation of one's life in the novitiate to conform to the principles of perfection after profession, the Church has seen fit to prescribe that all women religious and lay brothers who take perpetual vows should undergo a preparatory period known as the postulancy before their entrance into the novitiate. Certain obligations and rights in the matter of the postulancy belong to the Superior who is competent to admit candidates to the religious life.

A. The Admission of Postulants

Canon 539 requires the postulancy for prospective lay brothers and women religious of institutes wherein perpetual vows are pronounced. Fanfani defines the postulancy as a certain period of time extending from one's admission into a community as a candidate for the religious life and his admission to the novitiate, during which period the aspirant lives as a guest in the monastery and conforms his life to that of the other members of the community under the vigilance of the Superiors.[4] Canon 539 requires that this period be one of at least six months' duration preceding entrance to the novitiate. In communities wherein temporary vows alone are taken, it is left to particular law to determine the necessity and the duration of the postulancy.[5]

The Major Superior, or the Provincial, in the case of the Regular Orders, can prolong the period of this postulancy, but not beyond a semester. This law is comparatively new, although the postulancy was long required in the practise of some communities.[6] The norms of the Sacred Congregation of Bishops and Regulars of 1901 prescribed a period of six months' postulancy for aspirants to membership in insti-

[3] Can. 543.

[4] *De Iure Religiosorum*, n. 188.

[5] Can. 539, § 1.

[6] Wernz-Vidal, *De Religiosis*, pp. 191-192, n. 241.

tutes whose members take simple vows. They also required the permission of the Provincial or the General for entrance into the postulancy.[7] Pius X approved the general decree of the Sacred Congregation of Religious in 1911 that the prospective lay brothers in all communities with perpetual vows should submit to a postulancy of two years, but the following year he reduced this prescribed term to a minimum period of six moths.[8]

Canon 539 prescribes a minimum of six months for the duration of the postulancy, and therefore, particular law may prescribe a longer period of time.[9] Actually, there is no limit placed on the duration of the postulancy which the particular law may prescribe, although Biederlack-Führich (1845-1930)[10] and Augustine (1872-1943)[11] limited it to a year in virtue of the power of prorogation for six months which is granted to the Major Superior in the second paragraph of the canon. The better and common opinion, however, is that canon 539, § 1, does not indicate the maximum time of the postulancy at all.[12] Particular law, therefore, can prescribe any duration for the postulancy beyond a minimum of at least six months. Regardless of the duration beyond six months, the Provincial may prorogue the postulancy only for another six months. In doing so, he does not need to seek the consultation or the consent of his council.[13]

[7] *Normae*, nn. 63, 65.

[8] 1 ian., 1911—*AAS*, III (1911), 29-37; S. C. de Relig. decr. 15 aug., 1912, n. 2, 3—*AAS*, IV (1912), 565.

[9] Vermeersch-Creusen, *Epitome*, I, n. 666; Fanfani, *De Iure Religiosorum*, n. 189.

[10] *De Religiosis*, n. 62.

[11] *A Commentary on the New Code of Canon Law* (8 vols., Vol. II, 4. ed., 1923; Vol. III, 5. ed., 1938; Vol. IV, 2. ed., 1921; Vol. VI, 2. ed., 1923; Vol. VIII, 1922, St. Louis: Herder), III, 203 (hereafter this work will be cited as *Commentary*).

[12] Balzer, *The Computation of Time in a Canonical Novitiate*, The Catholic University of America Canon Law Studies, n. 212 (Washington, D. C.: The Catholic University of America Press, 1945), p. 86.

[13] Can. 539, § 2; Schaefer, *De Religiosis*, n. 216, p. 458.

The postulancy is not required for the validity of the novitiate.[14]

Furthermore, the period of the postulancy is to be spent in the novitiate house or a house of diligent observance, and the Provincial as the Ordinary of the province has the right to determine which shall be the house, as well as the right to determine the degree of its regular observance. Moreover, canon 540 requires the existence of a Master of postulants, and it is a matter of provincial interest to determine who this Master should be.

The Code has not determined whether the Major Superior alone or also the Local Superior is competent to receive postulants. Therefore, one must look to the particular law to see whether the Local Superior is competent.[15] However, if particular law is also silent on the matter, it seems that the act of receiving postulants should be reserved to the Major Superior of the province, namely, the Provincial. This conclusion is more in keeping with the earlier law, which saw in the reception of new members to the community a matter for the Provincial's interest. Similarly, the acceptance of candidates to the novitiate devolves upon the Provincial as the Major Superior, and it is thus his duty to see to it that the candidate has the requisite qualities.[16]

The Code does not specify in what this reception consists or what the qualities of the postulant should be. Acceptance to the postulancy begins at the moment the candidate freely and with the consent of the Superior begins to dwell in the house as an aspirant to the Order.[17] As for the qualities of the candidate, these are to be inferred from those

[14] Cf. cc. 11; 542.

[15] Fanfani, *De Iure Religiosorum,* n. 190.

[16] Beste, *Introductio,* p. 358; Maroto, "Annotationes"—*Commentarium pro Religiosis et Missionariis* (Romae: ab anno 1935; ante annum 1935, *Commentarium pro Religiosis*), XVI (1936), 226, nota 1 (hereafter referred to as *CpRM*); Schaefer, *De Religiosis,* p. 455, n. 215, 1; Berutti, *Institutiones,* III, n. 66.

[17] Fanfani, *De Iure Religiosorum,* n. 190.

required for entrance to the novitiate.[18] There is no prescription regarding the age of the postulant, but the prospective novice must have completed fifteen years before entering the novitiate.[19]

The duration of the postulancy prescribed by law should be considered in relation to this canonical age for the valid entrance to the novitiate. Ordinarily the postulancy should be begun at an age which makes it possible for the candidate to validly enter the novitiate at the conclusion of the postulancy. Canon 539, however, merely requires a period of postulancy before the novitiate; it does not require an immediate succession of the novitiate upon the completed period of the postulancy. The postulant may complete his period of postulancy and then continue in the religious life as a candidate for the novitiate.[20] Accordingly, the Provincial may, in unusual circumstances, admit to the postulancy one who at the time of its completion will lack the canonical age for admission to the novitiate. However, the entrance to the novitiate cannot ordinarily be deferred for a long time, and hence, proportionate reasons must justify the Provincial in acting in this manner since the postulant does not enjoy the rights and privileges of the Order,[21] and justice to a worthy candidate entitles him to entrance to the novitiate with its share in these, or else to a dismissal. Therefore, the Provincial, though not explicitly restricted with regard to the age of postulants, must be governed by the rules determining the age for admission to the novitiate.

When postulants are once accepted, although they fall directly under the more immediate jurisdiction of the Local Superior, they become subjects also of the Provincial, so that his jurisdictional powers can be exercised in the cases granted by the Code.[22] The dismissal of postulants is reserved to the Provincial.[23]

[18] Cf. can. 542.

[19] Can. 555, § 1, 1°.

[20] Fanfani, *De Iure Religiosorum*, n. 189.

[21] *AAS*, XXI (1929), 573.

[22] Cf. Clancy, *The Local Superior*, pp. 81-82.

[23] Schaefer, *De Religiosis*, p. 455, n. 215.

B. The Admission of Novices

Legislation pertaining to the novitiate is more abundant than that affecting the postulancy, since the institute of the novitiate is much older than that of the postulancy. Prior to an examination of the rights and duties of the Provincial regarding the novices, the presentation of some historical references will be useful.

1) Pre-Code Legislation

In the law of the Decretals, the reception of novices into an Order was a matter of concern for both the community and the province. Basing his opinion on a decretal of Innocent III (1198-1216),[24] Donatus stated that the reception of a subject to the habit and to profession pertained to the abbot and the community acting together.[25]

Later legislation dealt with the competence of the various Superiors to admit novices to the religious life. In the period before the Council of Trent, however, the particular law was the chief guide as to this competence. The constitutions of the various Orders were specific on the matter and the power to receive novices was uniformly placed by the particular law beyond the scope of power enjoyed by the Local Superior.[26]

Following the Council of Trent, Sixtus V (1585-1590) required that the reception of novices be made by the chapters of the province or of the Order.[27] In a later Constitution, however, he granted the right to the Provincial acting with the counsel of three other priests of the Order.[28] Gregory XIV (1590-1591) in 1591 confirmed this concession.[29] The

[24] C. 16, X, *de regularibus et transeuntibus ad religionem*, III, 31.

[25] "Recipere ad habitum et professionem, spectat ad abbatem, et conventum simul"—*Rerum Regularium Praxis*, Tom. III, qu. 17, tr. 12.

[26] Cf. c. 3, *de verborum significatione*, V, 12, in VI°, *Monumenta Carmelitana*, p. 64.

[27] Cf. const. *Cum de omnibus*, 26 nov. 1857, § 3—*Fontes*, n. 162.

[28] Cf. const. *Ad Romanum*, 21 oct. 1588, § 8,—*Fontes*, n. 164.

[29] Const. *Circumspecta*, 15 mart. 1591, § 5—*Fontes*, n. 170.

particular law of the individual Orders, however, was not prohibited from restricting this competence to the General.

Thus in the period after the Council of Trent, both the general and the particular law reserved the reception of candidates to the novitiate to the Major Superiors who, in accordance with their own constitutions, were required to obtain for this act the deliberative or consultative vote of a chapter or of a council.

2) Present Law

According to canon 543, the right of admitting the candidates to the novitiate pertains to the Major Superiors acting with the vote of the council or the chapter according to the norms of the constitutions of the Order. Under the present law, therefore, large scope is still granted to the constitutions of the Order. Since the term *Major Superiors* is indefinite, its specification is left to the constitutions. The Provincial as the Major Superior of the province will ordinarily be designated by them. The canon intends, through its requirement of the vote of the council or chapter, to restrict the right of the Major Superior in view of the importance of the act of accepting the candidates, but the decision as to the character and nature of the vote is reserved for the particular law of the Order.[30] If the particular law does not specify which Major Superior should exercise the right, then the Provincial certainly possesses the right since no distinction should be established when the law is silent on the point. In case the constitutions are thus silent on the question, the General cannot deprive the Provincial of this right, but he may for a just reason restrict the exercise of it.

Since the code does not establish the vote as a deliberative one, and since the requirement of it implies a limitation of the right of the Provincial, it can be presumed that simply

[30] Cf. Goyeneche, *De Religiosis*, p. 80; Vermeersch-Creusen, *Epitome*, I, n. 690; Fanfani, *De Iure Religiosorum*, n. 144; Schaefer, *De Religiosis*, pp. 485-487, n. 223.

a consultative vote is required in the event that the particular law does not specify.[31]

The validity of the subsequent novitiate of a candidate whom the Provincial has received without calling for a consultative vote is judged by the authors according to their views on canon 105, § 1, concerning the necessity of the previous act of consultation with reference to the validity or lawfulness of the Superior's act. Thus Goyeneche maintains[32] that the novitiate will be invalid, since canon 105, § 1, requires the obtaining of the consultative vote as an essential condition.[33] In virtue of canon 489, he says, constitutions which contravene this law of the Code are abrogated in this point. It has been seen above, however,[34] that there is a doubt of law concerning the interpretation of canon 105, § 1. Accordingly, Vermeersch and others who support the view that consultation is not an essential requirement maintain that the novitiate of one thus illicitly received would be valid.[35] Till the question is settled definitively to the contrary, the writer believes that this latter view may be accepted. It is to be noted that only the vote of the council is required by the Code. In consequence, unless particular law provides otherwise, a weighty reason will justify the Provincial's departure from the view submitted by the majority.

If the constitutions require a deliberative vote of the council or the chapter, a favorable majority vote is required before the Provincial can validly admit the candidate to the novitiate. However, the favorable vote of the council does not oblige the Provincial to accept the candidate, since the

[31] Cf. can. 11; Beste, *Introductio*, p. 162.

[32] "Consultationes"—*CpR*, III (1922), 265; and also *CpR*, IV (1923) 120.

[33] Blat, *Commentarium Textus Codicis Iuris Canonici* (5 vols. in 6, lib. II, *De Personis*, 2. ed., Romae, 1921), II, p. 599, n. 611, (hereafter cited *Commentarium*); Biederlack-Führich, *De Religiosis*, p. 126, n. 76; Coronata, *Institutiones*, I, p. 172, nota 8.

[34] Cf. *supra*, pp. 75-77.

[35] Cf. can. 15.

function of the council is simply one of assistance, while the function of the Provincial is really that of admitting the novices. If reason warrant his action, the Provincial may, despite the favorable vote, refuse to accept the candidate at all since canon 543 confers upon him the right of acceptance, although it restricts its exercise through the requirement of the vote.[36]

Coronata rejects the view of Vermeersch who contended that, if the particular law requires the deliberative vote of the chapter, the Provincial is not permitted to reject a candidate,[37] since this view would imply that the chapter together with the Provincial constitutes a collegiate moral person, which view is out of harmony with the obvious sense of canon 543, in which the right of acceptance is conferred, not on the chapter, but on the Superior.[38] Only for the acceptance of candidates to the novitiate must the Provincial have the vote of his council or chapter, but he is at all times free to reject a candidate by not accepting him.

In virtue of his right of receiving candidates, the Provincial is obliged to see that the novice satisfies all the qualifications for a valid and licit entrance to the novitiate,[39] which implies the receipt of the necessary documents as prescribed by the common and the particular law.[40] Violation

[36] Beste, *Introductio*, p. 364; Coronata, *Institutiones*, I, p. 716, n. 572; Goyeneche, *De Religiosis*, p. 47.

[37] "Annotationes"—*Periodica de Re canonica et Morali utili praesertim Religiosis* (Brugi, 1905—; ab anno 1927, *Periodica de Re Canonica, Morali, Liturgica*), XI (1922), 28 (hereafter cited as *Periodica*).

[38] Coronata, *ibid.*, p. 717, nota 7.

[39] Can. 542, § 1; Schaefer, *De Religiosis*, nn. 225-227, pp. 488-500.

[40] Can. 544. If the candidate has left a seminary, recourse must be had to the Sacred Congregation of Religious (*AAS*, XXIII [1941], 371). Cf. Hannan, "Ex-Seminarian and Novice"—*The Jurist*, II [1942], 61; Frison, "Ex-Seminarian and Novice: A Clarification"—*The Jurist*, VI (1946), 316-318. In the light of this latter article it seems safe to state that recourse need not be made when a seminarian, while still attached to the seminary, arranges to enter the religious

of these duties and the resultant admission of unworthy candidates renders the Provincial subject to the punishment called for in canon 2411.

It is the Provincial's right to preside personally or through a delegate at the reception of the habit, or at that analogous ceremony prescribed by the constitutions, which ordinarily signifies the canonical inception of the novitiate and the formal acceptance of the candidate by the competent Superior.[41] He can delegate another to perform this function, but not habitually, since this would point to a neglect of his official duties.[42]

Like the postulant, the novice is a subject of the Provincial's jurisdictional power, although he is more immediately within the sphere of authority of the Local Superior except in such matters as the canonical act of visitation.[43]

3) The Novice Master and the Training of Novices

Since the novitiate training is of fundamental importance for the religious growth of an Order, the obligation of the Provincial in its regard is grave. The law requires that the year of the novitiate be passed under the direction of the Novice Master, with reference to whose qualities[44] the present law is for the most part adopted from the decree *Cum ad Regularem* of Clement VII (1592-1605).[45] As the Code now does, so this decree provided for a *Socius* to assist the Novice Master whenever the large number of novices demanded such an arrangement. Both *Socius* and Novice Master were to be eminent for their faithfulness in the religious observance.

---

life. In the event, however, that he has left the seminary and only later decides to enter the religious life, recourse must be made.

[41] Can. 553. When the constitutions provide another manner of manifesting this formal acceptance, the Local Superior may have the right to preside at the investing ceremony.

[42] Schaefer, *De Religiosis*, p. 330, n. 265.

[43] Can. 561, § 1. [44] Can. 559, § 1.

[45] 19 mart. 1603—*Fontes*, n. 189.

The legislation of the Code regarding the qualities, duties and relationship of the Novice Master and the *Socius* to Superiors is almost identical with that of this decree. The Provincial must see that both are properly qualified for their posts, and that they fill their office properly. This duty is best discharged at the annual visitation, since the general discipline of the novitiate should be entrusted almost exclusively to the Novice Master. In fact, the Provincial is exhorted in some particular laws to visit the novitiate but rarely in the year, lest too frequent visits disturb the peace and recollection of the novitiate.

The obligation of the Novice Master to instruct his novices properly is a grave one.[46] In order that he may the better insure its fulfillment, he is to send periodic reports to the Provincial regarding the state of the novitiate, unless particular law requires him to send this report to the chapter.[47] The obligations to make such reports illustrate the importance of the duty of supervision over the novitiate thus vested in the Provincial. As Larraona noted,[48] the preliminary schema of the Code reveals that the legislators wished all the responsibility for and the government of the novitiate to be reposed in the Major Superior and the Novice Master to the exclusion of the Local Superior. The canons support this intention also for the present, with the exception that the jurisdiction of the Local Superior in ordinary routine affairs of the house is not restricted.

Novices represent potential members of the province. The question of their dismissal accordingly pertains to the general welfare of the province. Though the Code in canon 556 speaks simply of the dismissal of novices by the Superior, it appears that such action is reserved to the Provincial. Not only the fact that such action is beyond the sphere of local concern, but also the following reasons can be offered for this claim. Canon 543 confers the right of

[46] Can. 562.

[47] Can. 563.

[48] "Consultationes"—*CpR*, II (1921), 296.

admission of novices upon the Major Superior or the chapter. Similarly canon 572, § 2, confers the right of proroguing the novitiate upon the Major Superior or the chapter. Analogously, the right of dismissal pertains to the Major Superior or the chapter. Coronata agrees in stating that the word *"Superior"* refers to the Major Superior, since this view corresponds to the pre-Code teaching.[49] Particular law approved after the Code, however, may grant the right of dismissal to the Local Superior; or the special gravity and urgency of a case may demand immediate dismissal by the Local Superior in view of the analogy with the case of dismissal treated in canon 668. The Novice Master, however, does not possess this right, since he is subject, as well as the novices, to the Local Superior.[50]

Grave and urgent reasons, such as sickness or death in a family, are required that novices may be permitted to remain temporarily outside of the novitiate. The need of such permission is ordinarily unforeseen. Moreover, the period for which a permission is granted must be brief. Therefore, unless the particular law provides otherwise, recourse to the Provincial is normally uncalled for, and permission can be granted by the Local Superior.[51]

Extraordinary or unusual cases, so it seems to the writer, should be submitted, when circumstances permit, to the judgment of the Provincial if particular law makes no specifications regarding this point, since the common good of the province may be jeopardized by imprudence on the part of the Local Superior.

The general administration of the province pertains to the Provincial, and therefore the transfer of a novice from the house of the novitiate to another, as contemplated by canon 556, § 4, is likewise a matter of the Provincial's jurisdiction. Similarly, judgment as to the fitness of the novice for pro-

[49] *Institutiones*, I, p. 734, n. 582. Cf. Appeltern, *Compendium*, p. 59, qu. 64; Schaefer, *De Religiosis*, p. 521, n. 238.

[50] Can. 561, § 1.

[51] Cf. can. 556, § 3; Clancy, *The Local Superior*, p. 84.

fession pertains to him or to the provincial chapter if the prescriptions of particular law confer that right on him.[52] If the novice is found to be suited to the religious life, he has a right to profession and should be admitted. On the other hand, if a doubt as to his fitness remains, the Provincial, if the constitutions do not reserve the power to the General, may prorogue the novitiate period, but not beyond six months.[53] Ordinarily the judgment as to fitness of the novice will be sought from the Novice Master, the Local Superior and other members of the house of the novitiate, whose opinions should be heard prudently by the Provincial.[54]

Although the novices are subject to the jurisdictional powers of the Provincial, they are more immediately under the Local Superior. Accordingly the latter can dispense from or commute their private non-reserved vows,[55] their observance of fasts and holy-days,[56] and hear or delegate another to hear their confessions.[57]

In accordance with canon 569, the Provincial should provide that the novice arrange at some time before his profession for the administration of his temporal possessions and, unless the constitutions state otherwise, dispose freely of their use and usufruct. The canon places the obligation upon the novice, but the duty to see to its fulfillment devolves upon the Provincial as the Superior of the province to whose care the novice has been entrusted.

With regard to the requisite testimonial letters for the admission of the candidate to the novitiate, it is to be noted that the Provincial, upon whom the duty of seeking these letters devolves in virtue of his right to admit candidates to the novitiate, can delegate the Local Superior or any other priest to seek these letters for him. The petition of the delegated priest will then constitute a juridical petition, provided that the fact of delegation is clearly established, to which petition those who are obliged must respond accord-

[52] Can. 571, § 1.
[53] Can. 571, § 2.
[54] Cf. *supra*, pp. 74-75.
[55] Cans. 1312, 1313.
[56] Can. 1245, § 3.
[57] Can. 875, § 1.

ing to the prescriptions of canon 545, § 1.[58] Finally, a former novice or postulant seeking incardination in a diocese, or admission to another religious community, has need of testimonial letters which, according to canon 544, § 3, must be issued by the Provincial.

2. *Religious Profession*

One of the requisites for the validity of religious profession, whether simple or solemn, is that the subject be admitted to profession by the proper religious Superior.[59] The right of admitting subjects to profession, however, is reserved by canon 543 to the Major Superior acting with the vote of the council or chapter according to the norms of particular law. Therefore, as in the case of the reception of novices, the competent Superior for the act of admitting novices to profession is the Provincial unless the constitutions determine otherwise.

The terms of the Code affirming the right of the Provincial as Major Superior to admit novices to their first profession are more restrictive than those affirming his right to accept novices, or to admit professed religious to solemn or final simple profession. Whereas the character of the vote of the council or chapter is not specified in relation to the reception of novices, a *deliberative* vote is required with reference to the first profession, and a consultative vote with reference to the solemn or final simple profession.[60] Before the enactment of the law of the Code the deliberative vote now required with respect to the one who is to make his first profession was not uniformly necessary.[61] Contrary par-

[58] Cf. Clancy, *The Local Superior*, p. 86. [59] Can. 572, § 1, 2°.

[60] Cans. 543; 575, § 2. It is to be noted that perpetual profession, solemn or simple, must be taken immediately following the end of the novitiate in the case of a religious who has transferred from one community to another, if such a religious has already made profession of simple perpetual or of solemn vows. In this case the vote of the council is deliberative (*Pontificia Commissio ad Codicis Canones Authentice Interpretandos*, 14 iul. 1922, n. vii—*AAS*, XIV [1922], 528).

[61] Wernz-Vidal, *De Religiosis*, p. 270, n. 25.

ticular law is now abrogated so that the deliberative vote is required unless duly authoritative approval for contrary practice has been issued since the Code or privilege from before or after the Code has been retained. As in the case of the reception of novices, a favorable vote of the council or the chapter does not oblige the Provincial to admit a candidate to either temporary or perpetual profession, but the admission to first profession against their vote is invalid.[62] In the case of doubt on the part of the Provincial regarding a candidate's worthiness, or in the case of an unfavorable vote, he can prolong the period of the novitiate for six months,[63] and the period of temporary profession for another triennium.[64]

Since religious profession is the public act by which one formally embraces the religious state with its rights and obligations and is accepted thereto by the community, the Code properly distinguishes between the admission of a subject to that state[65] and the actual reception of the profession.[66] It is equally necessary for a binding contract, that one not only be admitted to profession by the proper representative of the community, but also that his profession actually be received by the proper authority. The admission to profession is the essential condition for validity, while the profession itself and its proper reception is the actual contract. Thus the Code states that it pertains to the validity of any profession that it be received by the proper Superior according to the norms of the constitutions.

Reception of the profession on the part of the Provincial is the actual incorporation of the subject in the Order after he has been judged fit and worthy. On the part of the Order, the Provincial accepts the candidate publicly and seals a mutual contract with him. That the profession ac-

[62] Larraona, "Consultationes"—*CpR,* I (1920), 368, nota 10; Goyeneche, "Consultationes"—*CpR,* III (1922), 53 sq.; Goyeneche, *De Religiosis,* p. 270.

[63] Can. 571, § 2.

[64] Can. 574, § 2.

[65] Can. 572, § 1, 2°.

[66] Can. 572, § 1, 6°.

tually be received by the Provincial is not demanded by the Code, which leaves the determination of the proper Superior for this act to the particular constitutions. Although the reception of the profession pertains essentially to the internal government of the Order, it can nevertheless be received by one not a Major Superior, even an outsider to the community, as long as he has been designated by the particular law of the community or delegated by the competent Superior to perform this juridical act in the name of the community.[67] In such a case, the person appointed by the particular law or delegated by the competent Superior to receive the profession is the lawful Superior mentioned in the canon, not indeed by his own right, but in virtue of the appointment by the particular law or in consequence of the delegation received from the community through the competent Superior.[68]

Although, as Coronata notes, the acts of admission to profession and of the reception of the profession can be performed by different persons,[69] such a procedure without the sanction of particular law cannot be upheld. The fact that in some communities the Local Superior receives the profession depends upon the particular law of the community. The right to admit candidates to the novitiate and to profession belongs radically to the Provincial or the General. Analogously, the reception of profession should be reserved to them, since the common good is vitally concerned in the contract of profession. In the absence of any particular law on this point, the valid reception of the vows must be regarded as an act which is to be exercised by the Provincial or the General, since the responsibility for the admission of the postulant, of the novice, and of the religious in temporary profession is vested alike in the Major Superior.

[67] *Loc. cit.*

[68] Coronata, *Institutiones*, I, p. 756, n. 591; cf. PCI, 1 mart. 1921—*AAS*, XIII (1921), 177.

[69] Coronata, *ibid.*, nota 2.

3. *Other Jurisdiction Regarding Religious Vows*

In connection with the actual profession of the subject, there are further obligations resting ultimately upon the Provincial, unless particular law rules otherwise. He must see that the novice, before simple profession, and the religious subject, before solemn profession, make the proper disposition of his material goods according to the canons.[70] The responsibility for the fulfillment of these canons can, of course, be delegated to the Local Superior, the Novice Master, or the Master of Clerics. Similarly, the Provincial must provide personally, or through a delegate, that the clerical novice present a written petition for profession as a Regular cleric,[71] and that the professed clerical religious before his solemn vows present a declaration signed and sworn to, attesting the fact that he is acting freely and that he intends to receive the subdiaconate.[72]

The obligation mentioned in canon 576, § 1, which ordains that the rite prescribed by the constitutions be carried out in the profession ceremony, likewise binds the Provincial as the proper Superior for the reception of the profession. This obligation, however, is transferred, if by particular law or in consequence of the delegation by the Provincial, the Local Superior receives the profession.[73]

[70] Cans. 569; 580; 581; 582; 583. Although these canons do not mention the Provincial, the ultimate obligation to provide for their fulfillment rests with him, who, as the competent Superior in the matter of admission to the religious life and to the subsequent profession, has the duty to see that the canonical prerequisites to profession be fulfilled.

[71] S. C. de Religiosis, instr. 1 dec. 1921, n. 14—*AAS*, XXIV (1932), 79-80.

[72] *Ibid.*, n. 18—*AAS*, XXIV (1922), 81.

[73] When one who is not a member of the community is designated by the particular law to receive the profession, it appears that the obligation likewise falls upon the Local Superior as the guardian of the constitutions in his particular house. The writer, however, has not found any instance of particular law among the Regulars whereby the reception of profession is entrusted to one who is not a member of the Order.

The same may be said of the document of profession which is to be signed by the religious and the Superior presiding at his reception. If the Provincial receives the profession, he is the Superior required to provide for the safekeeping of this document in the provincial archives, and to arrange that a record of solemn profession be sent to the pastor of the church of baptism of the professed.[74] If by delegation of the Provincial or by provision of particular law the Local Superior is authorized to receive the vows, the fulfillment of these obligations is the burden of the Local Superior.[75]

Regarding the period of temporary profession, the Provincial should see to the fulfillment of the law enacted in canon 574, § 1, in the case of those who lack the canonical age at the expiration of the three-year term.[76] This duty he can discharge by delegating the Novice Master to provide for the proper lengthening of the period for which temporary profession is made. Possible delays in the renewal of profession during which the religious would be bound by no vows are thus forestalled.[77]

The Provincial is the "lawful Superior" mentioned in canon 574, § 2, to whom is granted the right of prolonging the period of temporary profession for a period not exceeding three years. This is apparent from the following reasons: the Provincial exercises the right to admit candidates to first profession although he is restricted by the deliberative vote of the council or of the chapter; he has the

[74] Can. 576, § 2.

[75] Clancy, *The Local Superior*, pp. 88-89.

[76] Can. 573.

[77] With the expiration of his vows such a religious could licitly and validly change the disposal of his goods contrary to canon 580, § 3; give away all his possessions contrary to canon 583, § 1; make a new will contrary to canon 583. In the event of such a delay or interval between profession, however, the validity of the subsequent profession would not be affected (Goyeneche, "Consultationes"—*CpR,* IV [1923], 51-52). Cf. Schaefer, *De Religiosis,* p. 429, n. 200; Coronata, *Institutiones,* I, p. 757, n. 592.

right to admit candidates to solemn profession with the consultative vote of the council or of the chapter; he has the authority to prolong the period of postulancy in accordance with canon 539, § 2; according to canon 571, § 2, he has the authority to prolong the novitiate. In virtue, therefore, of all these specific rights with regard to his religious subjects, it would be inconsistent to give any other interpretation to canon 574, § 2, than that which confers upon him the right of prorogation spoken of in the canon.

However, the computation of the three-year period over which the profession can be prorogued has given rise to some discussion. Canon 574, § 1, requires that the temporary profession antecedent to solemn vows should be made for a three-year period unless the youthfulness of the candidate necessitates a longer period in order that the religious be of canonical age for solemn profession[78] at the expiration of his temporary vows. Vermeersch maintained that the total period of temporary profession is not to be in excess of six years, since the three-year prorogation is to be understood in relation to the three-year probationary period, so that a prorogation beyond six years is inadmissible.[79] Coronata, however, believes that the three-year prorogation is to be understood as beginning from the termination of the first temporary profession period, whether that was of three or more years. Thus, one whose first profession extended over a period of five years could have it prorogued for a period of three additional years.[80]

The wording of the canon justifies either opinion, although the more obvious opinion seems to be that of Coronata. Vermeersch argued from the mind of the Holy See, although the latter is not quite apparent in this case. This

[78] Can. 573.

[79] *Epitome*, I, n. 726. Cf. Oesterle, *Praelectiones Iuris Canonici* (Vol. I, Romae: apud Collegium S. Anselmi, 1931), I, 318.

[80] Coronata, *Institutiones*, I, p. 752, n. 591. Cf. Blat, *Commentarium*, II, p. 635, n. 644; Schaefer, *De Religiosis*, p. 584, n. 268; Fanfani, *De Iure Religiosorum*, p. 302, n. 265.

is not to deny that one who is not sufficiently approved after six years will hardly show himself more suitable after seven or more years. On the other hand, the conclusion is hardly justified that the right of prorogation should be denied as long as the doubt of law is not settled by the Holy See. It is to be noted that the right of the Provincial to prorogue the profession is not made dependent on a previous vote of the council or the chapter.

The Provincial may likewise anticipate the renewal of temporary profession for a just cause.[81] Convenience may dictate that the renewal of vows be anticipated by a month or less. According to canon 577, § 2, this is allowable. The anticipated profession takes effect on the day that the profession should have taken place.[82] But canon 577, § 2, grants only the power to anticipate the renewal of the temporary profession, and not also that of shortening the canonical period of temporary profession, i.e., the power to anticipate the perpetual profession, whether solemn or simple. For this the Provincial would need a special indult from the Holy See, since canon 572, § 2, requires for the validity of the solemn profession a previous temporary profession of three years or more according to the age of the subject, unless the subject be a religious already in solemn vows who has transferred from another community.[83]

The Provincial also possesses certain powers over the profession of a subject with regard to his dismissal prior to his perpetual profession.[84] This point, however, will be studied in a later chapter.

[81] Can. 577, § 2.

[82] Vermeersch-Creusen, *Epitome,* I, n. 728; Coronata, *Institutiones,* I, p. 758, n. 592.

[83] Can. 634. It is to be noted that the profession of solemn vows which has been postponed by the Provincial through a prorogation of the period of the simple vows may be anticipated at any time that the Provincial deems fitting, even though the period of prorogation has not expired (Fanfani, *De Iure Religiosorum,* p. 301, n. 265; Schaefer, *De Religiosis,* p. 588, n. 268).

[84] Can. 575.

4. *The Program of Studies*

Title XII of the tract on Religious in the Code is concerned with the program of studies for religious clerics who are candidates for Orders and whose fruitful clerical ministry depends upon a proper training and education for the reception of these Orders. Presupposing the requirements of the canons for the education of clerics in general[85] and of religious in particular,[86] this Title provides specific norms applicable to the houses of study of religious, the spiritual care of the students, the program of studies itself, and the increase and the development, subsequent to ordination, of the knowledge imparted in the course of studies. Serious obligations rest upon the Provincial and higher Superiors to see to the fulfillment of these canons which indicate the Church's concern for the training of her future ministers.

Many Popes, up to the very present, have stressed the importance of learning for clerics. Clement V (1305-1314) advocated a special master for the training and advancement of clerics in knowledge;[87] Clement VIII (1592-1605) in his Constitution *Nullus omnino* repeated the teachings of the Council of Trent that the Sacred Scriptures should be read in monasteries.[88] Pius X indicated in his *Motu Proprio* of June 24, 1914, the necessity of solid training in religious seminaries;[89] and even after the enactment of the Code Pius XI issued an extended commentary on this Title, as well as a defense of the religious state, in his letter *Unigenitus Dei Filius* of March 18, 1924.[90]

Canon 587, § 1 and § 3, prescribe that each Order and province shall have its seminary where clerics are to be trained. The seminaries are to be approved by the general chapter or the proper Superiors. Provision for a provincial seminary, where this is possible, is an obligation binding

[85] Cans. 1364-1366.

[86] Can. 589, § 1.

[87] C. 1, *de statu monachorum,* III, 10, in Clem.

[88] 25 iul. 1599—*Fontes,* n. 187.

[89] *AAS,* VI (1914), 333.

[90] *AAS,* XVI (1924), 133.

on the Provincial Superior or the provincial chapter. This conclusion follows from the parallel canon which governs the training of diocesan clerics and obliges the bishop to provide a major and a minor seminary in his diocese, or, if this is not possible, to send his students to another seminary, unless the Holy See has established a regional seminary.[91]

Since the establishment and approval of the provincial seminary is of major importance to the Order as a whole, the Provincial should at least consult the General and his council if particular law is silent on this point. The permission of the Ordinary of the diocese as well as the *beneplacitum* of the Holy See is required for the erection of a new house in a diocese.[92] The Ordinary of the place, therefore, may establish certain restrictions on the activities of the Provincial's subjects when he grants permission for the establishing of the house which is to serve as the seminary for the province. With regard to the seminary itself, however, the administration pertains exclusively to the internal government of the Order, and the Ordinary of the place cannot interfere. Similarly, a house already established in a diocese may be transformed into a seminary in such a way that, without prejudice to the laws of the foundation, the transformation affects only the internal régime and religious discipline of the house, so that the local Ordinary need not be consulted.[93]

Upon the Provincial rests the primary obligation to see that the perfect common life flourishes in the seminary; otherwise he cannot present his subjects for ordination. For this reason he should assign to this house only those priests who are noteworthy for faithfulness in the regular

[91] Can. 1354.

[92] Can. 497, § 1.

[93] Can. 497, § 4. Examples of such a change would be the transformation of a minor seminary for the junior professed into a house of theology for the more advanced seminarians; the addition to a seminary, or to a novitiate already established, of a convalescent home or house of retirement for sick and aged members of the province.

observance.[94] In addition to the canonical visitation he should, like the bishop in regard to the diocesan seminary,[95] frequently visit the seminary to exercise vigilance over the training and education imparted to the students, and to study the character, the piety, the signs of vocation and the progress of the seminarians. Unless particular law or the provincial chapter reserves the right of approval of the seminary statutes to itself, it is incumbent on the Provincial to discharge this duty, as well as to provide for the accurate fulfillment of the requirements of the canons affecting the curriculum of studies.[96]

The proper fulfillment of the pertinent canons requires that the students as well as the professors have sufficient time for study. Therefore the Provincial shall arrange that there will not be imposed upon them any duties which would withdraw them from their studies.[97] The fulfillment of this duty rests immediately upon the Local Superior who must provide that his students and professors are not engaged habitually in the works of the institute or in the active ministry to the detriment of their responsibilities in the seminary. At his visitation, especially, the Provincial is to inquire into the fulfillment of this prescription, as well as regarding the observance of the command of the Sacred Congregation of Religious that students ordained before the middle of their fourth year of Theology shall not engage in the work of the ministry, or in the care of souls.[98]

[94] Can. 554, § 3.

[95] Can. 1357, § 2.

[96] Cans. 589, § 2; 1364-1366.

[97] Can. 589, § 2.

[98] Declar. 27 oct. 1923: "... Sacrae Theologiae operam sedulo dare pergant, saltem usque dum praescriptum quadriennium rite compleatur, vetito interim quocumque animarum ministerio, idest, ne destinentur concionibus habendis aut audiendis confessionibus aut aliis exterioribus Religionis muniis; super quibus Superorum conscientia graviter onerata remaneat."—*AAS*, XV (1923), 549. Vermeersch noted, however, ("Annotationes,"—*Periodica*, XII [1923], 156) that to preach or to hear confessions once or twice is not the same as to be *destined* for the hearing of confessions or for preaching, and that if the other requisites are possessed by the student, such assignments are not necessarily to be prohibited absolutely, and hence may

Furthermore, at the time of his visitation the Provincial should inquire into the faithfulness of the regular observance in the house of studies, the fulfillment of the annual spiritual exercises, and the daily attendance at Holy Mass and at other religious exercises.[99] In individual cases, in the interest of study, he may dispense subjects from fulfilling certain of their duties, particularly the recitation of the nocturnal hours of the Divine Office.[100] Individual exemptions of this type, as well as those granted by particular law, need not be interpreted so strictly as to be effective only during school time; they may also be extended to vacation periods.[101]

If it is impossible to establish a seminary for the province, the Provincial should send his subjects to another well-regulated seminary, whether it be a seminary of the Order, a diocesan seminary, or a regional seminary established with pontifical approval. Coronata asserts that a mere lack of professors in the province does not relieve the Provincial of the duty of erecting a seminary, if the Order or the province can procure a sufficient number of professors, even outsiders, without grave inconvenience.[102] In the event that it is necessary for the Provincial to send his students to another seminary, the particular law or the statutes of the general chapter should provide for the details to be observed

---

be made occasionally (*per modum actus*). It seems, however, that the judgment regarding the necessity of such assignments should be reserved to the Provincial in view of the need of his approval of the priests who are thus to be commissioned occasionally. The opinion of Prümmer that such occasional ministerial work serves as a help rather than as a drawback for the study of theology may well influence the Provincial's judgment in cases where a need exists. (*Manuale Iuris Canonici in Usum Scholarum* [6. ed., Friburgi Brisgoviae: Herder, 1938], qu. 220, n. 5.

99 Can. 595.

100 Can. 589, § 2.

101 Coronata, *Institutiones*, I, p. 774, n. 596; Appeltern, *Compendium*, p. 212, qu. 210.

102 *Institutiones*, I, p. 775, n. 596.

by him. When these are lacking, the General should be sufficiently informed through his visitations and periodic reports on the status of the province, so that he may assist the Provincial with his counsel in this matter. Though the Code grants the right to the Provincial to permit his students to be absent from the province for periods beyond six months for purposes of study,[103] the choice of a seminary outside of the province for *all* his students is really a matter pertaining to the general welfare of the Order, and one in which the General, as the highest Superior, must be consulted.[104]

Canon 588 entrusts the spiritual care of the students in the seminary to the spiritual director. His office is best understood as the counterpart of that of the Novice Master for the formative years of the seminary life of the religious.[105] Usually, particular law will provide for his election or appointment at the provincial chapter. Since the religious and doctrinal spirit of a capable spiritual director, as well as his harmonious relationship with the Local Superior, will color the whole atmosphere of the seminary life, there is a particular need for the Provincial to know both of them well and to exercise discreet watchfulness over their fulfillment of duty.

Canons 590 and 591 are concerned with the fostering of the spirit of study after the completion of the seminary course. Unless particular law prescribes in a special way for their appointment, the examiners who are to administer the examinations to the junior clergy in accordance with canon 590 will be designated by the Provincial. The newly ordained priests are to be excused from the examinations during the five years immediately following the completion of their studies only in such circumstances in which their exemption is warranted by a grave cause to be judged by the

[103] Can. 606, § 2. [104] Can. 502.

[105] Canuto, "De regimine domus studiorum in religione clericali exempta ad normam can. 588."—*Apollinaris* (Romae, 1928——), IX (1936), 35-39.

Provincial. Junior clergy engaged in teaching Canon Law, Sacred Theology or Philosophy are excused by law. Those who teach the cognate sciences required in the theological course[106] are also exempt by law. Larraona cites as sufficient excusing cause the learning of one who is a University professor and a pressing occupation which entails a complete and constant attention.[107] The Provincial may judge the gravity of his obligation in reference to the junior clergy examinations from the fact that the Sacred Congregation of Religious requires, in the quinquennial report made to it, a statement of the reasons motivating any exemptions granted.[108] Certainly, an excessive readiness to exempt subjects or the reduction of these examinations to a mere formality is not the mind of the Church or the law of the Code. According to a response of the Commission for the Interpretation of the Code, when a Provincial neglects entirely to conduct these examinations, the Ordinary may not force the religious pastors or curates to undergo the parallel examination required of the diocesan junior clergy, but the matter should be referred to the Sacred Congregation of Religious.[109]

The grades made in the junior clergy examinations should, in accordance with the provisions of the parallel canon 130, § 2, be taken into account by the Provincial in making appointments in the province. It is thus that he will assure for the province the eventual service of capable and learned officials and Superiors.

The holding of the theological conferences prescribed by canon 591 primarily obliges the Local Superior, although his negligence in the matter is to be corrected by the Provincial, whose duty it is to see to the fulfillment of the duties

[106] From can. 1365, § 2, classes are required in Sacred Scripture, Church History, Sacred Eloquence, Gregorian Chant, Patrology and Liturgy.

[107] "Consultationes"—*CpR*, II (1921), 220, nota 11.

[108] Instr. 1 dec. 1931, n. 10—*AAS*, XXIV (1932), 78.

[109] PCI, 14 iul. 1922—*AAS*, XIV (1922), 526.

of office on the part of Superiors who are his subordinates.[110] Exemptions are to be determined by the particular law of the community.[111]

As to the curriculum, the Provincial must observe the provisions of canons 589 and 1365, which establish minimum requirements in philosophical and theological training; as to the teaching faculty, he must observe the prescription of canon 1380, which urges bishops to send priests selected for their piety and proficiency in these sciences to pontifical schools for the attainment of academic degrees in Theology, Canon Law and Philosophy. The Provincial should, therefore, according to the means and personnel of his province, provide that some of his priests pursue higher studies in these fields.

Necessity or utility will sometimes require that his subjects pursue higher studies in secular universities. The Church regards such cases with maternal concern, and has therefore established certain safeguards which oblige Provincials as well as bishops.[112] Only priests may be sent to such universities. Canon 590, which requires the junior clergy examinations, is to be applied all the more strictly in the case of young priests who pursue studies at such universities.

[110] Cf. Berutti, *Institutiones*, III, n. 106.

[111] Can. 591.

[112] S.C. Consist. decr. 30 apr. 1918—*AAS*, X (1918), 237-238.

CHAPTER VIII

THE PROVINCIAL SUPERIOR AND RELIGIOUS OBSERVANCE

The Provincial, as has already been noted, has the grave obligation of promoting the common good of the Order. Besides giving personal example in the faithful observance of his vows, the Rule and the constitutions,[1] he must strive to achieve the end of his office by promoting among his subjects the observance of the canons pertaining to the obligations of Religious as delineated in the Code in *Title XIII* of the tract *"De Religiosis."* The sources of these canons reveal the traditional character of the obligations imposed by them, as obligations resulting from the historical development of the clerical and religious states.

Through the profession of the three vows, religious embrace the state of evangelical perfection as their state in life.[2] In the interest of the spiritual perfection of clerics in general, the Code lists many duties binding them and flowing from the need for a greater measure of holiness in the clerical than in the lay state.[3] Religious, then, whose state of life is one which tends to perfection, are appropriately placed under the obligation of fulfilling the duties of clerics in general in so far as these duties are consonant with the religious state. Furthermore, they are obliged by their very profession to strive after perfection through the observance of the vows, the Rule, and the constitutions of their particular community.[4]

As the bishop is pastor of his diocese,[5] so the Provincial is pastor of the province. Consequently he must directly or indirectly insure the observance of duties deriving from the state of life of the subjects committed to his care. Accordingly the canons under *Title XIII* can be viewed as conducing to the observance of the three vows, of the Rule, of

[1] Can. 593.
[2] Can. 487.
[3] Cans. 124-142.
[4] Can. 593.
[5] Can. 334, § 1.

the obligation of striving for perfection, and of the common or special obligations imposed upon religious.

Pre-Code legislation illustrated the intention of the Church that religious Superiors promote the regular observance of their subjects. Alexander III (1159-1181) urged the Cistercian abbots to guarantee for their Rule its pristine vigor.[6] Under the threat of punishment, monks as well as clerics were commanded to avoid those activities which were unbecoming to the clerical state.[7]

The Council of Trent admonished Superiors to use all care and diligence to insure that their subjects would faithfully observe what pertained to the perfection of their state of life, namely the vows of obedience, poverty and chastity, as well as the preservation of the common life, especially in regard to food and clothing.[8] Clement VIII (1592-1605) was even more specific. He mentioned the chapter of faults as a means for promoting faithfulness in regular observance.[9] The Sacred Congregation of Bishops and Regulars issued a detailed decree in 1815 to the effect that religious observance be fostered in accordance with earlier decrees.[10]

Pius IX in his Encyclical *Nostis et Nobiscum* wrote that Major Superiors should spare no effort in working for the promotion of religious discipline through the observance of the vows of religion, of the Rule, and of the obligations of the particular institutes.[11] Finally, Pius IX in his Encyclical *Cum nuper* warned bishops to ordain only those who were worthy, and insisted that extreme watchfulness was

[6] C. 3, 4, 6, X, *de statu monachorum et canonicorum regularium,* III, 35.

[7] C. 1, 4, 6, X, *ne clerici vel monachi saecularibus negotiis se immisceant,* II, 50.

[8] Conc. Trident, sess. XXV, *de regularibus,* c. 1; Schroeder, *Canons and Decrees,* p. 218.

[9] Clemens VIII, decr. *Nullus omnino,* 25 iul. 1599, § 25—*Fontes,* n. 187.

[10] S. C.Ep. et Reg., decr. 22 aug. 1814, n. XI—*Fontes,* n. 1893.

[11] 8 dec. 1849, n. 26—*Fontes,* n. 508.

to be exercised over the junior clergy.[12] Although this encyclical was addressed to all the local Ordinaries of the Kingdom of Sicily, its application to religious candidates for the priesthood is seen in its citation among the sources of canon 593. Consequently its injunctions were to be applied to religious through their Ordinaries upon whom the responsibility of attesting to the worthiness of candidates for the priesthood among their subjects fell.

1. *The Observance of the Vows*

The obligation assumed by the religious in his profession of vows is a grave one. First of all, he submits his will to that of his Superiors, inclusive of the Provincial. They may accordingly impose gravely binding precepts on him in virtue of the vow of obedience. The Provincial obviously may do so, as well as the Local Superior and the Superior General. The precepts of the Provincial, however, as of other religious Superiors, bind in virtue of the vow of obedience only when they are imposed according to the Rule of the community.

Precepts which go contrary to, which reach beyond, or which are in no way contained even implicitly in the Rule, do not bind in virtue of the vow of obedience. Vermeersch stated that oligations which bind in virtue of the vow of obedience are usually stated as such in the particular law of religious institutes, and that it is ordinarily the presumption that such an obligation does not exist unless it is so expressed.[13] Ordinarily, therefore, it is not presumed that the Provincial commands in virtue of the vow of obedience unless he, or the nature of the case, clearly indicates this fact.

The vow of poverty touches the acts of proprietorship and administration. The relationship of the Provincial to the

[12] 20 ian. 1858—*Fontes*, n. 523.

[13] Cf. *supra*, pp. 37-42; Vermeersch, *Theologiae Moralis Principia, Responsa, Consilia* (4 vols., Romae: 1922-1924, III, p. 123, n. 139; Wernz-Vidal, *De Religiosis*, pp. 364-365, n. 363.

vow of poverty is discussed immediately below where special consideration is given to his duty to safeguard the common life.

The vow of chastity is protected by the religious cloister. The Provincial's relationship to it will be discussed in the study of his duty to safeguard the cloister.

A. The Common Life

One of the essential elements in the Code's definition of the religious life is that it is a firmly established manner of living in community.[14] The notion of the *"common life"* describes this idea of living together on a family or social basis. Accordingly, the Code forbids religious to live apart from the community except for reasons of study. In the event of an absence beyond six months for any other reason, a special indult must be obtained from the Holy See.[15]

More strictly, the *"common life"* in the canonical sense means living the life professed by persons who have taken the vow of poverty. It demands that all religious in common use the goods of the community, and possess nothing individually in the way of food, clothing, or furniture. It requires further that anything acquired by religious, even by Superiors, must be incorporated with the goods of the community.[16]

The Council of Trent commanded Superiors in their general and provincial chapters and in their visitations to insure that the essential elements of religious life, namely, the vows and the community of goods, food, and clothing, be accurately observed by all religious. It decreed that movable or immovable property should not be held in the individual's name, but should be incorporated with the goods of the convent to be administered solely by officials removable at the will of the Superiors.[17] To the Fathers of the Council of Trent, then, the *"common life"* was of such essential importance to the integrity of religious observance

[14] Can. 487. [15] Can. 606, § 2. [16] Can. 594, § 1, 2°.

[17] Conc. Trident., sess. XXV, *de regularibus*, cc. 1, 2.

that the responsibility for its preservation was imposed primarily on the Provincial and the General Superiors in their chapters and visitations. In turn, they were to insure it through the ministry of the Local Superiors.

Clement VIII in his Constitution *Nullus omnino* urged a perfect observance of the common life and denied the power to any Superior to interpret his decree in a contrary sense.[18] Similarly, various decrees of the Sacred Congregation for Bishops and Regulars[19] insisted upon the perfect observance of the common life and directed the attention of the higher Superiors to the law of the Council of Trent.

The requirement of canon 569, § 2, regarding the novice's disposition of goods aims at safeguarding the common life. Its observance must be insured by the Provincial personally, or through the Local Superior or the Novice Master. The gravity of the matter is indicated in canon 580, § 3, which provides that when a professed religious wishes to change the disposition of goods arranged in accordance with canon 569, § 2, he must have recourse to the General unless particular law specify otherwise.

In the eyes of the Church, the observance of the common life in religion is so important that those who violate it are to be warned canonically and, if the warning be to no avail, are to be punished with the privation of their vote and their eligibility for office or both, and with deposition from office.[20] This penal sanction evinces further evidence that the common life is of supreme importance to the integrity of the religious observance, that its furtherance and also the practise of personal compliance with it rests as a responsibility upon the Major Superior.[21]

[18] 25 iul. 1599—*Fontes*, n. 187.

[19] S.C. Ep. et Reg., *Pacten.*, 22 dec. 1579—*Fontes*, n. 1365; *Messanen.*, 1 mart. 1595—*Fontes*, n. 1534; decr. 22 aug. 1814, n. X—*Fontes*, n. 1893; decr. 22 apr. 1851—*Fontes*, n. 1959.

[20] Can. 2389.

[21] Pre-Code authors spoke of the *perfect common life* and the *less perfect common life.* The less perfect common life allowed the use of the *peculium*, that is, of the private and personal sums of money

B. The Cloister

Through canon 597 the law of the cloister is imposed upon Regulars. Experience proves that an unrestricted free communication with the outside world is not beneficial to monastic discipline. To safeguard the vow of chastity and to protect the peace and solitude of the religious house of regulars for recollection and prayer, this law prohibits the entrance of persons of the other sex[22] within certain limits of the monastery, and obliges religious to seek the proper permission before leaving the monastery. Custom, particular law and papal sanctions have been the source of the present law governing the cloister in monasteries of men religious.

The early sources listed in connection with canon 597 pertain to the cloister of nuns as imposed by Boniface VIII (1294-1303) in his Constitution *Periculoso*.[23] Pope St. Pius V (1566-1572) first imposed the general law of the cloister on monasteries of men and women religious through the Constitutions *Regularium*[24] and *Decet*.[25] Under the law of these Constitutions, women entering the monasteries of men were automatically (*ipso facto*) placed under an excommunication reserved to the Pope, and the Superior who ad-

---

accruing from one's estate or from the goods of the Order. Canon 594, § 2, is opposed to this private *peculium*. Chelodi correctly noted (*Ius de Personis*, p.461, n. 4) that the possibility of a lawfully tolerated immemorial custom to the contrary is not excluded by this canon. In the light of canon 5, however, the maintenance of such a custom is conditioned on the proper authority's judgment that the immemorial practice cannot be prudently set aside.

[22] A later consideration of the relationship of the Provincial to nuns subject to him will deal with his duties in reference to their cloister. In the present article the writer is concerned solely with the cloister of male religious. Further, since this study pertains only to Regulars who have the papal cloister, the writer will abstract from the consideration of the episcopal cloister throughout the discussion.

[23] C. un., *de statu regularium*, III, 16, in VI°; Conc. Trident., sess. XXV, *de regularibus*, c. 5.

[24] 24 oct. 1566—*Fontes*, n. 115.

[25] 16 iul. 1570—*Fontes*, n. 136.

mitted them was suspended and furthermore was to be deprived not only of his present office but also of his eligibility for a future office.

Benedict XIV (1740-1758) in his Constitution *Regularis* condemned and reprobated all privileges, exceptions or faculties contrary to the prohibition of Pope St. Pius.[26] Pius IX (1846-1878) renewed the excommunication incurred by women who entered the cloister and by Superiors who admitted them.[27] Clement VIII (1592-1605) had forbidden Regulars to leave their monasteries unaccompanied and without permission.[28] But no special penalty was established for offenders in the matter of unlawful egress other than that dictated by particular law or enacted by the Superior.

In the present law the establishment of the limits of the cloister pertains to the Provincial unless particular law reserves this act to the Superior General or the general chapter. However, the actual preservation of the law of the cloister pertains more immediately to the Local Superior. In accordance with the law of the cloister, a certain area within and about the religious house is so reserved for the religious that entrance by persons of the other sex is forbidden,[29] and permission from the Local Superior in communities of men religious is required for the egress of these religious.

The obligation of the law is a grave one and for this reason, the limits of the cloister are to be clearly indicated. The definition of the limits of the cloister gives rise not merely to local obligations, but likewise to general ones which affect everyone who comes to the religious. The act of setting the cloistral limits is accordingly a matter that relates to the common good and thus exceeds the scope of the Local Superior's jurisdiction. It is a major issue of which

[26] 3 ian. 1742—*Fontes*, n. 322.

[27] Const. *Apostolicae Sedis*, 12 oct. 1869, § 11, 7—*Fontes*, n. 552.

[28] Const. *Nullus omnino*, 25 iul. 1599, § 11—*Fontes*, n. 187.

[29] Can. 597, § 1, 2°.

the Code has taken cognizance in its designation of the Provincial as the competent authority for defining the limits of the cloister.

The Provincial, however, has not the optional power to accept or to reject the establishing of the papal cloister. Canon 597, § 1, imposes the obligation of the cloister upon all houses of Regulars regardless of the fully or only partially organized status of these houses.[30] Once the decree of erection of the house is drawn up according to canon 497, § 1, with the consent of the Ordinary and the *beneplacitum* of the Holy See, the obligation of the cloister arises. At that point, if not earlier, the Provincial is obliged to determine the boundaries of the cloister.

In the case of a new house, the proper planning of it will necessarily involve the element of a proper provision for the cloister. After the building is completed, it is the duty of the Provincial to determine the moment from which the law of the cloister will bind.[31] Failure on the part of the Provincial to determine the boundaries of the cloister is a serious lapse of duty. Once the proper permissions for the erecting of the house have been obtained, the obligation of the observance of the cloister binds all who live there, an obligation that they cannot properly fulfill unless the boundaries are determined.

On the other hand, the obligation of the cloister is not associated with residence at temporary dwellings, such as those which are used for vacation purposes alone, since these do not involve the element of stability or of permanence. Similarly, if religious must reside temporarily in a rented building until they acquire permanent quarters, there is lacking in that residence the stability postulated for giving rise to the cloistral obligation as connected with a house of Regulars, unless the temporary quarters be canonically erected as a religious house.[32] Ownership of the dwelling is

[30] Cf. can. 488, 5°, for a description of the *domus formata.*

[31] Vermeersch-Creusen, *Epitome,* I, n. 754.

[32] Nevertheless, care should be taken in the observance of the clois-

not a necessary condition for the canonical erection of a house of religious, since the stability inherent in the religious life is readily associated with rented quarters.

Just as the Provincial can define the limits of the cloister, so he can also change them.[33] However, the Code requires lawful reasons for such a step. Thus the enlarging or the reducing of the extent of the cloister according to the needs of the community, or the changing of the plan of the cloister to facilitate its better observance, would certainly warrant such a step. Care must be taken, however, that the evasion of canonical penalties is not the primary or perhaps even the exclusive purpose for the new arrangement of the cloistral boundaries.[34]

The proper custody of the cloister demands that its limits be clearly indicated, and that entrance into it be forbidden in accordance with the common and particular law. Its immediate custody will depend upon the Local Superior, who is to be watchful lest the advent of male visitors within it—should particular legislation not forbid their visits—frustrate the aim of the cloister in regard to religious silence and discipline. Within the authority which is not reserved to the Provincial he may, even through a delegate, grant permissions to leave the cloister. Generally the constitutions restrict this power so that he may not grant permission for an absence beyond three days.

The Provincial in turn is to be guided by canon 606, § 2, which requires a grave and just cause for an absence from the monastery for a period under six months, except for study; the permission of the Holy See is required for longer periods other than study.

---

tral obligation whenever possible even in temporary quarters. Schaaf noted that even in the cases of temporary residence, the particular law may enact penalties which the Provincial is to inflict for violations of the religious quarters (*The Cloister*, The Catholic University of America Canon Law Studies, n. 13 [Washington, D. C.: The Catholic University of America, 1921] p. 61).

[33] Can. 597, § 3.

[34] Schaaf, *The Cloister*, p. 73.

Since it is within the jurisdiction of the Provincial to assign the religious to the various houses of the province, it appears that his permission is required even in the case of religious who seek permission in some extraordinary case to reside in another house of the province for a period exceeding that specified in the constitutions as within the competence of the Local Superior. Particular law might, of course, provide otherwise.

As just noted, the special permission of the Holy See is required for absences from the cloister for a period beyond six months for causes other than that of pursuing studies.[35] The text of the canon in itself is quite severe. Vermeersch noted that its literal observance would introduce a new and severe obligation that could scarcely be harmonized with the works of many communities. Therefore, he concluded that the constant recourse of religious to the Holy See for permission to fulfill the very ministerial work of their vocation is not required by the Code. The writer subscribes to this view.[36]

But canon 606 does prohibit residence outside of the monastery for purposes foreign to the particular work of the religious. Thus a sick or convalescent religious who must reside for a period beyond six months at a resort or a sanitarium needs the permission of the Holy See. The Sacred Congregation of Religious warned Superiors that such permission must not be sought without sufficient reason, and obliged the Superiors, should the permission be granted, to insure that their subjects: 1) reside in a religious hospital or at least in a fitting place; 2) are faithful in wearing the habit; 3) avoid the frequenting of movies, theaters, games, etc.; and 4) obey these regulations under

[35] Can. 606.

[36] Vermeersch, "Dissertationes et Quaesita"—*Periodica*, X (1921), (36); Coronata, *Institutiones*, I, p. 796, n. 612; Schaefer, *De Religiosis*, p. 735, n. 364; Beste, *Introductio*, p. 411; Creusen, *Réligieux et Réligieuses d'après le Droit Ecclésiastique* (3. ed., Paris: Beauchesne, 1924), p. 215.

pain of serious punishment.[37] Furthermore, the Sacred Congregation of the Council in a similar letter concerning secular priests residing in such places instructed Ordinaries to be vigilant also with regard to religious, and to report them to their Major Superiors if they were guilty of misconduct.[38]

The obligation of seeking permission to reside outside the monastery in such conditions is most reasonable. It is difficult to see, however, that the canon would apply in the case of necessary confinement to a hospital or in an insane asylum. The purpose of the legislator in the present law is the observance of religious discipline and the avoidance of any deviation from the common life in a manner that would prove foreign to the religious profession, or that would be fraught with danger to the religious. Strict hospital cases or confinements to mental institutions are not envisioned in the scope of the law. When an illness is prolonged and postulates a long confinement of the religious, even as an invalid, the Provincial could apply for permission, but, in the opinion of the writer, he is hardly obliged to do so.

Coronata, Schaefer and Beste accept the opinion of Vermeersch that residence outside of the monastery for the performance of work conformable to the end and purpose of the institute is not prohibited.[39] Berutti, too, appears to accept this view, although he is not quite as specific as the former authors, and emphasizes the necessity of conformity with the particular law.[40] Accordingly, a religious engaged in the care of souls in a hospital, or in a parish, or in other work included within the purpose and end of his community, such as that of a chaplain in a seminary, does not require the

[37] S.C. de Religiosis, Litterae ad Moderatores Ordinum et Congregationum de religiosis qui, valetudinis causa, stationes balneares adeunt, 15 iul. 1926—*CpR*, VII (1926), 295.

[38] S. C. Conc., Litterae circulares ad omnes Ordinarios, 1 iul. 1926, n. 7—*AAS*, XVIII (1926), 312-313.

[39] Vermeersch, *loc. cit.;* Schaefer, *loc. cit.*; Coronata, *loc. cit.;* Beste, *Introductio*, 411.

[40] *Institutiones*, III, 270-271.

permission of the Holy See, since he dwells in the particular place as a subject of his lawful Superior, and by reason of his very vocation. Following the view of Vermeersch, the cited authors justify their opinion by alleging that such works are implicitly approved by the Holy See in the approval of the community and its works.

It seems to the present writer, however, that the implicit approval of the Holy See for the works of a community extends only to those works that can be done in conformity with community life itself and without any grave disturbance of the community life in favor of the work. Otherwise, every member of the community could live separately, provided, of course, that he was doing the work for which the community was approved. Obviously, community life would thus be destroyed, although the community might continue to pursue its approved work. In consequence, then, individual cases must be considered thoroughly by the Provincial and, in the opinion of the present writer, only in exceptional cases could the more liberal view be followed, in which case the Provincial's action might be justified, not by reason of the arguments alleged in its favor, but rather by reason of the authority of the authors who espouse this opinion.

The Provincial's responsibility requires him to judge prudently as to the necessity of each case and its compatibility with the religious state as obligatory in the specific institute. It may be found that, according to the mind of the legislator as well as the text of the law, an absence is justified, even beyond six months, but with certain limiting safeguards. Thus, in the cases of chaplaincies, the needs of the ministry may adequately be cared for through the rotation of service rendered by several members of the community after a periodic absence of short duration. When this is not feasible, a periodic return of the absent religious to the cloister may be demanded. Such expedients may even be obligatory on the Provincial in virtue of particular law.

Violations of the law of the cloister which prohibits the entrance of women are punished according to canon 2342,

2°. Women entering the cloister against the prohibition of the canon, with the exception of those specified in canon 598, § 2, and also those who admit women incur by that very act an excommunication whose absolution is reserved to the Holy See in a simple manner. Girls under twelve years of age, however, are not subject to the penalty;[41] on the other hand, those who admit them are subject to the penalty.[42] The gravity of the penalty indicates the serious nature of the law. The penalty imposed for the violation of the cloister follows only upon a violation interpreted in a strict sense. The penalty is not incurred, therefore, in the event that the cloister has not been defined, or if the obligation of observing it has not been officially imposed by the Provincial.

Although the local Ordinary is commissioned to watch over the observance of the cloister of nuns, even though they are subject to Regulars, the cloister of houses pertaining to Orders of men is under the jurisdiction, custody, and vigilance of the Regular Superiors alone.[43] Abuses in the observance of the cloister in houses of exempt male religious, however, can be noted by the local Ordinary and called to the attention of the Regular Superior, even as any abuse in the religious observance can be called to his attention.[44] In the event that the Superior does not correct the abuse, the local Ordinary still has no jurisdiction, but he can then inform the Holy See of the abuse.[45]

[41] Can. 2320.

[42] Schaaf, *The Cloister*, p. 99.

[43] O'Brien, *The Exemption of Religious*, p. 111.

[44] Can. 617, § 1. The canon does not specify which Superior is to be informed. The Ordinary may inform either the Local Superior or the Provincial.

[45] *Loc. cit.* In canon 617, § 1, there is to be noted a difference between the former and the present law in the matter of the smaller houses of Regulars. Formerly, only those houses at which the proper number of religious resided, six according to some, and twelve according to others, enjoyed the privilege of exemption. Now, by reason of canon 615, all houses of Regulars are exempt. Thus, even the partially organized houses (*domus non-formatae*) are exempt accord-

As the Provincial has the right to determine and to change the limits of the cloister, so he can also judge regarding the feasibility of reserving a special section of the house for the religious, when the house has annexed to it a boarding-school or some other project or enterprise of the community to which lay people must have access.[46] The Code advises this, and it is the Provincial who must settle the question in the various potential adaptations it involves. As Schaaf noted, however, the Code implicitly requires that a day-school be situated outside the enclosure.[47]

The law of the cloister is one means of restricting the relationship between the monastery and the world; other restrictions depend on particular law or provincial statutes.[48] In regard to letters, however, particular law cannot conflict with canon 611, which grants subjects the right to correspond freely with Superiors, inclusive of the Provincial, and to receive communications from them that are exempt from inspection.

2. *The Observance of the Rule and the Obligation to Strive after Perfection*

Superiors and subjects alike must faithfully observe their vows and, by conforming their lives to their particular Rule and constitutions, strive after perfection.[49] In this command of the Code the teaching of the Council of Trent is clearly reiterated.[50] Popes at all times have insisted upon

---

ing to the present law, although they are entrusted to the *vigilance* of the local Ordinary. Only when some scandalous abuses, in the eyes of the faithful, exist, can the local Ordinary act according to the present law. Moreover, his action is altogether of a provisional character until he has informed the Holy See of the abuse, in order that the Holy See itself may take action in the case. (Vermeersch-Creusen, *Epitome*, I, n. 777).

[46] Can. 599, § 1.

[47] *The Cloister*, p. 99.

[48] E.g., use of the radio, television, parlor calls, visits.

[49] Can. 593.

[50] Conc. Trident., sess. XXV, *de regularibus*, c. 1.

the observance of these obligations, since an Order prospers in the degree in which it is faithful to the end for which it was instituted, in the pursuit of which its Rule and constitutions are the guides. Through canon 593, independently of the binding force of the particular Rule or constitutions, a general obligation to conform one's life to them is now established in the Code for the individual religious.

The very nature of the office of Provincial requires the enforcement of law obligatory on his subjects, particularly that of the Rule and the constitutions. Particular law generally enlarges the extent of this obligation, an obligation the scope of which is broadened by reference to the analogous duties incumbent on a bishop in his diocese. The latter is instructed to enforce all ecclesiastical laws in his territory,[51] to be vigilant lest abuses creep in,[52] and to govern the diocese with legislative, judicial and coercive power. Similarly, then, the Provincial, as his counterpart in the government of religious, has parallel obligations, exclusive of legislative power, unless this latter right has been conferred by particular law. Usually the Provincial's obligations and rights are specifically itemized in the particular law.

The obligation which according to canon 593 requires religious to strive after perfection binds individual religious whether they are Superiors or subjects. Through the enforcement of religious discipline and the punishment of transgressions Superiors remove external difficulties and impediments, but the attainment of perfect charity is a goal to which the individual religious must strive himself. As Berutti states, this obligation does not bind the religious to perform heroic acts, to choose the more perfect action in every instance, or to make use of all the means by which perfection is achieved.[53] The religious is not presumed to be perfect, but he must strive for that goal.[54] Pius XI, in his

[51] Can. 336, § 1.

[52] Can. 336, § 2.

[53] *Institutiones*, III, 245.

[54] *Summa Theologica*, II-II, qu. 186.

letter *Unigenitus* of March 19, 1924,[55] stated that the best means for religious to strive after perfection is to become thoroughly imbued with the spirit of the Order. Any formal contempt of these means, permanent habits of serious sin, or grave delicts against one's religious state certainly constitute a violation of the injunction of canon 593.

The Provincial amply satisfies the obligation of canon 593 through giving in his own life an example of faithfulness to the spirit of the Order and through ceaselessly inculcating loyalty to it upon all his subjects.

3. *The Observance of Special Obligations*

By reason of his pastoral office, the diocesan bishop is obliged to enforce the general laws enacted for clerics in canons 124-142. All religious are equally obliged to the observance of these same laws in so far as they are conformable to their state of life.[56] The responsibility for the fulfillment of these obligations in the religious province resides primarily with the Provincial, although particular law and provincial government generally require their immediate enforcement by the Local Superiors. The general law as enacted for clerics, and as applicable to religious, requires of the latter a holier mode of life than that of the laity;[57] obedience and reverence to the diocesan bishop in so far as they are subject to him;[58] the pursuit of clerical studies after their ordination;[59] modesty in dress and personal appearance;[60] and abstinence from unbecoming pursuits, avocations, and amusements.[61]

Besides the fulfillment of these general obligations binding on clerics and religious alike, the Provincial as Ordinary should provide for the observance of the common and special obligations of religious. The immediate enforcement of these obligations should be effected by the Local Superior

[55] *AAS*, XVI, (1924), 133.
[56] Can. 592.
[57] Can. 124.
[58] Can. 127.
[59] Can. 129.
[60] Cans. 136, 142.
[61] Cans. 138, 139, 142.

under the supervision of the Provincial. It is the Provincial's duties in their regard, however, that will be treated in the following sections.

A. Pious Practices Incumbent on Religious

A comparison of canon 595 with the parallel canons affecting secular clerics leads to the conclusion that the responsibility for the fulfillment of the obligation of the yearly retreat and the other pious practices prescribed by canon 595 rests upon the Provincial Superior despite the use of the general term "Superiors." It is true that one should not distinguish when the law makes no distinction, but it requires no distinguishing to perceive that the fulfillment of the obligations of canon 595 is a matter affecting the general welfare of the province, and that the application to the Provincial of the analogous obligation for the diocesan bishop is accordingly justified.[62] Moreover, such a reservation implies no great diminution of the Local Superior's power, since the responsibility for the immediate fulfillment of the law resides with him by the very nature of his office.

The Code has not determined the duration of the yearly retreat for religious, but particular law frequently does. Canon 126 requires the Ordinary to determine the duration of the retreat for his subjects. Analogously, in the case of religious, if the particular law, the provincial statutes, and laudably established custom are silent on the matter, it is the Provincial who determines it. A norm may be drawn from the Encyclical *Mens Nostra* of Pius XI on fostering the practice of retreats among the classes of the faithful, religious, and clerics. The encyclical advocated a duration ranging from a few days to a month according to the circumstances of time, place, and individuals; but, according to the same encyclical, a rather narrow restriction of the duration of the retreat should not be adopted, lest the proper benefits expected of it be lost.[63]

[62] Cans. 125, 126.

[63] 20 dec. 1929—*AAS*, XXI (1929), 700-703.

Shortly after the issuance of this encyclical the appropriate duration of the retreats of religious was determined more precisely in a particular case in which the Sacred Congregation of Religious in 1931 prescribed a minimum of five full days for extern sisters in convents of nuns.[64] Though the determination of the duration of these exercises should be made by the Provincial in the absense of specific particular legislation,[65] details can be settled by the Local Superior with the approval of the Provincial, such as the schedule, the time of the year, and the choice of the Retreat-Master. By analogy with the competence of the local Ordinary, the exemption of a religious from the community retreat is reserved to the Provincial, unless particular law grants this right to the Local Superior. When such exemption is sought, the conditions of canon 126 should be present, namely, a just cause in a particular case and the express permission of the Provincial.

Assistance at daily Mass, mental prayer, and other religious practices are enumerated in canon 595, § 1, 2°, as pious practices the observance of which Superiors are required to promote, especially the Local Superior, although the Provincial, because of his responsibility for the spiritual status of his province, is required in the visitation to inquire into their fulfillment.[66]

The Local Superior will look to the fulfillment of the obligation of religious to receive the Sacrament of Penance weekly,[67] although both he and the Provincial have the right to question their subjects in regard to their faithfulness in this matter.[68]

[64] S.C. de Religiosis, instr. 16 iul. 1931—*AAS*, XXIII (1931), 380; *Apollinaris*, IV (1931), 345-360, n. 87.

[65] Cf. can. 126.

[66] The obligation of attendence at daily Mass will be discussed in the section pertaining to the conventual Mass, since Regulars who are obliged to choir duty are obliged to the celebration of the conventual Mass.

[67] Can. 595, § 1, 3°.

[68] The subject also has the obligation of manifesting to the Su-

Frequent and even daily reception of Holy Communion is to be promoted by Superiors among their subjects.[69] The fulfillment of this regulation is also the immediate concern of the Local Superior, although the Provincial's care for the spiritual welfare of the province requires that he direct the attention of his subjects to it when circumstances demand. Ordinarily, frequent and even daily Communion is quite generally practiced in religious communities. The Provincial must not overlook the Instruction of the Sacred Congregation of the Sacraments wherein local Ordinaries and Major Superiors of religious Orders are commanded to exhort subjects to frequent Communion, provided that the latter are properly disposed. On the other hand, the Superior should inform his subjects that it is not a matter of obligation to receive Communion daily.[70] The immediate fulfillment of this injunction is also primarily the concern of the Local Superior; but the Provincial should call his attention to the Instruction and solicit his care in fulfilling the wishes of the Sacred Congregation.

B. Wearing of the Religious Habit

The general obligation of clerics to wear an ecclesiastical garb according to the customs of the place and the prescriptions of their Ordinary[71] has also its counterpart for religious. Canon 596 prescribes the wearing of the proper religious habit within and outside the monastery, unless a grave cause, ordinarily to be judged by the Provincial, excuses the religious from compliance with this law.

It has always been the mind of the Church that religious should wear their proper habit. Thus Boniface VIII (1294-

---

perior who inquires whether he has an ordinary confessor, as well as when, and where, he confesses to him (Wernz-Vidal, *De Religiosis*, p. 381, nota 20).

[69] Can. 595, § 2.

[70] 8 dec. 1938, n. II, 1—Bouscaren, *The Canon Law Digest*, Supplement (Milwaukee: Bruce, 1941), pp. 97-104.

[71] Can. 136, § 1.

1313) imposed the penalty of excommunication upon those who laid aside their habit without a just cause;[72] and Clement V (1305-1314) decreed special penalties against those who refused without reason to wear the habit which their state required of them.[73] So serious was the fault of such religious, that the laying aside of the habit was sometimes considered a sign of apostasy. The Council of Trent declared that discontented religious who impugn the validity of their obligations and lay aside the habit should be returned to their monasteries and treated as apostates. Moreover, it was unlawful for a religious to wear his habit in a concealed manner.[74]

Although there is no penal sanction attached to the present law, the gravity of the obligation can be measured from the injunction that the judgment regarding the existence of an excusing cause should ordinarily be made by the Provincial. No power is hereby given to him to dispense with the wearing of the habit, but merely the faculty to judge the gravity of the excusing cause.[75] The faculty to dispense a religious from wearing the habit is reserved to the Holy Father, since it is so closely connected with the essential obligations of the religious.[76]

C. Choral Recitation of the Divine Office

The choral recitation of the Divine Office has long been of obligation among Regulars. Clement V (1305-1314) decreed that the canonical hours be recited in cathedral, Regular, and collegiate churches. Contemporaneously the particular law of the individual communities strongly urged it as a grave obligation. The Code states that the obligation of choir exists in those communities whose members are

[72] C. 2, *ne clerici vel monachi saecularibus negotiis se immisceant,* III, 24, in VI°.

[73] C. 2, *de vita et honestate clericorum,* III, 1, in Clem.

[74] Conc. Trident., sess, XXV, *de degularibus,* c. 19.

[75] Vermeersch-Creusen, *Epitome,* I, n. 754.

[76] Wernz-Vidal, *De Religiosis,* p. 381, n. 373.

bound to the choral recitation of the Divine Office whenever there are at least four religious actually present who are bound by it and are not lawfully impeded from fulfilling it. If particular law requires the obligation to be satisfied by less than four, this stricter provision supersedes that of the Code.[77]

From the beginning of the Mendicant history, the responsibility for the fulfillment of this obligation has been ascribed to the Local Superior in virtue of his office and its concomitant duties in regard to the regular observance.[78] The obligation imposed by the Code is a local and real one in every house where the necessary conditions are fulfilled. Though it is true that the Local Superior, in virtue of his office, is primarily obliged to insure the fulfillment of the community choral obligations, the same grave responsibility rests upon his subjects not to impede the fulfillment of the law through any unlawful absence from the choir.

In regard to choir duty, the Provincial's responsibility is a general one in relation to the whole province. He must investigate the choral observance at his visitations and provide for its proper fulfillment, at least in part, if the entire obligation cannot be satisfied owing to the inadequate number of religious residing in a given house, i.e., a number less than that required by general or particular law in the fulfillment of this obligation.[79] To fulfill this responsibility, he

[77] Can. 610, § 1. It should be noted that the Code requires the presence in choir of four religious to satisfy the obligation of choral recitation of the Divine Office. But novices are religious, at least in a broad sense, and hence they can be counted in the number present with reference to the satisfying of the obligation (Coronata, *Institutiones*, I, p. 810, n. 616; Piontek, "Choir Duty and Conventual Mass in Religious Communities"—*The Homiletic and Pastoral Review*, XLIII [1943], p. 804, note 10; Vermeersch-Creusen, *Epitome*, I, n. 768).

[78] Benedictus XII, const. *Redemptor Noster*, 28 iul. 1336, § 4—*Bull. Rom. Taur.*, IV, 392; Donatus, *Rerum Regularium Praxis*, Tom. IV, tr. XVIII, qu. XXVIII, n. 2; *ibid.*, Tom. III, tr. XVIII, qu. XXIII, n. 2.

[79] Cf. Goyeneche, "Consultationes"—*CpR*, VII (1926), 455-456.

can oblige by precept the members of religious houses, if they are not lawfully impeded, to be present in choir if their presence is required to make up the number necessary to satisfy the choral obligation. Even if less than four religious obliged to choir duty are available, he can still urge the recitation of the Office by them in choir. If he does this by precept in particular cases, the subjects are obliged to obey, although the obligation thus imposed, in the absence of special circumstances, would be grave only if the constitutions impose the choir obligation on less than four religious when the Provincial judges that number to suffice.

When four religious cannot be present for the recitation of all the hours because of ministerial or other lawful occupations, the Provincial would offend against community regularity if he urged the daily changing of the time for choir to harmonize with schedules that would release a sufficient number of religious for choir.[80] In this case the fulfillment of the obligation becomes morally impossible for the recitation of certain hours, although a probable opinion holds that two or three who are available may satisfy the obligation, even though by law they are not bound to do so.[81] Indeed, in these situations the Provincial can laudably urge the custom of reciting those hours in choir even with an inadequate number of religious in attendance. Where such a practice is customary, the fault of one who is unlawfully absent is only venial, and the Local Superior will need a less grave reason to excuse from the choir service a subject whose presence is necessary to constitute the canonical *quorum,* since in view of the probable opinion just noted there is moral certainty in both cases that the grave obligation will be fulfilled in spite of his absence.

The Provincial possesses no general dispensatory faculty over the law of the choral obligation, although his position as Ordinary empowers him to determine in particular cases

[80] Coronata, *Institutiones,* I, p. 810, n. 616.

[81] Fanfani, *De Iure Religiosorum,* p. 409; Goyeneche, "Consultationes"—*CpR,* (1925), 204-206.

the existence of the conditions that result in the obligation. It has been seen above, however,[82] that the Code does give him the power to dispense students and teachers in particular cases from the recitation of all or certain canonical hours in order that their studies may be fostered.[83]

With regard to the private recitation of the Office of those bound to it,[84] religious prelates possess many privileges. They may commute the obligation of the Divine Office to the recitation of seven Psalms, seven Our Fathers and the Apostles' Creed twice, for subjects engaged in or impeded by: a) works of the ministry; b) the teaching of Theology or Canon Law; or c) sickness which is not sufficient in itself to be an excusing cause.[85] Julius II granted regular prelates the privilege, still retained, of dispensing their subjects from the recitation of the Office, on condition that they impose some prayers to be said.[86]

Finally, religious Superiors can commute, into the recitation of the Little Office of the Blessed Virgin or other prayers, the obligation of the private recitation of the Office, for priests while engaged in mission work and those traveling to and from the place where they will be engaged in that work, as well as for those conducting retreats, novenas, tridua, or any continuous preaching assignment.[87]

D. Assistance at the Conventual Mass

Consistently with canon 413, § 2, the obligation to celebrate a conventual Mass corresponding to the Office of the day is imposed upon religious houses bound to the choral recitation of the Office.[88] Generally considered the phrase

[82] Cf. *supra*, p. 50. [83] Can. 589, § 2. [84] Cf. can. 610, § 3.

[85] Clemens VIII, const. *Dudum*, 7 Mart. 1533, § 2—*Bull. Rom. Taur.*, VI, 161.

[86] Julius II, const. *Etsi ad Universos*, 4 iun. 1507, § 34—*Bull. Rom. Taur.*, V, 444.

[87] Benedictus XIV, 13 iul. 1745; Pius VI, 16 iul. 1778; Gregorius XVI, 17 oct. 1834—Capobianco, *Privilegia et Facultates Ordinis Fratrum Minorum*, nn. § 150.

[88] Can. 610, § 2.

"choral obligations of Regulars" comprehends both the conventual Mass and the recitation of the Office. Thus, early legislation dealt simultaneously with both these obligations.[89]

The present canon on the conventual Mass incorporates into the Code the earlier Roman decrees which required its celebration in accordance with the Office of the day.[90] Among these decrees is that of the Sacred Congregation of Rites which in 1783 answered the question whether a Requiem Mass could be substituted for the required conventual Mass with the reply that the Mass corresponding to the Office could not be omitted.[91]

Since the celebration of the conventual Mass is an integral part of the choral obligations of the Regular house, the Local Superior must insure that the Mass is celebrated according to the norms of the general and particular law. On the part of the Provincial, corresponding to his obligation of enforcing choral recitation of the Office is his duty of providing against negligence in respect to or disregard of the conventual Mass in his province. The responsibility of both the Local and Provincial Superiors is a serious one, since it is also agreed that the obligation for the celebration of this Mass, given the required number of unimpeded religious who can be present, namely, a sufficient number for the choral recitation of the Office,[92] is a grave obligation.[93]

[89] C. 1, *de celebratione Missarum et aliis officiis*, III, 14, in Clem.

[90] S.C. Ep. et Reg., *Ianuen.*, 18 dec. 1618—*Fontes*, n. 1700; S.R.C., *Ordinis Minorum*, 13 febr. 1666, n. 6—*Decreta Authentica Congregationis Sacrorum Rituum* (6 vols., Romae: 1898-1927), n. 1332 (hereafter referred to as *Decr. Auth.*); *Ordinis Minorum Capuccinorum*, 7 dec. 1888, ad VII—*Decr. Auth.*, n. 3697; *Ordinis Fratrum Minorum Provinciae Apuliae*, 19 ian. 1906, ad II—*Decr. Auth.*, n. 4177.

[91] S.R.C., *Lusitana*, 20 dec. 1783, ad I: "Missa Conventualis de Officio currenti omitti non potest."—*Decr. Auth.*, n. 2524.

[92] Cf. *supra*, p. 129; Fanfani, *De Iure Religiosorum*, p. 410. Fanfani notes here that the celebrant is included in the computation of the requisite number.

[93] Schaefer, *De Religiosis*, p. 760, n. 378; Vermeersch-Creusen, *Epitome*, I, n. 701; Goyeneche, "Consultationes"—*CpR*, VII (1926), 37.

The choral obligations of a community bound to choir duty are divisible. A religious house may be bound to the Office, but excused from the Mass, inasmuch as a priest is not available for its celebration.[94]

On the other hand, the obligation of the conventual Mass is dependent upon the obligation of choir, so that if the latter obligation were to cease, the former would cease as well.[95] Accordingly the Provincial, but not the Local Superior without the approval of the Provincial, may determine that the priests of a particular house, for example, at a parish, cannot satisfy the obligation of the recitation of the morning hours, i.e., Prime, Terce, Sext and None, at the proper time without considerable inconvenience, although the community can easily be present at a much later hour in the morning. Here the Provincial may judge that the recitation of the "morning hours" cannot be fulfilled even at the reasonable hour, and thus may, in virtue of his privilege, dispense altogether from the obligation of reciting the morning hours. In this case, since the hours of which it is a concomitant element have been omitted, the obligation of the conventual Mass ceases. On the other hand, the Provincial may require the recitation in choir of the morning hours at the later convenient time, but dispense from the obligation of the conventual Mass, because of some serious inconvenience involved, or in view of the necessary performance of other works which require that all the priests of the house celebrate the Mass at an earlier hour.[96]

In virtue of canon 610, § 2, the obligation of attendance at daily Mass which rests on Regulars is more serious than that imposed by canon 595, § 1, on religious in general. In the latter canon religious Superiors are exhorted to see that

[94] Thus canon 610, § 2, obliges nuns to have this Mass celebrated "in so far as it is possible."

[95] Goyeneche, *ibid.*, p. 38.

[96] The conventual Mass should be celebrated inseparably from the proper morning hour according to the rite of the Office for the day.—Cf. S.R.C., decretum generale, 2 dec. 1891—*Decr. Auth.*, n. 3757.

their subjects who are not lawfully impeded attend daily Mass. Certainly on the part of the individual religious the obligation of attendance at the conventual Mass is not grave in itself. But, according to canon 610, § 2, a grave obligation rests upon the general body of religious in a given house to insure that the conventual Mass be not impeded by their illegitimate absence, since the Mass and the recitation of the Office are integral parts of the choral obligation of the community.[97]

Like the Office, the conventual Mass is established as a real and a local obligation, the fulfillment of which is the concern primarily of the Local and Provincial Superiors. But the individual members of the community who are not impeded or lawfully excused are not freed from all responsibility in this regard.[98] Nevertheless, if another Mass is celebrated in the choir at which those who are obliged to choir assist, their obligation seems to be satisfied, although in the strict liturgical sense this Mass is not the conventual Mass.[99] Ordinarily the conventual Mass of the community should be the principal Mass. But sometimes a sufficient reason will prompt the Provincial or the Local Superior to have another Mass celebrated as the principal Mass at which the members of the choir are required to assist. In such cases, then, he will not have to oblige them to assist as well at the conventual Mass, which, though celebrated, will not be the principal Mass in the choir.

[97] S.R.C., decretum generale, 2 dec. 1891—*Decr. Auth.*, n. 3757.

[98] Piontek, "An Application of the Principles"—*The Homiletic and Pastoral Review*, XLIII (1943), 927.

[99] Coronata, *Institutiones*, I, p. 813, n. 616, 3b., nota 7. In such a case, however, it seems to the writer that the obligation of celebrating the conventual Mass corresponding to the Office of the day has not ceased. Consequently this Mass should be celebrated by another priest. If another priest is not available, it seems that the conventual Mass may not be omitted. Therefore the assistance of the members of the choir at the other Mass can be justified only in consideration of the reasons prompting such a procedure, since the obligation must be fulfilled unless grave reasons excuse from it.

4. *The Censorship and the Prohibition of Books and Articles*

Although the censorship of books and of articles for periodicals and newspapers pertains to the public teaching office of the Church, it can also be discussed in relation to the religious observance in the province. The Provincial in virtue of his jurisdiction has certain duties in this regard, since he is not only the Major Superior of the province, but also a public official of the Church whose duty it is to supervise his subjects as members of it.

A. The Publication of Books and Articles

One of the limitations placed upon the exemption of religious Orders is verified in the matter of the publication of books and articles whether they be of a theological, a religious or a merely profane nature.[100] As public authorities in the Church, the Provincial and the local Ordinary both have the responsibility of guarding the integrity of doctrine through the regulation and supervision of the publications and the books of their subjects. Religious are forbidden to publish books, or to write articles for newspapers, public magazines and periodicals without the permission of both the Provincial and the Local Ordinary.[101] Moreover, if the books or articles treat of the matters enumerated in canon 1385, the religious have need not only of the permission of the Provincial but also of censorship by one of the local Ordinaries enumerated in the second paragraph of that canon. Similarly, the permission of both the local Ordinary and the Provincial is necessary if the religious wishes to fill some capacity in the direction or publication of any printed work publicly issued.[102]

B. The Prohibition of Books

The nature of certain books requires that the Church prohibit their use by the faithful. The public officials of

[100] Can. 615. [101] Can. 1386, § 1. [102] *Ibid.*

the Church must, therefore, be alert to forestall the effects of the pernicious teachings contained in such books. Ordinarily the right to prohibit a particular book in an Order is reserved to the General who with his council or chapter may act in this matter when a just cause requires it. However, if there be danger in delay, which may frequently be the case, the Provincial with his council or chapter may perform this duty with the added obligation of notifying the General immediately.[103] Both he and the Local Superior in virtue of their dominative power may, moreover, forbid a subject to read a certain book.[104]

Canon 1401 exempts the Provincial and any other Ordinary from the prohibitions of the canon law in the matter of reading forbidden books, except in so far as they are bound by the natural law to abstain from such reading. In urgent cases and for a just cause either can permit individual subjects to read individual books that have been forbidden by law or decree of the Holy See.[105] Since this is a right possessed by reason of his office, the Provincial can likewise delegate another to grant these permissions. He is warned by the Code, however, lest he grant permissions to subjects indiscriminately and without just and reasonable causes.

5. *The Care of Souls*

Certain obligations are binding upon religious Superiors in the matter of the care of souls. In order to determine the precise extent of these obligations, the particular law must be examined, since the performance of acts necessary for the exercise of parochial duties may be reserved now to the Local, now to the Provincial Superior.

The exercise by religious of the ministry of souls may occur in the following circumstances: 1) as assistance rendered to the diocesan clergy; 2) as parochial work in a parish united to the community in accordance with some

[103] Can. 1395, § 3.

[104] Goyeneche, "Consultationes"—*CpR,* IX (1928), 427.

[105] Can. 1402, § 1.

stipulation as mentioned in canon 1417; 3) as parochial work in the churches of religious. Canons 608 and 609 attempt to establish the mutual rights and duties between religious and the diocesan clergy in regard to this ministry, and to eliminate through adherence to these general laws as well as the particular law of the community the conflicts and strife which once marred the relations of religious and the diocesan clergy.

A. Assistance to the Diocesan Clergy

On condition that the regular discipline suffer no detriment, religious Superiors are urged to see that their subjects willingly assist the diocesan bishops and pastors who need their help in caring for the needs of the faithful, especially in the diocese in which the religious have their residence.[106] Similarly, the Ordinaries and pastors are urged to make use of the religious clergy, especially of those dwelling in the diocese, in the care of souls and particularly in the administering of the Sacrament of Penance.[107]

A distinction to be discussed more fully at a later time must briefly be anticipated here.[108] Religious priests require the approval of the proper Superior before they receive jurisdiction to be exercised in the Sacrament of Penance. Moreover, the proper Superior is required to present them to the diocesan Ordinary when diocesan jurisdiction for hearing the confessions of the faithful is needed.[109] The law of canon 608, § 2, presupposes: 1) the approval of the proper Superior given to the religious whose services are required for hearing the confessions of the laity; and 2) the presentation of the religious for the granting of diocesan jurisdiction to hear confessions and to preach by the proper Superior in accordance with canon 874, § 2.[110]

[106] Can. 608, § 1.

[107] Can. 608, § 2.

[108] Cf. *infra*, pp. 193-198.

[109] Can. 874, § 1, § 2.

[110] According to this canon, however, it is not essential, or in cases of necessity even required, that the proper Superior present the religious priest. Ordinarily, however, the bishop should not habitually

When necessity demands the assistance of religious priests, the duty to provide them devolves upon religious Superiors. The necessity spoken of in canon 608, § 1, may be the need of supplementary priests to offer Masses for the faithful, to preach, or to hear confessions. The use of the word "Superiors" in the law places no restrictions on the power of the Local Superiors. Moreover, canon 608, § 1, presupposes their approval of their subject, and, ordinarily, their presentation of him to the local Ordinary.

There is no reason why the fulfillment of this duty should rest with the Provincial to the exclusion of the Local Superior. Moreover, it seems that particular law should not reserve to the Provincial the right of supplying priests in cases like this, since the common good of the Church, namely, the welfare of souls, is at stake, and should not be unduly impeded by restrictions in the particular law of the Order. This conclusion is strictly applicable, of course, only to cases of necessity in which religious discipline suffers no detriment from the ministry of the religious outside the monastery.[111]

However, there are two notable exceptions to be taken to the view which concedes all rights to the Local Superior in the matter of furnishing assistance to the diocesan clergy. The first flows directly from the canon which speaks of the needs of the people *requiring* the assistance of the religious priest.

It may be argued that ordinarily the necessity for the assistance of *some* religious priests is always verified, if the needs of the faithful are to be satisfied in the best manner. Canon 608, § 2, indicates this with its particular reference to the Sacrament of Penance. As strangers to parochial affairs, religious priests offer greater liberty of conscience to the faithful, who at times may feel it less burdensome to

---

grant jurisdiction to religious priests who are not presented by the proper Superior (can. 874, § 2).

[111] This view is corroborated by Clancy in his study of the rights of the Local Superior.—Cf. *The Local Superior*, pp. 106-108.

confess to a priest who comes from outside the parish.[112] Moreover, their various jurisdictional privileges in the matters of absolving and of dispensing[113] can be of benefit to the faithful.

However, it is possible that there may be, in a given locality, no necessity for the assistance of religious priests in the parochial ministry. In such a case the Provincial may announce his judgment that the assistance of the priests of a particular house or territory is not necessary, and that its curtailment is therefore in order. He could arrive at this judgment more easily, if it was clear that the province, the Order or the Church would benefit by it. Moreover, he can limit the assistance to certain priests, prohibiting it to others. Canon 589, § 2, for instance, states that duties should not be imposed upon professors in houses of study if the performance of such duties is likely to occasion neglect of scholastic labors or distraction in the performance of their work.

A modicum of responsibility for the care of souls is not incompatible with this prohibition. However, the Provincial who is aware of the availability of a sufficient number of religious priests not thus engaged in teaching assignments who can care adequately for the needs of the faithful in a given locality may lawfully curtail or even prohibit, the occasional ministry of the priests mentioned in canon 589, § 2, in view of the ultimate greater good derived for the province and the Church from the total dedication of their time to seminary work.

The second exception to the power of the Local Superior is verified in the case of student priests who have not yet finished their studies. The declaration of the Sacred Congregation of Religious on October 27, 1923, placed a grave obligation upon Superiors not to make use of student priests in the care of souls.[114] Although the occasional use of stu-

[112] Vermeersch-Creusen, *Epitome*, I, n. 767.

[113] Cf. *infra*, p. 201.

[114] *AAS*, XV (1923), 549.

dent priests for such work can be permitted,[115] yet, since the matter is one of major importance, the granting of the permission is reserved to the Provincial Superior.

Without infringing upon the rights of the Local Superior in cases involving the needs of the faithful, the Provincial may rightfully and prudently have an understanding with the Local Superior, or determine a policy from the outset with regard to the assistance which the student priests of the province may be directed to furnish in the parochial ministry. Nothing, however, prevents the Provincial from appointing the Local Superior as his delegate, with the right to act according to the dictates of prudence.

B. Religious Parishes

The III Council of the Lateran (1179) permitted monks to exercise pastoral functions provided that they lived together with other monks during the time of their ministry and were subject to their proper prelates.[116] Frequently it happened that religious were placed in charge of benefices, and gradually certain benefices were reserved to the religious alone, to be administered according to special law.[117] The Council of Trent[118] and Benedict XIV (1740-1758)[119] confirmed this legislation on the reservation of certain benefices to Regulars.

In the present law the Provincial has rights and duties according to the type of union existing between the parish and the religious community. The Code recognizes three types of union between a parish and a community: a) a complete union in spiritual and temporal affairs; b) a union either in spiritual or in temporal affairs but not in both, or,

[115] Cf. *supra*, p. 104; Vermeersch, "Annotationes"—*Periodica*, XII (1923), 156.

[116] C. 2, X, *de statu monachorum et canonicorum regularium*, III, 35.

[117] C. 5, *de praebendis et dignitatibus*, III, 4, in VI°; C. 27, X, *de electione et electi potestate*, I, 6.

[118] Sess. XIV, *de ref.*, cc. 10, 11.

[119] Const. *Cum nuper*, 8 nov. 1751—*Fontes*, n. 417.

at least, not perpetually; c) a union in virtue of an indult by which a parish is committed to the care of a particular community of religious, after an agreement has taken place between the bishop and the community with regard to the manner of holding the parish. To determine the rights and duties of the Provincial with regard to parishes united to the community, each of the foregoing cases must be examined. A complete union (*pleno iure facta*) effected between a parish and a religious community involves a major issue in a religious province,[120] since it entails for a community grave obligations and administrative acts. These are such as fall within the competence of Major Superiors alone. The province, and even the Order, becomes responsible for the care of the parish involved, and therefore the Provincial, as the Major Superior of the province, should represent the Order personally, or through a delegate, in the preliminary measures. After the details and conditions have been arranged between the Provincial and the bishop, the council must be consulted before the Provincial accepts the deed in the name of the Order.[121]

When the instrument has been properly drawn up, copies are sent to the Sacred Congregation of the Council on the part of the bishop, and to the Sacred Congregation of Re-

[120] In this union the parish loses its own juridic personality, and is incorporated with that of the religious house to which it is united. The religious community becomes the pastor according to can. 452, § 1, with perpetual obligations necessitating the appointment of a vicar to care for the actual spiritual needs of the people which are to be administered under the care of the Ordinary of the place (can. 1425, § 2).

[121] The obligation to consult the council is deduced analogously from canon 1428, § 1, and also from the purpose of the council, which is to assist the Superior in matters of grave importance. Particular law will probably require its advice or consent, and also the permission of the General and his curia. Prudence dictates, however, that the Provincial consult the council. Even in the event that the vote of the General's council is not required, it will come to the attention of the General, at least when the Procurator General refers the document to the Sacred Congregation of Religious.

ligious on the part of the Provincial.[122] Through the permission of both these Sacred Congregations the parish becomes a religious parish, and the community of the house the *parochus habitualis*.[123]

Canon 471, § 1, requires the designation of one of the religious as vicar of the community in the exercise of the parochial duties. Moreover, the vicar is to be presented to the bishop of the diocese for canonical institution as acting pastor.[124] The Code does not exclude the Local Superior from designation by particular law as the Superior competent to present the candidate. Otherwise, the right belongs to the Provincial.[125] In the event that particular law concedes the right of presentation to the Local Superior, the Provincial retains the right to judge of the fitness of a candidate before his installation in office by the local Ordinary.[126]

If particular law is silent, as just noted, the presentation is to be made by the Provincial, upon whom the judgment of the candidate's fitness rests in any case. This conclusion follows *a fortiori* from the fact that Ordinaries are not habitually to grant diocesan jurisdiction for the hearing of confessions to religious unless they have been presented by their proper Superior,[127] who is the Provincial.[128]

The power to remove the vicar is a prerogative of the Provincial, unless particular law gives it to the Local Superior, since the Superior who makes the presentation is the one who is authorized to remove the vicar.[129]

Similarly, it is a right of the Superior who presents the vicar to the local Ordinary to consent to the choice of an econome made by the latter in the event of a vacancy in the

[122] This must be done through the Procurator General in accordance with canon 517.

[123] Cf. can. 452, § 2.

[124] Can. 456.

[125] Augustine, *Commentary*, II, 526.

[126] Can. 149.

[127] Can. 874, § 2.

[128] Cf. *supra*, p. 137, note [110].

[129] Cans. 454, § 5; 471, § 3.

parish caused by the death of the vicar.[130] Unless particular law determines otherwise, the Provincial's consent to the choice of the econome is required, because of his fundamental right to present and remove the vicar.[131]

If the religious vicar is to be absent from his parish for a few days, the permission of the Local Superior is sufficient, but both he and the Provincial have a responsibility to provide for the fulfillment of the needs of the faithful.[132] How-

[130] Can. 472, 1°. If particular law designates the Local Superior as the Superior competent to make the presentation of the candidate for the vicarage, then consistency demands that it specify the proper Superior both for his removal from office (can. 454, § 5) as well as for the consent that is given to the Ordinary's choice of an econome in the vacancy of the vicarage occasioned through the death of the acting pastor (can. 472, 1°). It is incongruous that one who is judged fit for institution by the Provincial should be removed at will by the Local Superior. Nevertheless, the Superior who presents the candidate for the office can likewise remove him, though the Superior must inform the Ordinary of the fact that the removal has been executed.

[131] In the matter of removing the vicar, the right to do so is attributed by canon 471, § 3, to the religious Superior without qualification as to whether it is the Major or Minor Superior who is authorized to act, since the determination of the proper Superior depends upon the designation of the Superior who has the right to present the vicar in the first place according to canon 456. Ordinarily the right of presentation involved in canon 456 will be reserved to the Provincial. Hence, ordinarily the right of removal mentioned in canons 471, § 3, and 454, § 5, belongs to him as well. It is clear that the Superior spoken of in canon 472, 1°, as competent to consent to the Ordinary's choice of a vicar econome is the Superior named in canon 456. However, in canon 472, 2°, the Code determines the Local Superior as the one to whom the government of the parish is confined before the appointment of an econome. It would be impractical to reserve this intervening administration to the Provincial who may not be accessible; the purpose of the law is to fill the breach in the parish as quickly as possible, even though only temporarily.

[132] Canon 465, § 6, obliges the pastor of a parish to provide adequately for the needs of the faithful. As Larraona notes, however, if a parochial church is united *pleno iure* to a religious house, a twofold consequence results, namely, the church becomes a *religious church*, and the parish becomes a *religious parish* in virtue of canon 1425, § 2. Since a *religious church* forms part of the religious house (can. 497,

ever, absence from the community for a period beyond three days generally requires the permission of the Provincial.[133]

If the absence is to be of a duration longer than a week, the Provincial is to approve another religious to be presented as the vicar substitute for the parish.[134] The approval of the substitute by the Provincial does not affect the validity of his appointment, so that jurisdictional acts that are performed by a parochial substitute approved only by the local Ordinary are valid.[135]

The other vicars, namely the parochial adjutants (*adiutores*) and assistants (*cooperatores*), are likewise to be presented to the local Ordinary by the Superior designated in the constitutions.[136] Ordinarily it is the Provincial who is thus designated, but if particular law designates another

---

§ 2), it is subject to the religious Superior of the house who is considered as its rector ("Consultationes"—*CpR*, II [1921], 181). As such, the Superior, as head of the community which is the *parochus habitualis*, must act for the moral person at times. When the vicar is negligent, the obligation of providing for the needs of the faithful devolves upon the community which is represented by the Superior. As head then of the moral person and as rector of the church, the Superior in such cases necessarily has the obligation of providing for the faithful.

[133] Cf. *supra*, p. 117.

[134] Can. 465, § 4. The canon uses the term "Superior" without qualification, but since all acts affecting the office of vicar are regularly reserved by the common law to the Provincial, there is no reason to make an exception in the approval of the vicar substitute. This reservation is the more apparent from canon 149, from which it can be concluded by way of analogy that the designation of a suitable substitute is a grave matter, and should be made, in accord with the provisions of that canon, i.e., with the approval of the Ordinary.

[135] Cf. PCI—*AAS*, XIV (1922), 527. Here the Pontifical Commission for the Interpretation of the Code ruled that the valid assistance at a marriage did not depend upon the previous approval of the vicar substitute by the religious Superior, provided that the local Ordinary had approved him. From this decision it appears that acts of jurisdiction placed by a substitute thus appointed are indeed valid but at the same time illicit.

[136] Cans. 475, 476.

Superior for the presentation, the approval of the Provincial, as religious Ordinary, is required before their presentation in accordance with canon 149 which requires the approval of one's proper Ordinary in such a case.

In the partial union of parishes with religious houses[137] the union effected pertains only to the temporalities, so that the religious house receives a portion of the revenues without the parochial office. A secular priest is presented to the local Ordinary by the proper religious Superior, and upon the approval of the former has the responsibility of fulfilling the parochial duties for a remuneration to be paid in the amount set by the local Ordinary. The consent to such a union as well as the presentation of the pastor are reserved to the Superior designated by the particular law.[138]

137 *Unio semi-pleno iure facta.*

138 This type of union is of rare occurrence at the present time, although it existed in the past as a method of supporting religious houses or colleges (Augustine, *Commentary,* VI, 505).

CHAPTER IX

THE PROVINCIAL SUPERIOR AND MEMBERS LEAVING THE ORDER

The rôle played by the Provincial Superior in the admission of members to an Order has already been studied.[1] It is in no way surprising, therefore, that his jurisdiction should enter into the processes involved in the departure of members from a religious Order. Titles XIV-XVI of the common law dealing with religious treat accordingly of the transfer, the departure, and the dismissal of religious.

1. *Transfer of Religious Within the Province and the Order*

Early legislation affecting the transfer of religious to different houses of the same province or Order is scarce. This was due, no doubt, to the prevalence of the monastic form of the religious life. The Mendicant constitutions did not adopt the principles of stability of the Order of St. Benedict whereby a religious dedicated himself to the pursuit of perfection in a particular Abbey or Congregation. In fact, one of the principal ideas embodied in them postulated that through his vow of obedience the religious made his services available for the Order wherever they were in demand. Consequently the particular laws of the Orders must be examined for a historical knowledge of the procedure of transfer with reference to the religious within a province. These laws ordinarily granted a right to the Provincial to effect this transfer. This legislation is in harmony with that of the Code, since the latter requires clerics and religious to undertake and faithfully to fulfill the duties imposed upon them by their Ordinaries as often as there is no excusing cause.[2] Over and above this obligation of the Code, however, there is the obligation of obedience to Superiors to whom the subject submits himself according to the laws

[1] Cf. *supra*, p. 82. [2] Can. 128.

of the institute, either as a candidate for the religious life, or as a subject by his religious profession. Thus all religious, lay as well as clerical, are obliged to obey according to the norms of the particular community. The dependence of religious upon the Provincial for their residence in a particular house is further indicated by the fact that permission for absence from the religious house for reasons other than duty is to be sought from the Provincial, if the duration of the absence is to exceed three days or the relatively short period designated by particular law.[3]

Moreover, the government of the province is committed to the Provincial with the obligation to provide for the common good and the observance of the religious discipline. The fulfillment of these aims necessitates the possession of the right to transfer subjects to different posts. These rights, however, are restricted to the houses and subjects of the Provincial, since his jurisdiction is limited inasmuch as it does not extend beyond these limits.

A similar power is granted to the General Superior by particular law with reference to the whole Order. He is the highest Superior of the Order and his jurisdiction is not limited to a particular house or province.[4] Thus all members of the Order are subject to him and he will have the right to transfer them according to the norms of particular law. Generally the religious profession will be made to him, considered as the Superior General, according to the norms of the particular law of the community. Consequently, in the event that the particular law is silent on the point of transfer, it seems that he could transfer subjects to any place in the Order.

The nature of the office of Local Superior, however, limits his jurisdiction to the subjects who are assigned to his house, and consequently he has no power to transfer a subject to another house.

[3] Cf. *supra*, p. 117.

[4] Cf. can. 502.

2. *Transfer of Religious to Another Order*

Legislation regarding the transfer of religious to other Orders or Congregations is found in Title XIV of Book II of the Code. Pre-Code law with regard to Mendicants can be traced almost to the time of their foundation as Orders in the Church. Martin IV (1281-1285) forbade Mendicants under pain of excommunication to transfer to communities of religious which were not communities of Mendicants.[5]

The Council of Vienne (1311-1312) decreed that Mendicants who transferred to non-Mendicant communities were to be deprived of their vote and their eligibility for office.[6] The Council of Trent (1545-1565) forbade Regulars to transfer to communities of a less rigorous Rule or observance regardless of privileges, permissions or faculties possessed by Superiors for making a transfer allowable.[7]

The Code requires the permission of the Holy See for all cases of transfer of religious from one community to another, or from one independent monastery to another.[8] The religious who with proper permission makes the transfer to another institute must make another novitiate. During the novitiate the obligations and rights attaching him to his particular community remain suspended, but he becomes subject to the Superiors of the new community.[9] Hence the jurisdiction of the Provincial extends to him as well as to the other members of the community, even by reason of his vows, so that the Provincial may lay obligations upon him by means of jurisdictional precepts. It is not within the scope of the Provincial's jurisdiction, however, to require or to permit a period of postulancy before he admits the re-

[5] C. 1, *de regularibus et transeuntibus ad religionem,* III, 8, in Extravag. com.

[6] C. 1, *de regularibus et transeuntibus ad religionem,* III, 9, in Clem.

[7] Sess. XXV, *de regularibus,* c. 19.

[8] Can. 632. Moreover, canon 542, 1°, provides that a person who is already bound by religious profession cannot validly enter the novitiate of another institute apart from a dispensation in the case.

[9] Can. 633, § 1. The novitiate is not required, if the transfer is made from one independent monastery to another (Can. 633, § 3).

ligious to the novitiate, since a professed religious is not subjected to the postulancy.[10]

As in the case of other candidates, canon 543 grants the Provincial the right to admit the religious to the novitiate with the consultative vote of the council or the chapter. The documents otherwise demanded for the admission of candidates to the novitiate[11] are not required in this case, provided that the religious candidate presents the papal rescript which allows the transfer and the testimonial letters of the Major Superior of the community to which the religious formerly belonged.[12] At the end of his novitiate the novice of solemn or perpetual vows is to be admitted by the Provincial to solemn profession immediately, but the vote of the community is deliberative. If doubt remains about the fitness of the novice the Provincial may prorogue his novitiate for a period not in excess of a year.[13]

A religious who has made profession of temporary vows which expired during the course of his novitiate in the community to which he has transferred can be received back again by the Provincial into the community to which he formerly belonged, without the repetition of a novitiate, since the juridic bond with the former Order is not completely severed. On the other hand, he is free to return to the world. If he makes profession in the new community or returns to the world, the Provincial of the institute to which he formerly belonged cannot receive the candidate again without an Apostolic indult.[14]

The Provincial of the institute to which the religious has transferred should see to the fulfillment of the common law

[10] Berutti, *Institutiones*, III, 319.

[11] Can. 544.

[12] Can. 544, § 5. A subject in an Order must likewise apply through the Provincial for permission to transfer to another Order or Congregation, and then obtain from him a testimonial letter which is to be presented with the papal rescript to the Provincial or proper Major Superior of the community in which he seeks admission.

[13] Can. 634.

[14] Can. 542, 1°; Berutti, *Institutiones*, III, 320.

affecting the property of the religious. The Order in which the original profession was made retains the temporal goods which the religious gained for it; but the Order in which the new novitiate is made has a title to a just recompense for the period of the novitiate if the constitutions or a contract justify it.[15] Otherwise there is no strict obligation in justice for the institute from which transfer has been made to pay these expenses, but it is fitting that it should do so if the transferred religious novice is lacking in funds.

If the religious had made a profession of merely simple vows in the institute from which he is transferred and thereupon makes a profession of simple vows in the new community, then the goods that he committed to the care and administration of the former institute must be restored to him. If the income was dedicated to the institute, the latter retains the interest that has already matured. In the event that goods are thus transmitted to the religious-novice of simple vows, he must make a new disposition and cession of their administration, and also make a last will, according to the norms of canon 569, § § 1, 3.[16] If the religious-novice is going to make a solemn profession, he must freely renounce or dispose of these goods beforehand.[17]

The religious in solemn vows who has disposed of his goods according to canon 581, § 1, does not recover their

[15] Cans. 635, § 2; 570, § 2.

[16] Through religious profession in the new institute all juridic bonds with the former institute are severed, and a true *discessus* in the sense of canon 580, § 3, is verified. Consequently the former disposition and cession of administration lose their juridic force, and no formalities are necessary to make similar arrangements anew. These are normally required, however, before profession, according to canon 569, § § 1, 3. It seems, therefore, that the religious-novice could confirm, without any special formalities, the arrangements he made before his profession in the former institute. However, if he desires to change them, it must be remembered that not all the juridic bonds have been severed with the former institute when he is in a state of incipient *departure.* Therefore, canon 583, 2°, seems to require that he seek the necessary permission for any change.

[17] Can. 581, § 1.

possession through a profession of simple vows in another community, although the renunciation of the right to acquire property ceases for the future.[18] The religious who makes simple profession must arrange for their administration, for the disposition of their use and income, and make a will according to canon 569.

Since the bond with the former institute is severed only by the new profession, whatever property the religious-novice who is in solemn vows may acquire before his profession in the community to which he transferred, is acquired for the community from which the transfer was made.[19]

Property acquired by a religious in simple vows, if not renounced before his solemn profession in the community to which the transfer is made, passes at his profession to the latter. However, property acquired for the institute belongs to the institute to which the religious returns, if he fails to make his profession in the institute to which the transfer was contemplated.[20]

In practice, the Provincial who accepts a candidate professed in another community can delegate the Novice Master, the Local Superior, or some other priest to supervise the fulfillment of the canons affecting the arrangements involving the property of the transferred religious.

3. *Departure of Religious*

Canon 637 affirms for the religious who was professed with temporary vows the explicit right to leave the religious

[18] Can. 636.

[19] Berutti, *Institutiones*, III, 322. This can be deduced from canon 633, § 1, which states that the religious-novice does not lose his obligations to the former community by entering another novitiate. They are suspended, however, and their complete lapse comes only with his new profession (Can. 635, 1°). Therefore, during the novitiate the religious is still juridically bound to the former community and the goods which accrue to him are acquired for that community.

[20] Cans. 633, § 1; 635, 1°; Berutti, *Institutiones*, III, 322.

community at the expiration of his vows.[21] The same canon, however, grants the Superior thus designated by the constitutions a right to deny or to delay the subsequent solemn profession for just reasons. Sickness occurring after the simple profession is not acknowledged in law as constituting a just reason in view of which the profession of solemn vows can be denied or delayed by the Superior.[22] The Superior to whom this right belongs, if the constitutions are silent, is the Provincial.[23]

In cases other than those involving the departure of religious at the expiration of his vows, the Provincial possesses rights and duties according as the departure is lawful or unlawful.

A. Lawful Departure

A twofold species of lawful departure from the community in virtue of a papal indult was recognized by pre-Code authors. The first was authorized by a dispensation from the vows. The power to dispense was reserved to the Holy Father personally, even in the case of religious bound only by simple vows.[24] The second was justified by an indult of secularization granted by the Sacred Congregation of Bishops and Regulars. This indult could be either perpetual or temporary. For this reason it corresponded, in a degree,

[21] Pius IX (1846-1878) decreed on March 19, 1859 that novices in Orders of men should make a simple profession for the duration of three years preceding their solemn profession (Bizzarri, *Collectanea in Usum Secretariae Sacrae Congregationis Episcoporum et Regularium* [2, ed., Romae: 1885], p. 906; hereafter referred to as *Collectanea*). Before the Code, these simple vows of a temporary duration were considered perpetual on the part of the religious who made them although the community was free to reject him (Declar., 12 iun. 1858, n. 1—Bizzarri, *loc. cit*).

[22] S.C. Ep. et Reg., declar., 12 iun., 1858, V—*Fontes*, n. 4383; *AAS*, XVI (1925), 107.

[23] Cf. *supra*, p. 95.

[24] Piat, *Praelectiones*, I, p. 183, qu. 186; S.C. Ep. et Reg., decr. 12 iun., 1858, n. II—Bizzarri, *Collectanea*, p. 907.

to both the indult of secularization and that of exclaustration, as recognized by the Code.[25]

Through the indult of secularization the religious was removed entirely from the jurisdiction of his Superiors, even in the matter of the Sacrament of Penance, although the vows were not dispensed. In this way, then, secularization differed from the indult granting a dispensation from the vows. Whereas the vows were suspended, as it were, through secularization, they were altogether cancelled through a dispensation.[26]

In regard to these dispensations and indults, the Provincial had no power. To the Sacred Congregation for Bishops and Regulars belonged the necessary competence and religious Superiors were bound to accept even doubtfully valid indults till the same Sacred Congregation declared them invalid.[27]

The present law does not grant to the Provincial any power of dispensation over the vows of religion. This authority is reserved to the Sacred Congregation of Religious. Temporary secularization is termed *exclaustration.*[28] Through this indult permission is granted to the religious to live outside of the monastery and free from the

[25] Cans. 639; 640; *Acta Sanctae Sedis* (41 vols., Romae: 1865-1908), IV (1868), 368 ss. Hereafter reference will be made to this pariodical with the abbreviation *ASS.* Cf. *Analecta Iuris Pontificii* (Romae: 1855-1869; Parisiis: 1872-1891), XVI (1877), 737.

[26] Piat, *Praelectiones*, I, p. 187, qu. 190. Secularization was ordinarily sought by a cleric religious in Major Orders. Hence a benevolent bishop was needed to receive the religious. The latter was obliged to obey the bishop in virtue of his vow of obedience. Wernz-Vidal stated that the indult of itself did not confer the right to proprietorship unless there was an express concession in it. Without this concession the secularized religious merely was granted the necessary use of property, but could not receive or convey title to it (*De Religiosis*, p. 460, n. 426, V).

[27] S. C. Ep. et Reg., declar., 15 febr. 1824—Bizzarri, *Collectanea*, p. 52; Piat, *Praelectiones*, I, p. 188, qu. 191.

[28] Can. 638.

jurisdiction of his religious Superiors.[29] By it a partial relaxation of the bond between the religious and the community is effected, although the subject remains a religious, and is obliged to return to the community at the expiration of the period of absence allowed in the indult.[30] While the indult endures, he is freed from his dependance upon his religious Superiors and is subject to the Ordinary of the territory in which he resides. Charity and justice, nevertheless, bind the Provincial to afford sufficient means to such a religious for an upright and decent livelihood, if the religious himself cannot provide adequately for his needs.[31]

Secularization, or the permanent separation of the religious from his Order and its attendant obligations, includes a dispensation from the vows with the exception of the obligations resulting from the previous reception of Sacred Orders.[32] Though the right to possess property is restored to the religious, neither any remuneration for past services nor any restoration of property acquired for the

[29] The indult of exclaustration differs from the indult mentioned in canon 606, § 2, whereby a religious obtains permission from the Holy See to live outside the monastery for a period beyond six months for purposes other than those of his religious vocation, while retaining the relation of a subject to his Superiors.

[30] Chelodi, *Ius de Personis*, n. 280, b.

[31] Berutti, *Institutiones*, III, 327. It seems more feasible to the writer that this obligation should be placed upon the Provincial, as a provincial responsibility, than upon the Local Superior, as the responsibility of the house in which the subject last resided. Particular law may specify with which of these two Superiors the responsibility will rest. In the event that it does not, this view is further supported by the fact that the Provincial is the proper pastor of the province, while the Local Superior has pastoral obligations and duties only in relation to those actually living in his house.

[32] Can. 640, § 1, 2°. Formerly the religious who obtained an indult of secularization remained bound by his vows although he was separated from the Order, unless a special concession was granted in the indult of permanent secularization. Piat (1815-1904) stated that rarely was there given in the indult the right to dispose of goods by will, and each indult had to be examined in the matters pertaining to the vow of poverty (*Praelectiones*, I, p. 187, qu. 190).

Order can be demanded by him from the Provincial or the Order.[33] Before the Provincial can receive such a candidate back into the Order, an Apostolic indult is required, and the novitiate must be repeated as in the case of candidates entering the Order for the first time.[34]

B. Unlawful Departure

As in the Code, flight from the monastery (*fuga*) and apostasy from the religious institute were considered as the types of unlawful departure of religious also in the legislation preceding the Code, and religious Superiors were gravely urged to take strong measures against subjects guilty of either.[35]

The first general legislation against apostate monks is found in the Council of Chalcedon (451), which decreed that excommunication was to be inflicted on them.[36] Till the time of the Code this was the chief penalty for apostasy itself, and no penalty existed for flight except those established by particular law. From the time of Boniface VIII (1294-1303), however, those who were guilty of either apostasy or flight accompanied by the laying aside of the habit incurred the penalty, a *latae sententiae* excommunication, i.e., by the very act of the violation of this penal law.[37] In 1911, the Sacred Congregation of Religious decreed that apostates

[33] Can. 643, § 1.

[34] Cans. 542, 1°; 640, § 2. Formerly, since the indult of secularization did not include a dispensation from the vows, the novitiate or profession was not repeated, if one who had become secularized was received again into the Order (Wernz-Vidal, *De Religiosis*, p. 460, n. 426, III).

[35] For a study of the history and canonical status of apostates and fugitives from religious institutes, the reader is referred to Riesner, *Apostates and Fugitives from Religious Institutes*, The Catholic University of America Canon Law Studies, n. 168 (Washington, D. C.: The Catholic University of America Press, 1942).

[36] C. 3, C. XX, q. 3; Mansi, VII, 362; Schroeder, *Disciplinary Decrees*, p. 96.

[37] C. 2, *ne clerici vel monachi negotiis se immisceant*, III, 24, in VI°.

who did not return to their monasteries within three months were subject to automatic dismissal from the institute.[38]

Religious Superiors have been urged at various times to seek out apostates either for the purpose of punishment or with a view to their reinstatement. Thus Paul IV (1555-1559) in 1559 forbade the bestowal of favors upon apostates, and urged Superiors to force their return to the monastery by means of censures and, if the case demanded, through recourse to the secular authority with the threat of major excommunication in the event of non-compliance.[39] A similar decree was issued by the Sacred Congregation of the Council in 1624.[40]

In the law of the Code, apostates incur an excommunication reserved to the proper Major Superior, who, in the absence of any divergent specification in particular law, is the Provincial. Moreover, the guilty party is punished with the loss of his vote and his eligibility for office forever, and with other penalties, in accordance with the constitutions, according to the gravity of his fault.[41]

Canon 2385 uses the general term "Superiors" in specifying the punishing authority competent to inflict the penalties or penances provided in particular law. Which Superiod is thereby rendered competent to inflict them? In the event that particular law is silent, it is the Provincial who is competent, since he is the religious Ordinary. This seems warranted by the fact that the excommunication of the religious mentioned in canon 2385 is reserved to him, and is corroborated by the terms of the following canon, which, in treating of fugitives, explicitly names the Major Superior as the proper Superior to mete out the punishment.[42]

[38] S.C. de Religiosis, decr. *Quum singulae*, 16 maii, 1911—*AAS*, III (1911), 236-238; *Fontes*, n. 4409.

[39] Const. *Postquam*, 20 iul. 1558—*Fontes*, n. 93.

[40] S. C. C., decr. 21 sept. 1624, n. 4—*Fontes*, n. 2454.

[41] Can. 2385.

[42] Can. 2386. Accordingly, fugitives incur a suspension reserved, in the absence of a different specification in particular law, to the Pro-

Since it is the common law that reserves both these censures to the Provincial, the extensive faculties of the confessor of men religious as noted in canon 519 do not cover these cases. Other than recourse to the Provincial or the higher Superior, the alternative for the confessor is to absolve the repentant religious according to the norms of canons 2250-2254.[43]

Canon 645, § 2, imposes a general obligation on religious Superiors to be solicitous in seeking out apostates or fugitives, and to receive them if they are truly penitent. Since the reception of these subjects pertains to the Provincial, so also the principal obligation of seeking them out pertains to him. Furthermore, it is his duty to adopt prudently the proper means of avoiding scandal in permitting their return to active service or in advising them to seek secularization in the event that a reconciliation is impossible. However, in petitioning for his re-admittance, it is the religous upon whom rests the burden of proof in establishing the fact of his amendment.[44] Regarding this the Provincial is authorized to render a prudent judgment. If the fact of amendment is not manifest, then in the interest of the common good the Provincial should not re-admit the religious. He should rather advise the subject to seek the proper Apostolic indult, or take measures for the dismissal of the religious from the institute.

4. *Dismissal of Religious*

A. *Ipso Facto* Effective Dismissal Enacted in Canon 646, § 1

With the exception of the crime of apostasy from the religious state for a period beyond three months, the cases involving an automatic dismissal by law from the religious state as listed in the decree *Quum singulae* of 1911 are re-

---

vincial, are deprived of their office if they hold one, and are subject to further punishment to be determined by the Provincial.

[43] Blat, *De Delictis et Poenis*, nn. 77, 228; Smith, *The Penal Law for Religious*, p. 98.

[44] Can. 645, § 2.

peated in canon 646, § 1. In these cases, in the absence of a specific reservation of the matter by the particular law to the exclusive competence of the General, the Provincial, in acting with the advice or the vote of his proper council, or of his chapter, needs only to issue a declaration of the fact of dismissal as already effected by the law itself, and then to preserve a record of the fact in the archives.

Before issuing the declaration of the fact, however, it is essential that the crime of the religious be evident, either from authentic documents or from the testimony of witnesses worthy of belief. The declaration of the fact is required as proof in the event that a recourse is made to the Holy See or that the juridic effects of dismissal are to be enforced in the external forum.[45] Since the religious who is guilty of one of these qualified crimes is dismissed by the law itself, no discretionary power is given to the Major Superior when the facts are evident. Though the declaration has no constitutive effect, the Superior should issue it both as a protection to the Order and as a safeguard against scandal.[46]

When the religious as dismissed by the law itself has also incurred an excommunication reserved by law to his proper Ordinary, i.e., to the Provincial,[47] the jurisdiction for the absolution of the censure still rests with the Provincial, since the juridic bond with the Order still affects the one under censure unless an Apostolic indult or a privilege based on particular law provide differently.[48]

[45] Berutti, *Institutiones*, III, 340.

[46] Goyeneche ("Consultationes"—*CpR*, XII [1931], 131) states that the Superior cannot delegate this duty.

[47] E.g., can. 2385.

[48] Can. 669, § 1. In those communities which have a privilege to the effect that dismissal includes also automatically (*ipso facto*) a dispensation from the vows, it seems that the excommunication enacted in canon 2385 is reserved not to the Superior who was the proper Ordinary of the religious at the time of the delict, i.e., to the Provincial, but to the Ordinary of the place, since the Superiors of the institute no longer have jurisdiction over the former religious (Riesner, *Apostates and Fugitives from Religious Institutes*, 81).

Though the Provincial retains the jurisdiction necessary for the absolution of the censure incurred through the delict mentioned in canon 646, § 1, 2°, in those cases wherein the institute does not possess any particular indult or privilege which associates an automatic dispensation from the vows along with the fact of automatic dismissal, this factor does not imply that the Provincial is obliged by canon 672, § 1, to receive the religious into the Order again.[49] In fact, the law does not contemplate the reinstatement of such a dismissed religious. The dismissal is effected by the law, and therefore a reinstatement is possible only through the intervention of the Holy See.[50]

B. Dismissal Effected According to the Norms of the Law

1) Dismissal by Decree of the Superior

In cases threatening grave and external scandal or harm to the community because of the actions of a religious, the Provincial with the consent of his council can immediately dismiss a religious to forestall scandal and to protect the community from injury.[51] Since the purpose of this extraordinary power is to avert scandal or imminent injury, the same power is extended to the Local Superior in the event that the Provincial is not available. In either case, however, the proper canonical process must be instituted im-

[49] PCI, 30 iul. 1934—*AAS*, XXVI (1934), 494.

[50] Because of the gravity of the offenses enumerated in canon 646, § 1, and the possibility of scandal through the reception of such a dismissed religious into the community again, this is not anly a *causa gravior* which affects the whole province, but a *causa gravissima* which affects the whole Order. Necessary means to avoid scandal may even entail a transfer of the religious to a distant province, and therefore the solution of the case pertains to the Holy See and the General. The case of a cleric who is not a priest, or of a solemnly professed brother, would hardly be contemplated, since his spiritual and temporal welfare can be safeguarded adequately through a dispensation from his vows and by means of a reduction to the lay state in the case of a cleric.

[51] Cans. 653; 668.

mediately, after the emergency action is taken, to effect the dismissal according to the canonical norms.

It is to be noted that even in the provisory dismissal, the Superior needs the consent of his council. Since the Code grants this extraordinary power for cases involving the dismissal of religious bound by perpetual profession, it follows *a fortiori* that it is available to the Provincial and the Local Superior in similar contingencies which involve a religious with temporary vows.[52]

2) Ordinary Dismissal of Religious in Temporary Vows

Canons 647 and 648 regulate the procedure of the Provincial in the dismissal of religious in temporary vows. The right of passing judgment on the reasons for dismissal resides with the General of the Order and his council, the members of which must manifest their view by secret ballot. Since profession confers an acquired right upon the religious which precludes arbitrary dismissal, the reasons for dismissal must be weighty. Moreover, they must be manifested to the subject who has the right to answer them.[53]

Ordinarily the General is dependent upon the Provincial and the Local Superior for the facts of the case. Since the tendency of the law is to reserve everything pertaining to the reception of postulants and novices and their profession to the Provincial, it follows that the responsibility for furnishing the facts and making the decision leading to the action of the General pertains to the Provincial. He, in

[52] Fanfani, *De Iure Religiosorum*, p. 497.

[53] The reasons must be grave, on the part either of the community or of the religious. Reasons that would be sufficient on the part of the Order are not determined in the Code. On the part of the religious, a serious lack of the religious spirit which is not amended despite repeated warnings is given in canon 647, § 1, 2°, as an example of such reasons. Wernz-Vidal stated that on the part of the community any cause in virtue of which the community will suffer a notable loss or grave inconvenience is sufficient, provided that it is not a matter of sickness contracted after simple profession (*De Religiosis*, p. 477, n. 439).

turn, will frequently be dependent upon the Local Superior or the Spiritual Director of the professed.

Since the religious in temporary vows is still on probation, no formal trial is necessary, and formal proof of the facts involved is not required. Against this decree of dismissal, the religious has the right of recourse to the Holy See, during which time the effect of the decree is suspended.[54]

3) Ordinary Dismissal of Religious in Solemn Vows

The dismissal of solemnly professed religious, with the exception of the cases seen above, is ordinarily accomplished according to a strict canonical process. Former privileges of Regulars to proceed in a summary fashion[55] are expressly revoked by canon 654. The competent tribunal is the General and his council or chapter, either of which must be comprised of at least four religious, or by an augmented number provided especially for the case by the president of the tribunal with the consent of the others. The presence in the process of the notary and the defender of the bond are likewise required. Dismissal can be effected only for the commission of grave, external delicts after two canonical warnings have been disregarded and the religious has given no signs of amendment.

The function of the Provincial is to draw up the case personally or through a delegate and to submit it to the General. The canonical warnings must be made by him or his delegate.[56] Before the warnings, however, it is necessary that the delicts be notorious or evident from extrajudicial confession or satisfactory proofs. Rumor or suspicion of crimes on the part of the religious may necessitate a judicial inquisition on the part of the Provincial according to the norms of canons 1939-1946. He can delegate this task to another, for example, to the Local Superior.

[54] Can. 647, 3°, 4°.

[55] Cf. *supra*, pp. 55-60.

[56] Can. 659.

There must be at least two admonitions, as required by canon 660, and to them may be added timely exhortations, corrections, penances or penal remedies. The purpose of the admonition is the correction and the amendment of the religious. Thus the Provincial may freely transfer a religious, in order the better to promote his amendment by removing him from the dangerous occasion. To each of the admonitions the Provincial must also attach a threat of punishment. Once the admonitions have been neglected and the Provincial has decided to take up the process which may lead to the dismissal of the subject, he should arrange the facts of the case and transmit them to the General.[57] Only after the decision has been confirmed by the Sacred Congregation of Religious can the sentence be executed.

It may happen, in cases warranted by the common law, that the General, with the consent of his council or chapter, will delegate at least three religious to form a tribunal to proceed in the dismissal of a religious. This is usually done when, according to canon 667, the distances are great between the General's tribunal and the residence of the religious involved in the case at issue. Usually the Provincial is then delegated to conduct the trial, although this is not necessarily the case. When he is thus delegated, the process is carried out according to law; he and the other judges decide the question; then he transmits their decision to Rome for confirmation by the Sacred Congregation of Religious.

[57] Can. 663.

CHAPTER X

THE PROVINCIAL SUPERIOR AS ADMINISTRATOR OF TEMPORAL GOODS

Canon 531 states that the religious province has the same rights as other moral persons to acquire and possess temporal goods, unless its rights have been restricted or excluded by the particular laws of the Order. Originally the Mendicant Orders were unable to possess goods in common, but the Council of Trent decreed that monasteries of men and women, with the exception of the houses of the brethren of St. Francis, namely the Capuchins and the Minor Observants among the Franciscans, could in the future possess immovable property.[1] Though the Code retains the name of Mendicants, the Pontifical Commission for the Interpretation of the Code has distinguished the Mendicant Orders into Mendicants in the strict sense and Mendicants in the broad sense, to distinguish those which are permitted the ownership of immovable property in common from those which do not have such a permission.[2]

It is required that administrators be appointed for the safeguarding of the interests of the convent, the province and the Order, and that those who are appointed for this purpose function according to the norms of the law.[3]

The Provincial Superior has rights and duties over the common property of the province as well as over that of the individual houses. He exercises these rights and duties according to the norms of the common and the particular law.

1. *The Acquisition of Goods*

The general principle governing the acquisition of goods by religious is that the religious province can acquire goods

[1] Conc. Trident. sess. XXV, *de regularibus*, c. 3; Schroeder, *Canons and Decrees*, p. 219.

[2] PCI, 16 oct. 1919—*AAS*, XI (1919), 478.

[3] Can. 531.

in any way that is lawful for other moral or physical persons. The Provincial's position in reference to this acquisition of property is analogous to that of the Ordinary of a diocese.[4] Hence there are dependent upon his judgment the determination of the amount of the endowment of a pious foundation before it can be accepted,[5] the written permission granting subjects the right to accept pious foundations,[6] and the designation of a safe place for the depositing and the investing of the endowment.[7] He is also to obtain and preserve in his archives a record of all the pious foundations of the province, so that he can effectively supervise their fulfillment.[8] As executor of the pious foundations of the province he must see to their fulfillment, especially in his visitation of the province when he receives an account regarding them from their immediate administrators.[9]

The Provincial also possesses certain limited rights in accordance with canon 1517, § 2. When the fulfillment of the obligations imposed by a will has become impossible through no fault of the administrator, the Provincial may, with the counsel of the interested parties, and, provided that he fulfill the wish of the donor in so far as it is possible, diminish the obligations involved in all bequests other than Mass obligations. With regard to the latter, their reduction is always reserved to the Holy See.[10] Any inheritance involving for the community perpetual or grave obligations over a long period of time must be referred to him before its acceptance, since such are tantamount to pious foundations.[11]

Subjects who wish to become trustees or executors of pious bequests need the Provincial's permission. If the

[4] Cans. 1499, § 1; 1550.

[5] Can. 1545.

[6] Can. 1546, § 1.

[7] Can. 1547.

[8] Cans. 1548; 1514.

[9] Cans. 1514, 1°, 2°; 1549, § 2.

[10] Can. 1517, § 2. It is to be noted that the Provincial may make this reduction himself if the articles of the foundation expressly permit this freedom to him.—PCI, 14 iul. 1922, ad IX—*AAS*, XIV (1922), 529.

[11] Pejška, *Ius Canonicum Religiosorum*, p. 64.

donor refuses to permit that the Provincial be informed of the matter, or that the Provincial may control the fiduciary activity of the religious, the religious may not accept the position of trustee or executor.[12] The Provincial should see to the fulfillment of the laws governing the cession of administration and the disposition of the use and of the income of their property by novices before profession, and to the execution of their will. In urgent cases he can permit the latter to change their will without having recourse to the Holy See.[13]

The relations of subjects to property and its acquisition are further subjected to the Provincial in that he is required to be vigilant against unlawful business ventures. Offenses, particularly in regard to the fulfillment of the obligations of Mass stipends, are to be punished by him.[14]

As to the collection of alms, in view of canons 621-624 only mature and senior religious who are not engaged in studies should be permitted to go out in public in quest of them, and the regulations of the Holy See in the matter are to be followed carefully.[15] It seems, moreover, that the choice of the subjects for this work is a matter for the judgment of the Provincial, unless particular law grants the right to the Local Superior. The basis for this opinion is that there is involved an absence from the community for

[12] Can. 1515. Under canon 139, § 3, the acceptance of such a fiduciary relation in regard to profane or secular bequests also requires the Provincial's permission.

[13] Can. 583, § 2; cf. can. 569, § 1-3.

[14] Cans. 142; 1539, § 2; 2324; 2380.

[15] S.C. de Religiosis, decr. 21 nov. 1908, n. I, 1°. This decree requires that the offerings be sought by the religious personally and not through seculars. They should have proper credentials in writing. Except in the case of a religious who is well known and esteemed, it is not permitted that religious go in quest of alms alone or unaccompanied; rather, they must go in pairs. In their own diocese they should not remain away from the religious house beyond a month; elsewhere the absence should not be prolonged beyond two months. Upon returning to the monastery they should not be sent on the quest again until after the lapse of one or two months.—*Fontes*, n. 4391.

a long period, and the Provincial is presumed to have a better knowledge of the religious who can be best permitted to remain outside the religious house for the period required. It seems particularly warranted that his permission is required in the case wherein Mendicants in the broad sense go on quest of alms in virtue of an Apostolic indult[16] since the latter need the permission of the diocesan Ordinary unless the indult provides otherwise.[17]

The degree to which the individual moral persons (local houses) of the province may own goods depends upon the particular law, upon privilege, and upon the current general custom.[18] The law of the Code in itself is strict in reserving to the local houses an exclusive right of ownership even as against the province. Authors agree that certain taxes can be levied upon all the houses for provincial and general expenses of the Order. Beyond these taxes, one must examine the particular law of the institute for determining what additional rights the province may enjoy in reference to the houses established within its limits.[19] In itself the law of the Code points to an arrangement that is somewhat parallel to that of the parishes of a diocese in relation to the bishop. The parishes may be taxed, but their surplus funds cannot be taken by the bishop; each parish is a unit in itself. Deviations from this arrangement must be sanctioned by papal approval.

The particular law of centralized institutes, based on canon 531 which permits the particular law to restrict the property rights of local houses, may provide that the necessities of the individual house shall first be met, and that superfluous funds shall be devoted to the necessities of the province and of the Order.[20]

[16] I.e., Mendicants possessing property in common—PCI, 16 oct. 1919—*AAS*, XI (1919), 478.

[17] Cf., however, Clancy, *The Local Superior*, p. 68.

[18] Berutti, *Institutiones*, III, 112; Vermeersch-Creusen, *Epitome*, I, n. 654.

[19] Berutti, *loc. cit.;* Schaefer, *De Religiosis*, p. 409, n. 187.

[20] Privilege or lawful custom may also sanction this allocation of

Particular law, however, could not, it seems take away entirely the rights of the individual local houses of the province. This is indicated by the fact that the Generals of Congregations of simple vows must, in the quinquennial report to the Holy See, state specifically the amounts of superfluous goods contributed to the common treasury yearly by the individual houses, and explain whether the houses made these contributions freely or unwillingly.[21]

2. *The Administration of Goods*

In order to understand the rights and duties of the Provincial in relation to the administration of goods, it is essential to know what the Code means by the phrase. Administration of goods includes all those acts which are intended for preserving and improving temporal goods according to their purposes and their nature.[22] It comprehends acts of two distinct species, namely, of ordinary and of extraordinary administration. The former includes all acts which pertain to the ordinary day-to-day conservation and substantial improvement of goods already acquired, or to the lawful acquisition, conservation, improvement, or application of the revenue derived from them.[23]

Extraordinary administration, on the other hand, embraces the idea of the expenditure of money for the extra-

---

goods. The justifiable restriction of the property rights of local houses through the particular law is probably based on the fact that the inequality of funded capital in the different houses might result in an unequal standard of living, a relaxed regard for poverty, and even a possible discontent. Accordingly, the present Constitutions of the Carmelite Order, for example, contain arrangements for an economic equality among local houses to be effected through the arrangements of the Provincial with his council.

[21] S.C. de Religiosis, decr. 25 mart. 1922, qq. 62-63—*AAS,* XIV (1922), 282.

[22] Creusen, *Religious Men and Women in the Code,* translated by Garesché, 4. Eng. ed. by Ellis (Milwaukee: Bruce Publishing Co., 1942), p. 116.

[23] Wernz-Vidal, *De Religiosis,* p. 171, n. 218.

ordinary conservation or improvement of the temporal goods of the moral person, such as extraordinary repairs of a building, as well as the canonical concept of *alienation.* The latter term signifies any act or acts by which the right of ownership is transferred in whole or in part. It includes purchases or transfers of property, the making of onerous contracts, and the contracting of debts and financial obligations. Briefly, any transaction which renders the position of the ecclesiastical moral person less secure is termed alienation.[24]

Since alienation in the strict sense affects only stable capital, it is necessary to advert to the distinction between *stable* and *unstable capital.* Stable capital is that money which is invested or restricted in some manner, so that it cannot be used primarily as a means of exchange. Money that has not been designated or invested as stable capital, but is used for ordinary administration, is called unstable capital, and remains such until designated as stable capital by the proper Superior of the community or province with the respective council's vote or consent.[25]

Since canon 1523, 4°, requires administrators to invest, with the permission of the Ordinary, the surplus funds of the church which have been entrusted to their care, it follows that surplus provincial funds are to be invested with the permission of the Provincial. Similarly, Local Superiors are to see to the investment of surplus funds in accordance with the particular law of the community, which may frequently necessitate the permission of the Provincial. Through investment, however, the surplus goods become stable, regardless of how they are invested.[26] Thus the

[24] Doheny, *Practical Problems in Church Finance* (Milwaukee: Bruce Publishing Co., 1941), p. 21.

[25] Heston, "Stable Capital in Temporal Administration"—*The Jurist,* II (1942), 130-131.

[26] Thus the goods may be used for the purchase of stocks and of bonds, or of real estate, or the goods may be set aside for some specific purpose such as a building fund.

designation of funds as stable capital is either directly or indirectly contingent upon the consent of the Provincial according to the norms of the particular law which may require the additional consent or advice of the council.

Canon 516, § 2, arranges for the administration of the temporalities of each house and province. The provincial procurator is designated as charged with the administration of the goods of the province under the supervision of the Provincial. As Pejška notes, the administration of goods pertains to the Regular prelate,[27] but procurators are appointed to act under the prelate's supervision because of his many other duties. The law of the Code is derived from the Council of Trent which required their appointment.[28] In the case of the Provincial, the performance of the duties of his office and the simultaneous fulfillment of those of the provincial procurator are incompatible with reference to the same person, and consequently the double performance of these duties is explicitly prohibited by the Code.[29]

A. Temporal Goods of Individual Houses

The very nature of the office of Provincial requires his supervision over the administration of the temporal goods of local houses. Particular law generally specifies the nature and the extent of this supervision. It may, for instance, require that periodic financial reports be made to the Provincial or to the provincial procurator. Beyond this authorized supervision of the acts of ordinary administration, the Provincial is not permitted to interfere in the ordinary administration of the individual houses, since each is a moral person with its own rights that are to be exercised by officials under the immediate supervision of the Local Su-

[27] *Ius Canonicum Religiosorum*, p. 68.

[28] Conc. Trident., sess. XXV, *de regularibus*, c. 2.

[29] Can. 516, § 3. Vermeersch-Creusen state that the provincial procurator is subject to the direction of the Provincial alone, and not to that of the Provincial's council, although accounts of his administration are to be rendered to the latter (*Epitome*, I, n. 635).

perior. Within the limits of the ordinary administration both the local procurator and the Local Superior act validly.[30]

If particular law should establish that permission be sought from the Provincial for all expenditures in excess of a certain amount, the latter amount marks the limit of the ordinary administration.[31] Particular law usually requires the consent of the Provincial and of his council for acts of extraordinary administration even when they do not constitute alienation. The relation of the Provincial, then, to this extraordinary administration of the property of the individual houses exceeds the limits of supervision. If the extraordinary administration of the particular house involves alienation, the rights of even the Provincial are restricted by the requirement that the community obtain an Apostolic indult in cases involving a notable amount.[32]

[30] Can. 532, § 2.

[31] It may be that the particular law is silent as to the extent of expenditures that the various Superiors can lawfully make without reference to the higher Superior. Larraona believes ("Commentarium Codicis"—*CpR*, XIV [1933], 170) that a norm may be borrowed from canons 1532 and 1541, *congrua congruis referendo*, or from the former law and the specifications of the Instruction *Inter ea* of July 30th, 1909, issued by the Sacred Congregation of Religious with regard to the contracting of debts and obligations by religious communities (*AAS*, I [1909], 696-699). According to this Instruction (II), *a notable amount* which requires the consent of the council in relation to individual houses is one that exceeds 500 francs but is less than 1000. In relation to provinces, a notable amount is one in excess of 1000 francs but less than 5000. In relation to the General and his council, a notable amount is one in excess of 5000 francs and less than 10,000 francs. In the event of a sum greater than the latter amount, the *beneplacitum* of the Holy See was also required. Larraona argues that since the Code has raised the amount of the sum which calls for an Apostolic indult from 10,000 francs to 30,000 francs, the intermediate sums should likewise be raised proportionately.

[32] Alienation of ecclesiastical goods was declared invalid in the law of Gratian (cc. 18-21, C. XII, q. 2). Later it was held to be lawful for an abbot to exchange the goods of two churches subject to him, with their consent, although priests were forbidden to alienate church

The necessity of an Apostolic indult will be examined further in relation to the Provincial's authority over the temporal goods of the province. The Provincial's permission is frequently required for every alienation, even when an Apostolic indult is not necessary. This requirement extends to donations, which under canon 537 may be made for a just cause with the permission of the proper Superior. Formerly it was necessary for religious to have the permission of the general chapter to make donations.[33] Later law allowed the making of donations with the permission of the proper Superior,[34] and in 1909 the Sacred Congregation of Religious instructed religious to conform to the general and the particular law in the making of donations.[35]

In summary it may be said, then, that the duties of the Provincial in relation to the temporal goods of the individual houses consist of the following, derived from either the common or the particular law:

1) supervision over the ordinary administration in all its phases;
2) supervision and immediate control, in virtue of particular law, over certain matters of extraordinary administration, even when alienation is not involved;

---

property under pain of nullified action as well as of ecclesiastical censure (c. 1, X, *de rebus ecclesiae non alienandis*, III, 13). In cases of necessity and with the consent of the proper prelate, the procurator was authorized to make certain alienations (c. 1, *de rebus ecclesiae non alienandis*, III, 4, in Clem.). Paul II (1464-1471) inflicted the penalty of excommunication upon anyone who performed an act of unlawful alienation, and also upon anyone who received the goods thus alienated (c. un., *de rebus ecclesiae non alienandis*, III, 4, in Extravag. com.). The Council of Trent and pre-Code authors likewise condemned the unlawful alienation of ecclesiastical goods (Conc. Trident., sess. XXV, *de regularibus*, cc. 2, 3; Suarez, *De Religione*, Lib. II, Cap. XIV, n. 20).

[33] Clemens VIII, const. *Religiosae congregationes*, § 4—*Fontes*, n. 178.

[34] Urban VIII, const. *Nuper*, 16 oct., 1640, § 1—*Fontes*, n. 220.

[35] S.C. de Religiosis, instr. *Inter ea*, 30 iul. 1909, n. XIII—*Fontes*, n. 4394; *AAS*, I (1909), 698.

3) supervision and immediate control over matters involving alienation both when an Apostolic indult is necessary and, usually under particular law, also when such an indult is not needed.

B. Temporal Goods of the Province

It is left by the Code to particular law to determine what goods of the province are common provincial goods, and what relation in the matter of temporalities is to exist between the individual houses and the province. It is, furthermore, the function of particular law, if the common law is silent on the matter, to specify the cases in which the Provincial needs the consent or the advice of his council.

The intervention of the council is usually not required for acts of ordinary administration.[36] However, the Provincial's habitual exercise of the acts of ordinary administration is illicit in virtue of canon 516, § 3, which requires that a provincial procurator be appointed for the performance of these duties under the Provincial's supervision. Within the scope of the ordinary administration of the property of the province the following acts can be included:

1) those affecting the domestic economy of the Provincial's house;
2) those involving the acceptance of rents and annual receipts from creditors;
3) the payment of current bills and taxes and other sales or purchases necessary for the daily maintenance of the provincial property;
4) acts involving the employment of funds not designated as part of the stable capital of the province, provided that they do not exceed the limits established by the particular law; and
5) the making of leases when the annual rental accruing from them does not exceed one thousand francs (gold)

[36] Cf. can. 532, § 2.

and their period does not extend beyond a period of nine years.[37]

Particular law may restrict the right of the Provincial to make donations from current surplus funds without the advice or the consent of his council, or also of the General.

In the matter of extraordinary administration the rights of the Provincial may be restricted by particular law even as those of the Local Superior may be restricted. Particular law may require the consent or the advice of the Provincial's council, or even the permission of the General and his curia for extraordinary expenditures of certain grave amounts. In the absence of particular legislation, the advice of the council should be sought if the sum involved is equal to that specified by the general law as determining the need of the council's advice or consent for alienation.[38] If alienation is involved, the general norms of the Code governing it must be observed. Accordingly, the value of the object is to be determined by expert appraisal; there must be a just cause for the alienation;[39] the property must be sold to the highest bidder at, or beyond, the price of appraisal;[40] and the money acquired from the investment must be safely invested.

The foregoing norms pertain to the licitness of the action; the validity itself depends upon the permission of the proper

[37] The gold franc was equivalent to .193 of the gold dollar of the United States, and daily usage considered the exchange to be five francs for an American dollar at the time of the promulgation of the Code. Hence, the thousand francs above mentioned were the equivalent of $200.00, which amount has become extended to $338.00 in view of the devaluation of the American dollar to 59.06 cents, which devaluation set in with the Presidential Proclamation of President Roosevelt on January 31, 1934 (Doheny, *Practical Problems in Church Finance*, pp. 41-42. Cf. Larraona, "Commentarium Codicis"—*CpR*, XIV (1933), 169; Vromant, *De Bonis Ecclesiae Temporalibus* (Louvain, 1932), p. 185, n. 173).

[38] Can. 1532, § 1, 2°, 3°.

[39] Can. 1530, § 1, 1°, 2°.

[40] Can. 1531, § § 1, 2.

Superior with the advice or the consent of his council expressed through secret ballot.[41] Moreover, this permission must be given in writing according to canon 534, § 1, which in the clause "written permission is required and suffices" equivalently includes the invalidating clause of canon 1530, § 1, 3°. Furthermore, an Apostolic indult is required for the validity of the transaction if the value of the object of alienation exceeds six thousand dollars (gold).[42] An Apostolic indult is also needed according to canon 534, § 1, for the alienation of precious objects[43] of notable value,[44] or to contract debts or obligations beyond the sum of six thousand dollars (gold).

Doheny cites the letter of the Most Reverend Apostolic Delegate to the United States of November 13, 1936,[45] written under the authority of the Sacred Congregation of Religious, and stating that the two following systems of collecting money are governed by the law of canon 534: 1) the issuance of bonds or debentures upon ecclesiastical property and their sale; and 2) annuity plans providing for the payments of a stipulated annuity sum during the lifetime of the donor. Under both these systems economic obligations are undertaken by the moral person, and have to be met at a certain time. Thus any attempt to raise money in either way would be invalid without a papal indult, whenever the sums of money accruing from one or both systems or from a

[41] Cans. 1530, § 1, 3°; 534, § 1.

[42] Can. 534, § 1. The Holy See considers any alienation of property valued at this figure to be of major importance for the economic status of the moral person. Particular law may also require the previous consent of the General with the advice or the consent of his council.

[43] Can. 1497, § 2, describes as *precious* those objects which have a special intrinsic, artistic or historic value. Cf. Vermeersch-Creusen, *Epitome*, II, n. 819.

[44] S.C.C., 12 iul. 1919—The alienation of precious objects is reserved only when they have a notable value (*AAS* XI [1919], 417). From the accompanying discussion of the Sacred Congregation of the Council, it is made evident that the amount of a notable value can be placed, as a minimum, at two-hundred dollars (gold)—*ibid.*, p. 418.

[45] Bouscaren, *The Canon Law Digest*, Supplement (1941), p. 78.

combination of several operations at the same or different times accumulate in a sum greater than six thousand dollars (gold).[46]

To serve as a guide for determining when the permissions required by canon 534 will be necessary, the following classes of acts verifying either the notion or alienation or of contractual obligations resembling alienation can be listed:

1) the *sale* of property belonging to stable capital;
2) *donations* from stable capital;
3) *leases* of property belonging to stable capital when the leases extend beyond nine years;
4) *rentals* of property comprised in the stable capital when the rentals continue for over nine years;
5) *exchange* of property included in the stable capital, with due allowance for the faculty given in canon 1539, § 2, for the exchange of securities;
6) *compromise* in financial disputes over goods pertaining to stable capital.
7) *mortgaging by special mortgage* of goods already under the full ownership of the church organization;
8) *payment of debts* with funds taken from the stable capital;
9) *surety for others* with funds belonging to permanent assets.[47]

C. Investments

The investment of money means the disposition of it in such a manner as to assure that it will be preserved, at least in an equivalent form, or that it will produce revenue.[48] Unless it be a temporary investment of current funds, it is an act of extraordinary administration, though it entails no notion of alienation requiring the *beneplacitum* of higher Superiors or of the Holy See.[49] Investment is distinguished

[46] Doheny, *Practical Problems in Church Finance*, p. 68.

[47] Heston, "Stable Capital in Temporal Administration"—*The Jurist*, II (1942), 130.

[48] Creusen, *Religious Men and Women in the Code*, p. 116.

[49] S.C. Prop. de Fide, 7 iul. 1893—*Fontes*, n. 4925.

from the mere depositing of money in banks at a low rate of interest and with liberty to withdraw the funds at any time. Money placed in the bank is not affixed to the stable capital by the mere fact of its being deposited. It should not be left there permanently, if it is true surplus capital, but should be affixed to the stable capital and invested in fruitful capital goods. This follows analogously from the requirement that money acquired from the sale of stable capital goods, including land, must be invested.[50]

When money is invested, the presumption arises that it is aggregated to the stable capital of the moral person, and subject to the rules governing the alienation of stable capital. It is this act which canon 533 envisages, namely, the consumption of surplus funds for the acquiring of fruitful, immovable goods. These goods may be property, stocks, bonds, bank notes and the like, but once they have been acquired, they are likened, as stable capital, to immovable property.[51]

The Provincial's consent is needed by the provincial procurator in the investment of the surplus funds of the province. There may be other regulations of the particular law which must also be fulfilled by him or by the Provincial, v.g., the obtaining of the advice or the consent of the Provincial's council. The Provincial's consent for the investment of the stable capital of the local houses is also needed, subject to whatever other provisions particular law contains.

For the greater security of the moral person canon 533 gives a list of cases in which the local Ordinary must be consulted in the investment of funds entrusted to religious institutes. In the administration and investment of their own stable capital Regulars are exempt from the jurisdiction or supervision of the local Ordinary. However, money

[50] Can. 1531, § 3.

[51] Berutti, *Institutiones*, III, 116; Doheny, *Practical Problems in Finance*, p. 44; S.C. Prop. Fide, Epistola, Appendix, n. XVI—*AAS*, XIV (1922), 307.

given to a religious or to a religious institute for the benefit of a diocesan parish or mission cannot be invested, or its investment changed, without the previous consent of the local Ordinary.[52]

D. Debts and Obligations

The prescriptions of the general and the particular law regarding the administration of temporal goods are intended to avert economic tragedies, and to promote the economic security of the moral person. Canon 536 aims at the removal of doubts and controversies over the question of responsibility for debts and obligations. From it the responsibility of the Provincial and of the moral person he represents can be determined.

If the Provincial contracts debts or obligations in the name of the province and in accordance with all the norms of law, he contracts validly and licitly.[53] Accordingly actions which require the *beneplacitum* of the Holy See and, under particular law, of the General, cannot be validly transacted by the Provincial without such requisite permissions. The proper permission to assume debts or obligations up to the amount requiring the *beneplacitum* of the Holy See[54] obliges him to first secure the consent of his council or his chapter by secret vote in accordance with canon 534, § 1.

On the other hand, the licitness of the action is governed by the prescriptions of the common law which regulate the licitness of acts of alienation, as well as by the particular prescriptions established by the law of the institute.[55] If

[52] Can. 533, § 1, 4°, § 2.

[53] Can. 532, § 2. Thus Fanfani states that the moral person is responsible if one who has been lawfully instituted as Superior formally acts as such in assuming debts or obligations within the limits of his office and within the scope of the ordinary administration (*De Iure Religiosorum*, p. 175.).

[54] I.e., $6,000.00 (gold) or the equivalent of the 30,000 francs mentioned in canon 534, § 1.

[55] Cf. cans. 1530, § 1, 1°, 2°; 1531, § § 1, 2, 3; 1530, § 2; Fanfani, *De Iure Religiosorum*, pp. 178; 184-185.

his contract is merely illicit, e.g., in view of his neglect to obtain the proper assurance that the interest and debt can be met in accordance with the injunction of canon 536, § 5, but fulfills the essential conditions for validity, the contract is valid and the province is responsible, although the Provincial may be punished by the General. If the contract is not only illicit, but also invalid, Fanfani teaches that the Provincial alone is responsible, since he has overstepped the limits of his office.[56] It seems, however, that the law of canon 1527, § 2, would apply, so that the province would be responsible to the extent to which the contract has been a benefit to it.

Individual moral persons, i.e., local houses, within the province are responsible for their own obligations. Two exceptions to this rule can, however, be established: 1) if the province has given security for the debt of the local house; and 2) if a particular house has been declared incapable of responsibility in temporal matters, so that the Superior of that house, in granting permission for debts, has been constituted to represent the province as the moral person responsible.[57]

If the local house through its Superior or procurator acted without the permission of the Provincial when this is required, neither the Provincial nor the province are responsible, since the inferiors have also exceeded the limits of their office and are therefore personally responsible, just as when the Provincial transgresses the limits of his office in like manner. Again, however, through an application of canon 1527, § 2, it seems that the province would be responsible in the event of benefit to itself, and to the extent of that benefit.[58]

[56] *De Iure Religiosorum*, p. 176.

[57] McManus, *The Administration of Temporal Goods in Religious Institutes*, The Catholic University of America Canon Law Studies, n. 109 (Washington, D. C.: The Catholic University of America, 1937), pp. 165-166.

[58] Fanfani, *loc. cit.*

Individual religious can validly contract debts and obligations with the express, tacit or presumed permission of the Superior. When the religious contracts debts in such a way with the permission of the Provincial, the province is responsible, since tacit and presumed permissions suffice, as in the case in which a religious publicly and notoriously enters a contract in a matter which only the Provincial can authorize. Previous knowledge of his contemplated act on the part of the Provincial is, of course, postulated, as well as the Provincial's freedom to forbid it. In this case there is every reason for supposing a tacit or presumed permission, and accordingly the obligations are contracted by the province.[59]

Although canon 536, § 2, states that a religious who enters a contract with the permission of his Superior contracts in such a way that the moral person represented by the Superior is responsible, the canon must nevertheless be understood in connection with canon 532, § 2, which establishes the conditions within which the Superior can validly contract for the moral person. As has already been seen in the preceding paragraphs, a Superior who exceeds the limits of his office in contracting debts is personally responsible instead of the moral person which he has been designated to represent within the limits of the law. Therefore a Superior who gives permission to a subject to contract in a matter in which the Superior himself is incompetent becomes responsible himself, since in authorizing the subject's action he has at the same time exceeded the limits of his office.[60]

The same conclusion would be warranted with regard to the Local Superior's permission within the scope of his authority. On the other hand, if a religious enters a contract without any permission of the Superior, either Local or Provincial, he alone is obliged.[61]

[59] Berutti, *Institutiones*, III, 127.

[60] Fanfani, *De Iure Religiosorum*, p. 176.

[61] Can. 536, § 3.

E. Sanctions Invoked by Law Against Violations

The Code does not, but particular law may, establish penalties to be inflicted or declared by the Provincial for maladministration in matters of ordinary administration or of extraordinary administration not involving alienation.

Violations of the law regarding the alienation of temporal goods are punished with certain penal sanctions in canon 2347. Thus, acts of those who presume to effect an unlawful alienation are invalid. Moreover, there is imposed on the possessor of goods thus alienated an obligation, which can be enforced with ecclesiastical censures, to restore the goods unlawfully acquired and to repair the damage which has resulted. Similarly, those who give consent to acts of alienation contrary to canons 534, § 1, and 1532 can be obliged to repair the injuries suffered as a consequence by the moral person. Moreover, the Provincial should punish those guilty of minor violations involving a sum not exceeding two-hundred dollars (gold).

The procurator, or Superior, or both, are to be deprived of their office and their eligibility for office, and are to be subject to other fitting penalties for violations which involve a sum exceeding $200.00 (gold). It is to be remembered, however, that the delict is committed only if it is motivated with presumptuousness, and hence a diminution in the imputability will lessen the penalty which remains to be inflicted, although it will not excuse from it entirely.[62] Finally, canon 2347, 3°, states that, when the obtaining of the *beneplacitum* of the Holy See has been *knowingly* passed over,[63] then all who are guilty in giving, receiving, or granting consent in-

[62] Can. 2347, 1°, 2°. It is to be noted that the canon postulates presumptuousness for the incurring of the penalties. Canon 2229, § 2, according to its rule would excuse from the incurring of a *latae sententiae penalty* in cases wherein any diminution of imputability was verified.

[63] Cf. canon 2229, § 2, for the necessity of a complete imputability before a *latae sententiae* penalty will be incurred if presumptuousness is postulated as inherent in the delict.

cur a *latae sententiae* excommunication which is not reserved to any one. Beyond this penal sanction of the common law, the Sacred Congregation of Religious issued an Instruction which was communicated to Ordinaries and religious Superiors of the United States through a Letter of the Most Reverend Apostolic Delegate, dated November 13, 1936, wherein it was stated that the Sacred Congregation would inflict the above-mentioned penalties as stated in canon 2347 when the case warranted such action. Moreover, the Congregation would inflict other severe penalties according to its discretion, not excluding the penalty of privation of office.[64]

[64] The text of this Letter is quoted in full by Doheny, *Practical Problems in Church Finance*, Appendix, II, pp. 93-98.

CHAPTER XI

THE PROVINCIAL SUPERIOR AND THE SACRAMENTS

Many of the pastoral rights and duties connected with the administration of the Sacraments in their relation to the spiritual life of religious subjects are possessed by the Local Superiors and primarily exercised by them. Yet, the superior jurisdictional position of the Provincial suggests that he is the true pastor of the province. In order that his inability to be present in all the local houses might not result in spiritual harm to his subjects, the exercise of many sacramental functions has been conceded by the common law to the Local Superior. Though many of these are possessed cumulatively by the Provincial, the latter cannot lawfully reserve to himself rights granted to Local Superiors, unless a just cause warrants his action. On the other hand, certain powers in relation to the Sacraments of Penance and of Holy Orders are reserved by the common law to the Provincial. Before examining the latter powers, the position of the Provincial in relation to the other Sacraments will be briefly treated.

1. *Baptism and Confirmation*

The right to permit novices or professed religious to act as sponsors in the administration of Baptism or of Confirmation is explicitly granted to the Local Superior whenever a sufficient reason justifies such a permission.[1] There is no reason to think that this canon grants this right exclusively to the Local Superior.[2] Consequently the Provincial is authorized to grant the same permission to any of his subjects and, for a just reason, to overrule a contrary decision of the Local Superior. Moreover, canon 766, 4°,

[1] Cans. 766, 4°; 796, 3°; 765, 4°.

[2] Reg. 53, R. J., in VI°.

requires *at least* the permission of the Local Superior.[3] Particular law, therefore, may even restrict the right of the Local Superior in this matter by reserving the permission to the Provincial. Indeed, the next number of canon 766 actually requires the permission of the Provincial in the case of a religious in sacred Orders, since it states that the permission of one's proper Ordinary is necessary for one in sacred Orders to act as sponsor.[4]

2. *Matrimony*

The exercise of jurisdiction in relation to this Sacrament is not distinctly within the sphere of the Provincial's relationship to his subjects. Yet, he indirectly touches on the functions related to this Sacrament through his presentation to the local Ordinary of a priest for appointment as pastor or as parochial assistant. Although the licitness of the act of assistance at a marriage by an exempt priest religious depends upon the previous permission or approval of the Provincial, the validity of the act is not open to question when the authorization has been derived directly or indirectly from the competent pastor or from the Local Ordinary.[5]

3. *The Holy Eucharist and Extreme Unction*

The rights of the Provincial in administering Holy Communion and Extreme Unction to his subjects are possessed cumulatively with the Local Superiors of the province. Particular law may specify certain of these cumulative rights as exclusively those of the Provincial in the event that both Superiors are present at the time when these Sacraments

[3] "Ut autem quis licite patrinus admittatur, oportet: in nulla religione sit novitius vel professus, nisi necessitas urgeat et expressa habeatur venia Superioris saltem localis."

[4] Can. 766, 5°: "Ut autem quis licite patrinus admittatur, oportet: in sacris ordinibus non sit constitutus, nisi accedat expressa Ordinarii proprii licentia."

[5] Cf. PCI, 20 maii, 1923—*AAS*, XVI (1924), 114.

are to be administered, but no discrimination is made in the Code.

Since the time of the Council of Chalcedon (451), legislation prescribed the furnishing of a testimonial letter, i.e., of a *celebret,* by a cleric before the exercise of the sacerdotal ministry outside his own city.[6] Canon 804 requires a priest religious to exhibit a *celebret* from his Superior, if he seeks permission to celebrate Mass outside his monastery. It is certain that the Provincial can issue the *celebret* to his subjects in view of his position as Ordinary, although the Local Superior can also issue it.[7]

It has been seen above that the fulfillment of the spiritual exercises prescribed by canon 595, § 1, 2°, 3° is fundamentally a responsibility of the Provincial, although the insurance of their fulfillment rests immediately with the Local Superior.[8] The Provincial is required to check upon the observance of this canon particularly at the time of visitation. Similarly the proximate responsibility for the fulfillment of the obligation enacted in canon 805, which urges Superiors to see that priests under their jurisdiction celebrate Mass at least on Sundays and Holy Days, rests with the Local Superior. However, because the Provincial is responsible for the religious observance in the province, he should also keep a check upon this matter at the time of his visitation, and, when necessary, exact from his subject the fulfillment of the obligation in question.

It has been seen above that charity, and perhaps also the particular law, will oblige the Provincial to celebrate Mass occasionally for his subjects.[9]

Canon 842 confers on Superiors the right and the duty of insuring that the laws of the Church concerning Mass sti-

[6] C. 7, D. LXXI; Conc. Trident., sess. XXII, *de observandis et evitandis in celebratione Missae;* sess. XXIII, *de ref.*, c. 16; S.C.S. Off., decr. 11 aug. 1649—*Fontes,* n. 729.

[7] Clancy, *The Local Superior,* pp. 131-133.

[8] Cf. *supra,* p. 126.

[9] Cf. *supra,* p. 73.

pends and regarding the fulfillment of Mass obligations are complied with by the responsible parties. In the absence of reservation which in the particular law connects this duty with the office of the Provincial, it will remain primarily the concern of the Local Superior to attend to its fulfillment. Attention is called to the fact that pious foundations must be referred to the Provincial before their acceptance.[10] The Local Superior must present, at least annually, to the Provincial or his delegate, an account of the actual fulfillment of the obligations of the Mass intentions of the particular church or community.[11] Thus the Code renews the law of Innocent XII (1691-1700), which required that not only the rectors of churches but also the intermediate religious Superiors keep accurate record of the fulfillment of these obligations, and render an annual account to their Superiors.[12]

The Local Superior is obliged to transmit to the Provincial a record of the Mass obligations that remain to be satisfied at the end of each year in accordance with the law of canon 841, § § 1, 2. Thus quasi-manual Masses (*Missae ad instar manualium*) which have not been satisfied at the end of the calendar year during which they should have been celebrated are to be transmitted to the Provincial in the manner which he prescribes. Manual Masses, however, need not be transmitted to him until a year from the date on which the obligation was assumed, unless the intention of the donor specifies a shorter period of time during which the Masses are to be celebrated. Prudence dictates that if only a few obligations remain unsatisfied at the end of the year, since they can be satisfied more quickly by retaining them, they need not be sent to the Provincial.[13]

Originally the rights of Regulars to distribute Holy Communion were quite restricted, but by the time of the Code,

[10] Cf. *supra*, p. 164.
[11] Can. 843, § 2.
[12] Const. *Nuper*, 23 dec. 1797, § 19—*Fontes*, n. 260.
[13] Vermeersch-Creusen, *Epitome*, II, n. 106.

certain privileges and subsequent legislation entitled religious priests to administer Holy Communion to all the faithful.[14] Canon 846 permits any priest to administer Holy Communion according to the norms indicated in that canon. When it is necessary to administer Holy Communion, Holy Viaticum or Extreme Unction to subjects who are sick, either the Local or the Provincial Superior is competent according to canon 514, § 1. Neither, however, can lawfully infringe upon the parochial rights of a pastor by administering Extreme Unction to a pastor's subjects without his permission, or by carrying Communion or Viaticum *publicly* even to a subject religious confined in a hospital committed to the care of a territorial pastor.[15]

Matters pertaining to dispensation from the Eucharistic fast for priests or religious not confined to bed[16] must be referred through the Provincial to the Holy Office, or to the Ordinary of the place if he possesses proper faculties from the Holy Office.[17]

[14] Clancy, *The Local Superior*, pp. 136-137.

[15] PCI, 16 iun. 1931—*AAS*, XXIII (1931), 353; Clancy, *The Local Superior*, p. 140. The presumed permission of the local pastor suffices for the carrying of Holy Viaticum publicly to novices or religious outside their monastery unless the particular law of the territory should provide otherwise. But it is to be noted that, though canon 514, § 1, includes as authorized for the receiving of the last Sacraments from the clerical Superior both the *familiares* and those who are present in the religious house, the clerical religious Superiors are not, outside of a case of necessity or apart from at least the presumed permission of the local pastor or Ordinary, entitled to administer the last Sacraments to them when they are confined by illness outside of the religious house.

[16] Cf. can. 858, § 2.

[17] The petition must contain a statement regarding the age, office and duty of the subject of the dispensation; regarding his physical condition as attested in a certificate from a reliable physician; regarding the need of and the manner of taking liquid nourishment or medicine; regarding the number of Masses the priest must celebrate on Sundays or on the days of precept; regarding the hour at which the Mass or Masses must be celebrated, telling whether the Masses are to be celebrated in the same church or in different churches, and

4. *Penance*

A. Appointment and Approval of Confessors

1) Pre-Code Legislation

For the period before the Council of Trent there are conflicting opinions as to the source of the jurisdiction of Regular confessors, namely, whether the jurisdiction came directly from the Holy See or from the local Ordinaries.[18] Reasons for the discussion can be found in the fact that some papal documents seem to indicate that the Regulars obtained confessional jurisdiction directly from the Holy See and independently of the local Ordinaries, provided that they were approved by the proper Superior designated by particular law.[19]

Boniface VIII (1294-1303), indeed, demanded the approval of the local Ordinary despite the previous approval by the religious Superior.[20] But Benedict XI (1303-1304) reversed this teaching only a short time later and removed the obligation of the presentation of Regular confessors to the local Ordinary for approval when they had been approved by their proper Superior.[21] Clement V (1305-1314)

---

whether it is possible to substitute another priest for the celebration of them. The petition must be submitted by the Major Superior, and if the religious seeks the dispensation for the sake of functioning in the parochial ministry, then the petition must be signed by the local Ordinary (S.C.S. Off., Litterae ad Ordinarios locorum de ieiunio Eucharistico ante Missam, 22 mart. 1923—*AAS*, XV (1923), 151; Beste, *Introductio*, pp. 485-486.

[18] Cf. Donatus, *Rerum Regularium Praxis*, Tom. IV, tr. IV, qq. 31-33; Piat, *Praelectiones*, II, p. 181, qu. 225.

[19] Gregorius IX, const. *Quoniam abundavit*, 10 maii, 1227—*Bullarium Ordinis FF. Praedicatorum* (ed. a T. Ripoll, recognitum a A. Brémond, 8 vols., Romae: 1729-1740), I, 19 (hereafter cited as *Bull. Praed.*); Potthast, *Regesta*, n. 7896; Celestinus V, const. *Ad fructus uberes*, 27 nov. 1294—*Bullarium Ordinis Eremitarum S. Augustini* (ed L. Empoli, Romae: 1628), p. 103.

[20] Const. *Super cathedram*, 18 febr. 1300—c. 2, *de sepulturis*, III, 7, in Clem.

[21] Const. *Inter cunctas*, 17 febr. 1304—c. 1, *de privilegiis*, V, 7, in Extravag, com.

in turn abrogated this Constitution in the Council of Vienne (1311-1312), and the Constitution of Boniface VIII which had required the presentation of the confessors to the local Ordinary was restored.[22] This teaching appears to have remained the constant one for the following years, although Pope Leo X (1513-1521) apparently saw a need to renew the obligation of religious Superiors to present confessors to the local Ordinaries, if the latter requested such presentation.[23] The Council of Trent decreed that no Regular confessor could hear the confessions of the laity unless he held a parochial benefice or was approved by the bishop.[24]

This brief historical sketch of the source of jurisdiction of Regular confessors is but a necessary preliminary to the question of which Superior was the proper one for the approval of confessors. In cases wherein it seems that the jurisdiction was conferred through the approval of the confessors by the religious Superiors, the point of interest regards the determination of the Superior who enjoyed the necessary competence for granting such approval.[25]

During the period before the Council of Trent the approbation of religious priests of exempt Orders which was spoken of in the papal documents as necessary before they could hear confessions appears to have been contingent

[22] Const. *Dudum*, 6 maii 1312—c. 2, *de sepulturis* III, 7, in Clem.

[23] Const. *Dum intra*, 19 dec. 1516, § 6—*Fontes*, n. 72.

[24] Sess. XXIII, *de ref.*, c. 15.

[25] It is to be noted that the Council of Trent (Sess. XXIII, *de ref.*, c. 15) actually abstracted from the question regarding the source of jurisdiction of Regular confessors. It did not state that the local Ordinary conferred this jurisdiction nor did it state that it came directly from the Holy See. It merely demanded that Regular confessors be *presented* to the local Ordinary for approval. "Quamvis presbyteri in sua ordinatione a peccatis absolvendi potestatem accipiant, decernit tamen sancta synodus, nullum, etiam regularem, posse confessiones saecularium, etiam sacerdotum, audire, nec ad id idoneum reputari, nisi aut parochiale beneficium, aut ab episcopis per examen, si illis videbitur esse necessarium, aut alias idoneus judicetur, et approbationem, quae gratis detur, obtineat; privilegiis et consuetudine quacumque, etiam immemorabili, non obstantibus."

upon the Provincial or the provincial chapter, unless particular law ruled otherwise. Thus, independently of the question of the source of jurisdiction, it appears that previous approbation of the Regular Superior was necessary.[26]

Various papal documents support this view. Thus Celestine V (1294) permitted all priests of exempt Orders to hear confessions and to preach everywhere provided they were approved for such work by their provincial chapters.[27] Boniface VIII (1294-1303) in his Constitution *Super Cathedram* instructed Provincials to select priests of their community whom they deemed fit for the hearing of confessions, and to present them to the local Ordinary for his approbation.[28] Benedict XI (1303-1304)[29] and Clement V (1311-1312)[30] confirmed the necessity of the Provincial's approval of such confessors.[31]

With regard to the confessors of the religious themselves, similar difficulties exist as to the determination of the competent Superior for their approval. Canon 21 of the IV General Council of the Lateran (1215) prescribed that confessions be made to one's *proper priest* or, with his permission, to some other priest.[32] But since Regular prelates were the proper priests of religious,[33] it was in virtue of this

[26] Piat, *Praelectiones*, I, p. 416, qu. 434.

[27] Const. *Ad fructus uberes*, 27 nov. 1294—*Bullarium Ordinis Eremitarum S. Augustini*, p. 103.

[28] 18 febr. 1300—c. 2, *de sepulturis*, III, 7, in Clem.

[29] Const. *Inter cunctas*, 17 febr. 1304—c. 1, *de privilegiis*, V, 7, in Extravag. com.

[30] C. 2, *de sepulturis*, III, 7, in Clem.

[31] Particular law of the Orders also shows the necessity of approval given by the Provincial or by the Provincial and the provincial chapter. Thus the Carmelite Constitutions reserved the right of approval of confessors to the Provincial and his definitors at the provincial chapter or to the Provincial alone outside of the chapter (*Monumenta Carmelitana*, I, 37ss).

[32] C. 12, X, *de poenitentiis et remissionibus*, V, 38; Mansi, XXII, 1001; Schroeder, *Disciplinary Decrees*, p. 259.

[33] Donatus, *Rerum Regularium Praxis*, Tom. IV, tr. V, qu. 12, nn. 1-2.

same prescription that it became their duty to appoint confessors. Thus Provincials were authorized to appoint confessors in a province for their religious subjects. Moreover, as Superior over the entire province, the Provincial possessed jurisdiction also over the "famuli" of the monasteries within the province.[34] In regard to the confessors for nuns subject to Orders of men, the appointment of these confessors seems also to have been reserved to the Provincial, since it was to the latter that the nuns seem to have been subject, rather than to a Local Superior, whose jurisdiction by the very nature of his office was restricted to subjects actually residing within or assigned to his house.[35]

Against the general conclusion that in the period before the Council of Trent Regular confessors required the approbation of their Provincial it might be objected that occasionally the sources speak of *priors* as entitled to perform this function.[36] However, it seems warranted to infer that with this term reference was made to the Provincial, in accordance with the teaching of the common and the particular law, since he was known also as the *Prior Provincial.*[37]

In virtue of their quasi-episcopal position, Provincials and, *a fortiori*, Generals, retained the right of approving the confessors of their own subjects, which right had been enjoyed by them previous to the Council.[38] Clement VIII (1592-1605) commanded Superiors to approve and appoint

[34] Innocentius IV, const. *Qui Deum*, 5 febr. 1244—*Bull. Praed.* I, 131; Potthast, *Regesta*, n. 11240; Shuhler, *Privileges of Regulars to Absolve and Dispense*, The Catholic University of America Canon Law Studies, n. 186 (Washington, D.C.: The Catholic University of America Press, 1943), p. 16.

[35] Cf. *supra*, pp. 18-19.

[36] Innocentius IV, const. *Licet olim*, 4 apr. 1246—*Bull, Praed.*, I, 161; Potthast, *Regesta*, n. 12055.

[37] *Monumenta Carmelitana*, I, 64.

[38] Suarez, *De Religione*, Lib. II, Cap. XV, n. 4; Donatus, *Rerum Regularium Praxis*, Tom. III, Pars V, cap. 1; Ferraris, *Prompta Bibliotheca Canonica, Iuridica, Moralis, Theologica, necnon Ascetica, Polemica, Rubricistica, Historica* (11 vols., Venetiis, 1782-1794), s.v.,

several confessors for their subjects in order to afford full liberty of conscience to the latter.[39] Although Clement VIII did not restrict the term Superiors in such a manner as to make it extend only to Major Superiors, he seems rather to have presupposed an initial approval by the proper Superior whereby the priest had been judged fit for the office of confessor. Moreover, his later Constitution *Nullus omnino* actually prescribed that confessors be approved by examiners appointed at the provincial or general chapters, which fact seems to preclude the Local Superior from enjoying in this matter a power equal to that of the Provincial.[40] However, it was also recognized[41] that outside of these chapters the Provincial and the General could approve confessors without any intervention from others.

Since the Provincial had the power to depute confessors for the Order, he enjoyed the corresponding right to revoke their jurisdiction for a just cause,[42] for the very consideration of justice demanded such a cause lest the good name of the religious be injured.

Although the Superiors designated by particular law were to appoint confessors for their subjects who by delegation would possess the jurisdiction and the faculties enjoyed by the Superiors themselves for absolving from reserved cases, the subjection of religious to their prelates was emphasized in the fact that the former were permitted to confess only to the priests who had been delegated by their Superiors.[43] On

---

"*approbatio*", n. 23 (hereafter cited *Prompta Bibliotheca*); Appeltern, *Compendium*, p. 271.

39 Decr. *Sanctissimus*, 26 maii 1593—*Fontes*, n. 177.

40 Clemens VIII, 20 mart. 1601, § 24,—*Bull. Rom. Taur.*, X, 666.

41 Cf. *supra*, p. 189.

42 Cf. S.C. Ep. et Reg., *Clericorum Regularium*, 2 iul. 1627—*Fontes*, n. 1729; *Ordinis Praedicatorum*, 2 mart. 1866—*Fontes*, n. 1996; Bizzarri, *Collectanea*, p. 811; Piat, *Praelectiones*, I, p. 420, qu. 444.

43 Urbanus VIII (1623-1644), const. *In specula*, 19 iun. 1630—*Bull. Rom. Taur.*, XIV, 144; Pius VI (1775-1799), const. *Pastoris Aeterni*, 18 iul. 1783—apud Molitor, *Religiosi Iuris Capita Selecta*, p. 280, n. 195.

the other hand, once in a lifetime, and also on certain feasts, the religious were permitted, with the permission of their Superiors, to choose a confessor who enjoyed the faculty to absolve from reserved cases.[44] Appeltern stated that it was commonly held that these privileges were enjoyed by all Regulars through their participation in the original grant by reason of the favor of the intercommunication of privileges which Regulars enjoyed.[45]

With regard to the confessors of nuns subject to the Regular Provincial, the Council of Trent did not revoke the former right of Regular Superiors to grant them delegation.[46] Despite all previously granted rights or privileges to the contrary, Gregory XV (1621-1623) demanded episcopal approbation of them, though they might still be presented by the Major Superior.[47] This prescription was renewed by Clement X (1670-1676),[48] and the revocation of all contrary privileges or customs was emphasized by Innocent XIII (1721-1724).[49] In 1742 Benedict XIV (1740-1758) confirmed the obligation imposed by these Constitutions.[50]

The Council of Trent and the subsequent Roman Pontiffs required that the confessors of those who were not subject to the Regular Superior be presented to the local Ordinary by the Provincial or the General for episcopal approbation.[51]

[44] Sixtus IV, const. *Sacri Praedicatorum et Minorum*, 26 iul. 1479, § V—*Bull. Rom. Taur.* V, 280.

[45] *Compendium*, p. 293.

[46] McCormick, *Confessors of Religious*, The Catholic University of America Canon Law Studies, n. 33 (Washington, D.C.: The Catholic University of America, 1926), p. 84.

[47] Const. *Inscrutabili*, 5 febr. 1622—*Fontes*, n. 197; *Bull. Rom. Taur.*, XII, 656.

[48] Const. *Superna*, 21 iun. 1670—*Fontes*, n. 246; *Bull. Rom. Taur.*, XVIII, 55.

[49] Const. *Apostolici ministerii*, 23 maii, 1723—*Fontes*, n. 280; *Bull. Rom. Taur.*, XXI, 231.

[50] Const. *Ad militantis*, 30 mart. 1742—*Fontes*, n. 326.

[51] Sess. XXIII, *de ref.*, c. 15; S. Pius V, const. *Romani Pontificis*, 6 aug. 1571—*Fontes*, n. 139; Gregorius XV, const. *Inscrutabili*, 5 febr. 1622—*Fontes*, n. 197; Clement X, const. *Superna*, 21 iun. 1670—

However, seculars who lived at the monasteries and *belonged to the household* (*famuli*) were still within the jurisdiction of the Provincial Superior, and confessors, though they had solely his approval, could hear their confessions.[52]

2) Present Law

The guiding principle that the particular law of the individual institute must be kept in view when one seeks to determine the rights and duties of the Provincial is particularly true in the case of the legislation of the Code on jurisdictional matters touching on the Sacrament of Penance. Various questions frequently controverted in the past are now settled quite simply in line with the general terms wherewith the Code makes allowances for the more specific qualifications which may be invoked in the particular law of a given religious Order or institute.

All religious Superiors of exempt clerical communities, including Local Superiors, are explicitly granted ordinary jurisdiction for hearing the confessions of their subjects, according to the norms of their constitutions.[53] The only restriction placed by the common law is that of canon 518, § 2, which warns Superiors not to hear the confessions of their subjects regularly, even though they are permitted to hear the confessions of those who freely and wilfully seek their service.

In accordance with canon 199, § 1, this jurisdiction can, therefore, be delegated unless the law itself expressly prescribes the contrary. In the period before the Council of Trent it was generally held that the approbation of religious

Fontes, n. 246; Benedictus XIII, const. *Pastoralis officii*, 27 mart. 1726 —*Fontes*, n. 289; S.C. Ep. et Reg., *Zagabrien.*, 14 dec. 1674—*Fontes*, n. 1809; S.C. Ep. et Reg., *Ordinis Praedicatorum*, 2 mart. 1866—*Fontes*, n. 1996.

[52] Con. Trident., sess. XXIII, *de ref.*, c. 11; S.C.C., *Parisien.*, 30 mart. 1594—*Fontes*, n. 2266; Clemens X, const. *Superna*, 21 ian. 1670 —*Fontes*, n. 246; Ferraris, *Prompta Bibliotheca*, s.v., "*approbatio*", nn. 64-68.

[53] Can. 873, § § 1, 2.

priests for the hearing of confessions depended upon the Provincial or Major Superiors of the Order unless the particular law stated otherwise. The present law states that jurisdiction or permission to hear confessions should not be conferred except upon priests who have been found suitable through an examination or in some other manner. It uses the general term "Superiors" as the counterpart, in the matter of delegation, of local Ordinaries, upon whom in the same canon it imposes the same obligation.[54] In the absence of particular legislation, the unqualified term does not refer exclusively to the Provincial, but can also include the Local Superior.[55]

The essential character of this previous approbation in relation to the validity of the Sacrament is not indicated by the Code and can only be determined from the particular law. In keeping with canon 11, the law of canon 877, § 1, does not invalidate the jurisdictional acts of a subject who receives jurisdiction without previous approval or from a Superior incapable of granting such approval. The same is true of the particular law when it is merely hortatory. Though according to the premises the exercise of jurisdiction would be illicit, the Sacrament would be validly conferred.

Canon 875, § 1, in naming those who can delegate jurisdiction for the confessions of religious, of novices, and of certain other persons who reside within religious houses, employs the general term "Superiors." Particular law, however, may specify the Superiors authorized to grant this delegation. Thus the Franciscan Local Superiors, in virtue of a restriction of the particular law, are forbidden to delegate jurisdiction to priests for the confessions of the professed, the novices,[56] and those included within the scope of

[54] Can. 877, § 1.

[55] The Carmelite Constitutions, however, prescribe an examination in the presence of examiners appointed by the Provincial for those about to be approved (*Constitutiones O. Carm.*, art. 232).

[56] Cf. can. 875, § 1.

canon 514, § 1.[57] In the absence of a restriction of this kind in the particular law[58] it cannot be said that the right to delegate priests for the confessions of subjects in a particular house is reserved to the Provincial, for the whole tendency of the Church's present legislation in the matter of the confessions of religious is one of clemency.[59]

Two or more priests are to be appointed as ordinary confessors in each house of men religious.[60] The number should be determined according to the number of religious resident in the house. The confessors are to be given jurisdiction over cases reserved in the Order.[61] The constitutions may reserve to the Provincial the right of delegating these ordinary confessors, as in the Francisan Order.[62] If they do not, it seems that even the Local Superior is competent to delegate them.

The Code has definitely solved the legal question formerly involved in the notions of approbation and jurisdiction, i.e., whether the approbation of the local Ordinary was necessary for the validity of the absolution conferred on those who were not subject to the religious Superior.[63]

[57] Capobianco, *Privilegia et Facultates Ordinis Fratrum Minorum*, n. 93. Canon 514, § 1, includes within the scope of the jurisdiction of the Superior of the house the professed subjects, novices, those dwelling day and night in the house in virtue of participation in its administration, and those dwelling there in like manner for the purpose of education or health.

[58] The Carmelite Constitutions (*Constitutiones O. Carm.*, Art. 233) specifically mention the Local Superior as included within the terms of this canon.

[59] Cf. Blat, *Commentarium*, II, n. 220.

[60] The Code does not specifically determine the number of confessors. Coronata states that there should be at least two (*Institutiones*, I, p. 673, n. 544).

[61] Can. 518, § 1.

[62] Capobianco, *Privilegia et Facultates Ordinis Fratrum Minorum*, n. 91.

[63] Cf. Gregorius IX, const. *Quoniam*, 10 maii, 1227—*Bull. Praed.*, I, 19; Bonifatius VIII, const. *Super cathedram*, 18 febr. 1300—c. 2, *de sepulturis*, III, 7, in Clem.; Conc. Trident., sess. XXIII, *de ref.*, c. 15.

Canon 874, § 1, explicitly states that jurisdiction for the hearing of the confessions of these subjects as also of religious is delegated both to secular priests and even to exempt religious priests by the local Ordinary. Canon 875, § 1, limits the delegating power of the religious Superior to the cases of confessions of those who are subject to the institute, inclusive of those who have residence in the religious house. In this restriction the question is solved with the effect of a real curtailment of the rights of the Provincial.

On the other hand, the local Ordinary should not regularly confer jurisdiction upon religious who have not been presented by the proper Superior.[64] Whether the term *proper Superior* refers exclusively to the Provincial or also includes the Local Superior is to be determined from the constitutions.[65]

Formerly the Provincial had the power to delegate confessors for nuns subject to him, but this right has been abolished by the Code.[66] Today the delegation of the confessors for nuns, whether or not they be subject to the Provincial, must be obtained from the local Ordinary. However, if the nuns are immediately subject to the Provincial, he is the proper Superior to present the confessors to the local Ordinary for the obtaining of jurisdiction, unless the particular law specifies another Superior as enjoying the right of presentation mentioned in canon 525.[67]

Moreover, if religious priests are to be given jurisdiction as ordinary or extraordinary confessors of women religious, they need the permission of their Superior.[68] There seems to be no reason for placing a restriction here on the comprehensive meaning which can attach to the general term

[64] Can. 874, § 2.

[65] Blat, *Commentarium*, lib. III, pars I, 219.

[66] Can. 875, § § 1, 2.

[67] Even this right can be superseded, however, by the local Ordinary in a case of negligence on the part of the religious prelate to present the confessors.

[68] Can. 524, § 1.

"Superior" as used in canon 524, § 1. Accordingly, the permission of the Local Superior is sufficient, unless, of course, the particular law reserves to a higher Superior the right of granting this permission.[69]

The jurisdiction delegated by the local Ordinary extends not only to the confessions of all religious as well as of seculars, but likewise to the cases reserved within the Order to the confessional jurisdiction of any of the Major Superiors.[70] The lawful exercise of diocesan jurisdiction by a religious priest, however, implies the necessity of the permission, at least presumed, of the proper religious Superior, either Provincial, or Local, according to the particular law.[71] Yet the necessity for this permission does not affect the validity of the delegated exercise of confessional jurisdiction at all, but only renders it illicit if performed without this previously obtained permission.[72] Moreover, if a priest religious possesses jurisdiction both from his Provincial and from the local Ordinary, the limitations placed by either of these authorities will not affect the jurisdiction granted by the other.[73] Thus, even the suspension of jurisdiction for the hearing of confessions when inflicted by one authority does not affect the validity of a confession heard in virtue of jurisdiction obtained from the other authority, and the priest in exercising the confessional jurisdiction does not incur an irregularity. Accordingly, a religious who enjoys jurisdiction from both sources, if suspended by his Provincial, nevertheless validly absolves a penitent in virtue of diocesan faculties, although his action will perhaps be illicit.[74] Coronata states that a priest religious who uses

[69] Cf. Blat, *Commentarium*, lib. III, pars I, 219.

[70] Cans. 874, § 1; 519.

[71] Can. 874, § 1.

[72] Cf. S.C. Ep. et Reg., *Ordinis Praedicatorum*, 2 mart. 1866—*Fontes*, n. 1996.

[73] Fanfani, *De Iure Religiosorum*, n. 145, p. 163; Blat, *Commentarium*, lib. III, pars I, 219 ss.

[74] S.C. Ep. et Reg., *Ordinis Praedicatorum*, 2 mart. 1866—*Fontes*, n. 1996.

diocesan jurisdiction to absolve a religious who approaches him in the circumstances contemplated in canon 519 acts *validly* and *licitly*, despite the fact that his proper Superior has suspended his jurisdiction for hearing confessions.[75]

B. Absolution from Reserved Sins and Censures

1.) Pre-Code Legislation

In the period before the Council of Trent the Provincial could absolve his subjects from certain reserved sins in view of his rank as a prelate. His jurisdiction extended to all cases not reserved to the Pope, to all minor excommunications, and to all non-reserved major excommunications.[76] The penalty for striking a cleric which was reserved in a simple manner to the Holy See could be absolved by prelates in virtue of the papal privilege granted by Alexander III (1159-1189), and later enjoyed by all Regulars through the intercommunication of privileges among the various religious Orders.[77]

Since recourse to Rome, whenever necessary, had to be made in person, the jurisdiction of Regular prelates was extended also to the cases reserved to the Holy See, so that they could absolve their subjects, who as religious were impeded from making this journey.[78]

In virtue of papal privileges, Regular prelates also possessed jurisdiction to absolve from all sins reserved by the

[75] Coronata, *Institutiones*, I, p. 673, n. 544.

[76] Lezana, *Summa Quaestionum Regularium*, Vol. I, Pars I, cap. XIX, n. 14; c. 29, X, *de sententia excommunicationis*, V, 39.

[77] C. 2, 50, X, *de sententia excommunicationis*, V, 39; Potthast, *Regesta*, n. 7854. With regard to the dates of the general grants of privileges to the individual Mendicant Orders whereby they were entitled to participate in all the privileges, past, present, or future, of the other Orders, the reader is referred to Shuhler, *Privileges of Regulars to Absolve and Dispense*, pp. 18-23.

[78] C. 36, X, *de sententia excommunicationis*, V, 39; c. 22, *de sententia excommunicationis*, V, 11, in VI°.

common law to the local Ordinary.[79] The Provincial or other Regular prelate could delegate another to absolve subjects in such cases.[80] However, sins and censures which the bishop reserved to himself, or which were reserved to him in his capacity as a delegate of the Holy See, were beyond the jurisdiction of the Provincial according to the common law.[81] Nevertheless in the period before the penitential reforms of Clement VIII (1592-1605) various privileges were granted to different Orders, and in these privileges the various Orders participated, so that Regulars enjoyed faculties in general to absolve from episcopal reservations.[82] On the other hand, sins and censures reserved within the Order to prelates in general were within the jurisdiction of the Provincial.[83] Moreover, in relation to his own subjects the Provincial's competence extended to all the reserved cases over which the local Ordinary possessed competence in favor of his diocesan subjects.

The Council of Trent empowered bishops to absolve from all occult cases, even if they were reserved to the Holy See, or if they entailed the guilt of heresy.[84] The Constitution *Romani Pontificis* (July 21, 1571) of St. Pius V (1566-1572) reaffirmed the Regular prelate's equality with the bishop in the matter of penitential jurisdiction over his own

[79] Cf. Shuhler, *Privileges of Regulars to Absolve and Dispense*, pp. 72-73.

[80] Piat, *Praelectiones*, I, qu. 488.

[81] Lezana, *Summa Quaestionum Regularium*, Vol. I, Pars I, cap. XIX, n. 14.

[82] Cf. Paulus III, const. *Cum inter cunctas*, 3 iun. 1545—Augustinus a Virgine Maria, *Compendium Privilegiorum Omnium Religionum* (Lugduni, 1661), p. 150. Though the extensive privilege listed here was granted to the Society of Jesus for its members, it was likewise shared by the other Orders in virtue of the Constitution *Dum indefessae* of Pope St. Pius V (7 iul. 1571—*Bull. Rom. Taur. VII*, 923). Cf. also, Shuhler, *Privileges of Regulars to Absolve and Dispense*, p. 73, note 24.

[83] Passerinus, *Tractatus de Electione Canonica*, Cap. XXVI, n. 10.

[84] Sess. XXIV, *de ref.*, c. 6.

religious subjects.[85] Therefore in virtue of this competence it was clear that the Provincial, and even the Local Superior, could absolve in cases of the same nature as those in which absolution could be given by bishops according to the concession of the Council of Trent. Regular prelates enjoyed this jurisdiction in virtue of their office, and therefore could delegate it to another, since in the papal Constitution there was no restriction regarding the matter of possible delegation.

Clement VIII (1592-1605) prescribed that Superiors should appoint for their subjects confessors who by delegation would possess the jurisdiction and the faculties enjoyed by the Superiors themselves for absolving from reserved cases.[86] At his request the Sacred Congregation of Bishops and Regulars in 1601 issued a decree whereby all privileges which Regulars claimed or possessed for the absolution of cases reserved by bishops to themselves were abolished.[87]

With regard to the reservation of sins by Regular prelates, the power to establish reservations was restricted by the decree *Sanctissimus* of Clement. Yet there were authors who held that the individual privileges of certain Orders in this regard were not revoked.[88]

The Constitution *Apostolicae Sedis* of Pius IX (1846-1878) reorganized the discipline of the Church on censures enacted as *latae sententiae* penalties.[89] In reference to the penalties contained in this Constitution, it may be stated that competence of Regular prelates was the following:

1) Regular prelates could not absolve subjects from censures which as enacted in the Constitution were reserved even in a simple manner to the Holy See.[90]

[85] *Bull. Praed.* V, 283.

[86] Decr. *Sanctissimus*, 26 maii 1593—*Fontes*, n. 177.

[87] 9 ian. 1601—*Fontes*, n. 1596.

[88] Cf. Donatus, *Rerum Regularium Praxis*, Tom. IV, tr. V, qu. 5, n. 2; Suarez, *De Religione*, Lib. II, Cap. XVIII, n. 14.

[89] 12 oct. 1869—*Fontes*, n. 552.

[90] S. Poenit., 5 dec. 1873: "An praelati regulares post Constitutionem

2) Regular prelates could absolve their subjects from occult cases involving censures reserved in the papal Constitutions to the local Ordinary. This faculty, however, was not peculiar to the office of prelate alone, but was enjoyed by all Regular confessors who had been approved by their Superior, and, when there was question of the confessions of seculars, had been presented to the local Ordinary for his approbation.[91]

It is to be noted that this privilege is not expressly abrogated in the Code. According to the more probable opinion this privilege can be safely and licitly used by any Regular confessor who has been approved by his Superior and has been presented to the local Ordinary for his approbation and faculties.[92] This faculty extends, however, only to occult cases. Moreover, if the local Ordinary should also reserve the precise case to himself *ratione peccati,* the faculties of the Provincial or of any Regular, as a Regular confessor, would not apply. But the norms of canon 900 would de-

---

Apostolicae Sedis iisdem privilegiis gaudeant quibus antea, id est, possint nec ne suos subditos absolvere a casibus papalibus in dicta Constitutione simpliciter reservatis?—S. Poenitentiaria proposito dubio respondet: "*Negative,* salvis illis facultatibus quae promanant ex rescriptis particularibus ad tempus concessis."—*Fontes,* n. 6431. Moreover, the reservation to the Holy See of all classes of censures reserved to the Holy See is clear from the words of the Constitution itself, which in speaking of past privileges or future concessions of the Holy See stated: "... nullo modo ac rationi intelligi unquam debere, aut posse comprehendi facultatem absolvendi a casibus, et censuris quibuslibet Romano Pontifici reservatis, nisi de iis formalis, explicita, ac in individuo mentio facta fuerit ....." (*Fontes,* n. 552, § VI, n. 2.)

[91] The common opinion prior to the time of the Constitution *Apostolicae Sedis* maintained that Regular confessors could absolve in such cases, and it continued to retain probability even after the promulgation of this Constitution, since the abrogations therein contained affected only such censures as were reserved to the Holy See (Shuhler, *Privileges of Regulars to Absolve and Dispense,* pp. 94-95).

[92] Cf. Noldin-Schönegger, *De Censuris* (31. ed., Oeniponte, 1937), n. 95; Fanfani, *De Iure Religiosorum,* n. 365, p. 382; Prümmer, *Manuale Iuris Canonici in Usum Scholarum* (6. ed., Friburgi-Brisgoviae, 1922), n. 324.

termine the cessation of the reservation in certain circumstances.[93]

Accordingly the reservation would cease: for the sick who, while unable to leave the house, make their confession while thus confined; for those who make their confession in preparation for the contracting of marriage; as often as the proper ecclesiastical Superior denies the necessary faculties for a particular case; when in the judgment of the confessor the Superior cannot be approached without grave inconvenience or danger to the seal of confession; and, finally, when the confession is made outside the territory of the one who established the reservation, even when the subject has left the territory for the simple purpose of gaining absolution.

3) Regular prelates could absolve their subjects, or delegate others to absolve them, from censures pertaining to the internal administration of the Order, if no mention of their reservation was contained in the papal Constitution.[94]

In view of a reply of the Holy Office in 1886, it was apparent that Regular prelates could no longer absolve subjects who were impeded from going to Rome, but the subject, the confessor, or the Superior were required to make recourse to the Sacred Penitentiary. If the case was to be treated as an urgent one, then there was implied the obligation of making recourse after the absolution.[95]

2) Present Law

With the decree of the Sacred Congregation of Bishops and Regulars in 1601 the privileges of Regulars over cases which local Ordinaries had reserved to themselves were abrogated,[96] and in the Constitution *Apostolicae Sedis* the privileges of Regulars with regard to absolving censures reserved to the Holy See were revoked. Neither of these

[93] Beste, *Introductio*, p. 498.

[94] S.C.S. Off., decr.—*apud Nouvelle Révue Théologique*, XXVI (1894), 318; Appeltern, *Compendium*, p. 294, n. 3.

[95] S.C.S. Off., 23 iun. 1886—*Fontes*, n. 1102.

[96] Cf. *supra*, p. 200.

former privileges can any longer be invoked in virtue of canon 4.[97]

Nevertheless, the Code itself gives the Provincial, as religious Ordinary in regard to his subjects, competence in occult cases which entail *latae sententiae* penalties established by the common law, with the exception of censures which are reserved in a most special or in a special manner to the Holy See. Moreover, since this is ordinary competence, he can delegate it.[98] Thus the privileges formerly possessed by the Provincial as a Regular to absolve the faithful from censures reserved to the Holy See, and which were abrogated by the Constitution *Apostolicae Sedis,* have now been restored in a limited degree, not as privileges but as rights of the common law to be exercised over his subjects in occult cases in virtue of his position as an Ordinary. If the Provincial possesses diocesan jurisdiction for the hearing of the confessions of the faithful,[99] he does not thereby cease to enjoy the privileges which he holds as a Regular confessor. Thus, as was noted above,[100] according to the more probable opinion he can safely and licitly absolve the faithful from censures reserved by law to the Ordinary in occult cases, unless the Ordinary has also reserved the case to himself *ratione peccati.*

[97] Actually the abrogation of the Provincial's faculties to absolve subjects from episcopal reservations, which abrogation was introduced with the decree of 1601 in the Clementine penitential reforms, affected the condition of Regulars but little in practice, since it is commonly held by authors that Regulars are not affected by episcopal censures, unless there be question of preaching without proper permission or against the will of the local Ordinary (Coronata, *Institutiones,* I, p. 821, n. 619 *bis*). Moreover, exempt religious are generally not considered as subject to the penal laws established by local Ordinaries, even in matters in which they are subject to him, unless their subjection to the law is *expressly* stated by the Ordinary (Coronata, *ibid.,* p. 831, n. 626; Davis, *Moral and Pastoral Theology* [4 vols., New York: Sheed and Ward, Inc., 1935], III, 439. Cf., however, Voltas, "De Reservatione Episcopali quoad Regulares"—*CpR,* III [1922], 69-77).

[98] Cans. 2237, § 2; 199, § 1. [99] Can. 874, § 1. [100] Cf. *supra,* p. 201.

The Code also grants the Provincial, as Ordinary, authority to absolve his subjects from *latae sententiae* penalties in public cases, but with the following exceptions as enumerated in canon 2237, § 1:

1) public cases that have been introduced into court;[101]
2) public cases involving censures reserved to the Holy See;
3) public cases entailing an incapacitation for offices, benefices, dignities, functions in the Church, the right in an ecclesiastical election to vote and to have others vote for him, or the deprivation of any or all of these claims; the penalties of perpetual suspension, of legal infamy, of the privation of the right of patronage, and of the dispossession of any privilege or favor granted by the Holy See.

The competence for the remission of penalties thus granted to the Provincial by the Code in virtue of his position as Ordinary is his by reason of his office. Consequently this competence can be delegated habitually,[102] and is to be interpreted broadly.[103] The Provincial's jurisdiction as Ordinary is limited, however, to his subjects, since he bears this relation to them alone.[104] But all those who receive mention in canon 514, § 1, namely, the professed subjects of the province, the novices, and the laity staying in the monastery as part of the household, as students, as guests, or as convalescents, are included within the scope of his ordinary jurisdiction.[105]

C. Power to Reserve Sins

1) Pre-Code Legislation

In the period before the Council of Trent, references to the power of the Provincial to reserve sins are quite scarce. What references there are, are found in the particular law.

[101] I.e., after the citation according to canon 1725 has taken place.—Coronata, *Institutiones*, IV, p. 141, n. 1737.

[102] Can. 199, § 1. [103] Can. 200, § 1. [104] Can. 198, § 1.

[105] Cappello, *Tractatus Canonico-Moralis de Censuris iuxta Codicem Iuris Canonici* (3. ed. recognita et emendata, Taurinorum Augustae: Marietti, 1933), n. 123 (hereafter cited *De Censuris*).

The quasi-episcopal power which he exercised seemed sufficient warrant for the exercise of this power.[106] The Council of Trent affirmed the power of bishops to reserve certain sins,[107] and Piat stated that the Sacred Congregation of the Council declared that this power belonged also to the Major Superiors of Regulars.[108]

Clement VIII (1592-1605) restricted the powers of Regular prelates in such manner that, independently of their chapters, they could not reserve any cases other than those listed in the decree *Sanctissimus*.[109] Some authors held that the delicts enumerated in this document could be reserved also by Local Superiors. However, particular law usually restricted the power of the Local Superior in this matter.[110]

Cases other than those mentioned in the decree *Sanctissimus* of Clement VIII could be reserved only with the due deliberation of the Provincial and his chapter.[111]

[106] Cf. *Monumenta Carmelitana*, p. 39.

[107] Sess. XIV, *de penitentia*, c. 11.

[108] *Praelectiones*, I, pp. 450-451, qu. 493.

[109] 26 maii 1593—*Fontes*, n. 177. For the sake of convenience, the delicts enumerated in the first paragraph of this decree as falling within the competence of the Regular prelates for prospective reservation are here listed:

1. Veneficia, incantationes, sortilegia;
2. Apostasia a religione . . . ;
3. Proprietas contra votum paupertatis, quae sit peccatum mortale iuramentum falsum in iudicio regulari, seu legitimo;
4. Procuratio, auxilium, seu consilium ad abortum faciendum . . . etiam effectu non sequuto;
5. Falsificatio manus aut sigilli . . . ;
6. Lapsus carnis voluntarius opere consummatus;
7. Occisio, aut vulneratio, seu gravis percussio cuiuscumque personae;
8. Violatio litterarum Superiorum;
9. Peccatum grave contra religionem, interveniente tamen matura discussione et consensu sive Generalis Capituli in toto Ordine, sive Provincialis in provincia.

[110] Piat, *Praelectiones*, I, p. 452, qu. 494.

[111] *Ibid.*, p. 453, qu. 497.

2) Present Law

With the present law the Provincial has lost all power to reserve sins, since this right is now to be exercised only by the General with his council.[112] Even this right as possessed by the General is shorn of much of its practical import through the faculties which canon 518 requires the General to give to the confessors for religious.[113] Moreover, the confessor who possesses diocesan jurisdiction has competence to absolve from cases reserved in a religious Order in the event that for his peace and tranquility of conscience a religious approaches him in the tribunal of penance.[114] In either case the confessor has the necessary faculties to absolve from the sin: the religious confessor by mandatory delegated power, and the secular confessor by a delegated power which transcends all limitations invoked by the religious Superior.

D. Power to Dispense from Irregularities

1) Pre-Code Legislation

In order to preserve the dignity of the priesthood, the Church at an early age created barriers, known as irregularities, to impede the reception or the exercise of Orders by subjects who, either through defects of a physical or of a moral nature, or through grave personal faults, were considered as unworthy ministers of priestly Orders. The setting up of irregularities was primarily intended for the common good, namely to preserve the public esteem and reverence for the priesthood. Dispensations from irregularities were properly reserved to the Pope, although cer-

[112] Can. 896.

[113] Can. 518, § 1: "In singulis religionis clericalis domibus deputentur plures pro sodalium numero confessarii legitime approbati, cum potestate, si agatur de religione exempta, absolvendi etiam a casibus in religione reservatis." Confessors, therefore, who have been appointed for exempt clerical communities must be endowed with the faculties necessary to absolve from sins reserved in the Order (*Vermeersch-Creusen*, *Epitome*, I, 638).

[114] Can. 519.

tain powers of dispensation were granted to bishops, and certain privileges to the Superiors of Regulars.

In view of the rule of the participation of all Regulars in whatever privileges had been granted to one Order without a specific exclusion of the others, Provincials and Generals of all Orders shared in a privilege granted by Sixtus IV (1471-1484) to the Dominican Order. In virtue of this privilege these Superiors could dispense their subjects from irregularities resulting from illegitimacy as well as those resulting from crime, with the exception of voluntary homicide,[115] public bigamy[116] and self-mutilation.[117]

[115] Piat (*Praelectiones*, I, p. 615, qu. 757) implied the existence of a controversy among the authors with regard to whether an irregularity resulted from criminal abortion. Some considered such a crime to be the same as voluntary homicide, and therefore that an irregularity was incurred, the dispensation of which was reserved. After the Council of Trent, however, Sixtus V (1585-1590) removed all doubt in the matter when he declared that those guilty of such a crime incurred an irregularity, the dispensation from which was reserved to himself (Const. *Effraenatam*, 29 oct. 1588—*Fontes*, n. 165). Later, Gregory XIV (1590-1591) decreed that the irregularity was incurred only in the case of the abortion of a living human fetus (Const. *Sedes Apostolica*, 31 maii 1591—*Fontes*, n. 173).

[116] Bigamy was distinguished into two species: *bigamia successiva* (the marrying of two wives successively) and *bigamia similitudinaria* (the attempted marriage of a religious in solemn vows). It is not clear which species of bigamy was intended. It seems, however, that the *bigamia similitudinaria* was intended, since the reservations were apparently invoked in view of the enormity or the special gravity of the crimes involved. Those who were guilty of this offense, if the crime were public, were considered suspect of heresy, and the irregularity was not within the bishop's power to dispense from it (Piat, *Praelectiones*, I, p. 614, qu. 757). If the case was occult, however, bishops could grant a dispensation in virtue of the faculties accorded them by the Council of Trent, and Regular Superiors also could grant a dispensation in virtue of the Constitution *Romani Pontificis* of Pope St. Pius V (Piat, *loc. cit.*).

[117] Probable opinions maintained that the Provincial could dispense subjects in occult cases of self-mutilation and in similar cases of casual homicide. Cf. Shuhler, *Privileges of Regulars to Absolve and Dispense*, pp. 153-159; Piat, *Praelectiones*, *loc. cit.*

Thus, before the Council of Trent the Provincial possessed faculties to dispense from all irregularities resulting from crime, with the three exceptions just mentioned. Moreover, his faculties extended to all cases, whether public, notorious, or occult, and could be used either with a view to the reception of Sacred Orders, or with a view to the exercise of Orders already received. These faculties could also be delegated,[118] so that Local Superiors, to whom it seems they were not directly granted, could receive delegation for particular cases.[119]

The Council of Trent granted bishops the power to dispense subjects from all irregularities resulting from occult crime with the exception of irregularities resulting from voluntary homicide or from a crime that had been brought before a court.[120] The Council, thus specifying the faculties of bishops under the common law, did not revoke the previous privileges enjoyed by the Provincial. By reason, however, of their quasi-episcopal power, Local Superiors received under the Constitution *Romani Pontificis* of Pope St. Pius V (1566-1572) a right equal to that of bishops in regard to the dispensation of irregularities, but it was to be exercised in the forum of conscience.[121]

The privileges of the Provincial which have been examined thus far were privileges that could be exercised in the external forum in relation to his subjects. In addition to his power over irregularities, derived from his office of Provincial, the latter was further empowered in the capacity of a confessor of the faithful, to exercise the faculties acquired by Regular confessors through pre-Code privileges, which have not been revoked by the Code. In virtue of these he could dispense the faithful, in the sacramental forum, from

[118] Cf. Innocentius VIII, const. *Tuis supplicationibus*, 16 febr. 1486—*Bullarium Ordinis Eremitarum S. Augustini*, p. 193.

[119] Shuhler, *Privileges of Regulars to Absolve and Dispense*, pp. 147-153.

[120] Sess. XXIV, *de ref.*, c. 6.

[121] 21 iul. 1571—*Bull. Rom. Taur.*, VII, 931.

all irregularities from which the Ordinary could dispense, namely, those resulting from occult delicts with the exception of irregularities arising from vountary homicide, effectively procured abortion, and cases called to the judicial forum. Moreover, these faculties he could use not only to permit promotion to Orders but also to allow the exercise of Orders already received.[122]

Sixtus V (1585-1590) barred from the religious life the offspring of incestuous and sacrilegious unions. Moreover, he required that other candidates of illegitimate birth should undergo a severe probation before their admission to the religious life.[123] However, Gregory XIV (1590-1591) entirely modified this legislation, and restored the pre-Tridentine law, in virtue of which Generals and Provincials could dispense and receive persons of illegitimate birth, except in cases in which the father of the applicant was already a member of the community. In addition, through a restored privilege, the General with the general chapter, or the Provincial with the provincial chapter, could dispense members of illegitimate birth in order to permit them to receive dignities in the Order.[124] These faculties could be used outside of the forum of confession, unless the contrary was prescribed through special decree or particular law.

In summary, then, the pre-Code privileges of the Provincial in regard to the dispensation of his subjects from irregularities may be set down as the following. He possessed faculties through privileges granted to Regulars to dispense from all irregularities incurred by his subjects by

[122] Cf. Leo XII, const. *Plura inter*, 11 iul. 1826—*Bullarii Romani Continuatio Summorum Pontificum* (19 vols., Prati, 1835-1858), XIII, 437. Shuhler states that the privilege granted by this Constitution to the Society of Jesus was shared by religious Orders in virtue of their enjoying the privilege of participated communication in the privilege of the Society of Jesus (*Privileges of Regulars to Absolve and Dispense*, p. 162).

[123] Const. *Cum de omnibus*, 26 nov. 1587—*Fontes*, n. 162.

[124] Gregorius XIV, const. *Illius qui*, 21 sept. 1591—*Bull. Rom. Taur.*, IX, 479.

reason of canonical delicts, with the exception of those resulting from voluntary homicide, self-multilation, effiectively procured abortion, and public bigamy, while a probable opinion maintained that he could also dispense subjects in occult cases of self-mutilation. If he was approved by the bishop for the confessions of seculars, he also enjoyed the privileges of all Regular confessors, so that he could dispense the faithful, in the forum of conscience, from all irregularities from which the Ordinary could dispense, namely, those resulting from occult delicts, with the exception of irregularities arising from voluntary homicide, effectively procured abortion, and cases called to the judicial forum. This latter competence was granted to the Provincial and other Regular confessors in such a manner that they could not only permit the reception of Orders but also allow the lawful exercise of Orders already received.

2) Present Law

The canons of the Code pertaining to irregularities[125] do not revoke the privileges of the Provincial or of Regular confessors which were possessed before its promulgation. In keeping therefore with canon 4, the privileges noted above in the summary remain intact. Some rights of dispensation from irregularities formerly enjoyed by the Provincial only as privileges are now explicitly granted him by the common law in virtue of his position as Ordinary. Thus he has ordinary jurisdiction to dispense his subjects from all irregularities resulting from a secret crime (*ex delicto occulto*), with the exceptions of voluntary homicide, effectively procured abortion, or crimes already introduced into the judicial forum. Thus, under the common law he can dispense from the irregularity resulting from the occult delict of self-mutilation, to which his erstwhile privilege did not extend with certainty.[126] This faculty given him by

[125] Cans. 983-991.

[126] The pre-Code probable opinion concerning the Provincial's faculties to dispense from the irregularity incurred through self-mutilation

the common law may be used in the external forum with a view either to the reception of Orders or to the exercise of Holy Orders previously received.

Since canon 984, 1°, states that solemn profession removes the irregularity of illegitimacy, the Provincial in an Order can lawfully according to his own good judgment receive a candidate laboring under that irregularity, without regard to the condition of canon 542, 2°, in this matter.[127] One who is legitimated through the subsequent marriage of his parents is considered legitimate and is not subject to the irregularity. Such a one, moreover, is eligible for the office of Major Superior,[128] but one who is dispensed from the irregularity of illegitimacy by means of an indult, or in consequence of solemn profession in virtue of the norm enacted in canon 984, 1°, is by no means eligible for that office, so far as the common law is concerned.[129] He may be dispensed, however, by the Provincial and his chapter, or by the General and his chapter, in virtue of the privilege of Gregory XIV, if his own particular law permits this.[130] If such a dispensation, however, is not given to the applicant from the beginning, but rather at the time of possible eligibilty to office, it would seem more fitting that such a dispensation should come from the General and his chapter, since the dispensation would actually be concerned with his appointment to the post of Provincial.

In addition to these faculties derived from his office of Provincial, the latter is further empowered, in the capacity of a confessor of the faithful, to exercise the faculties acquired by Regular confessors through pre-Code privileges which have not been revoked by the Code. In virtue of

---

is now explicitly granted for occult cases through canons 990, § 1, and 985, 5°.

[127] Particular law may require the permission of the General or of the council in such cases. Cf. Coronata, *Institutiones*, I, p. 715, n. 571, 5°.

[128] Can. 504.

[129] Fanfani, *De Iure Religiosorum*, n. 48, A, p. 58.

[130] Cf. *supra*, p. 209.

these, as confessor, he can dispense the faithful from all irregularities from which the Ordinary can dispense, namely, those resulting from occult delicts, with the exception of irregularities arising from voluntary homicide, effectively procured abortion and cases called to the judicial forum. Thus, as all Regular confessors, he possesses more extensive power over irregularities than the ordinary diocesan confessor possesses in virtue of the Code,[131] since he can use his pre-Code privileges, which have not been revoked, even in a case that is not urgent, and thus can permit not only the exercise of Orders already received, but also the licit reception of Orders.[132]

5. *Holy Orders*

1) Pre-Code Legislation

Matters pertaining to the ordination of Regulars were generally reserved by particular law to the Provincial or General Superiors as issues touching upon the general welfare of the province of the Order. Especially in questions concerning this Sacrament, the rights and duties of the Provincial exceeded those of the Local Superior, and formed a basis for the early distinction between Major and Minor Superiors.[133]

The general law before the Council of Trent required that Regulars should be ordained by their *proper* bishop,

[131] Can. 990, § 2.

[132] Shuhler, *Privileges of Regulars to Absolve and Dispense*, p. 168.

[133] It has been seen above (Chapter II, pp. 6-9) that the differentiation of the spheres of jurisdiction on the part of Regular prelates was not clear in the pre-Code law, although many authors accepted the distinction of Major and Minor prelates. It is not surprising to note that some authors attributed to the Local Superior the right to issue dimissorial letters, to forbid subjects to receive Orders, and to dispense from certain irregularities *provided* that the particular law did not forbid it (Cf. Clancy, *The Local Superior*, p. 64). The pre-Code restrictions generally inserted in the particular law are now incorporated in the Code. All matters pertaining to the ordination of a religious are thus reserved by the Code to Major Superiors.

who was considered to be the bishop of the place in which their monastery was located, but many Regulars possessed privileges enabling them to be ordained by any bishop.[134] From the beginning the Mendicants were recipients of such privileges from the Holy See.[135]

Although the Council of Trent decreed that religious should be ordained by the bishop of the place of their monastery,[136] Pope St. Pius V (1566-1572) in the Constitution *Etsi Mendicantium* expressly declared that these decrees did not apply to Regulars.[137] Gregory XIII (1572-1585) later applied the law of the Council of Trent to all religious,[138] and required the permission of the Local Ordinary before religious could be ordained by another bishop. Sixtus V (1585-1590) approved this teaching,[139] and Benedict XIV (1740-1758), in turn, limited the privileges of Regulars in regard to ordination when he declared that only those privileges which had been granted directly to Orders since the Council of Trent were to remain in force.[140] The general law thus imposed was by no means universally followed, for the Mendicants had secured privileges after the Council of Trent, whereby they could send their subjects to any bishop for ordination, and these retained their effect in virtue of Benedict XIV's exception.[141]

The dimissorial letters of the Provincial for the ordination of his subjects were required by the Constitution of

[134] Cf. Wernz-Vidal, *De Rebus*, p. 216, n. 197; Piat, *Praelectiones*, II, p. 276, qu. 350.

[135] Clemens IV, const. *Virtute conspicuos*, 21 iul. 1265, § 7—*Bull Rom. Taur.*, III, 735; Sixtus IV, const. *Regimini universalis*, 31 aug. 1474, § 7—*Bull. Rom. Taur.*, V, 218.

[136] Sess. XXIII, *de ref.*, c. 8: "Unusquisque autem a proprio episcopo ordinatur."

[137] 16 maii, 1567, § 2, n. 7—*Fontes*, n. 121.

[138] Const. *In tanta rerum*, 1 mart. 1583—apud Benedictum XIV, const. *Impositi Nobis*, 27 febr. 1747, § 3—*Fontes*, n. 376.

[139] *Ibid.*, § 4—*Fontes*, n. 376.

[140] Const. *Impositi nobis*, 27 febr. 1747, § 3,—*Fontes*, n. 376.

[141] Cf. O'Brien, *The Exemption of Religious in Church Law*, p. 186.

Benedict XIV, who, however, made provision for two exceptional cases, namely, if the Local Ordinary was absent, or was not to hold ordinations at the next proper time.[142] In these cases the Provincial was permitted to send his subjects to any bishop for ordination.[143] If the subject was sent to another bishop for ordination, the dimissorial letters were to state the reason for the absence of the proper bishop, or why he was not holding ordinations.[144] Moreover, in this case there was also required an official attestation by the local Ordinary, or by his delegate, that the exceptional circumstances existed.[145]

It was commonly taught that a Superior could not transfer a subject to another house for ordination, merely for the sake of evading the law that the candidate be presented to the local Ordinary.[146] Benedict, moreover, renewed the penalties decreed by Clement VIII (1592-1605)[147] against Regular Superiors who violated the laws concerning ordinations. He stated that they were to be penalized with the privation of their office, and that in ecclesiastical elections they were to be excluded from the right to vote or to have others vote for them as candidates for any office or function.[148]

Regulars who were presented for ordination by the Provincial were subject to examination by the ordaining bishop unless they had a privilege to the contrary.[149] An examination, however, was not necessary when the bishop could ac-

[142] *Ibid.*, § 12—*Fontes*, n. 376.

[143] *Loc. cit.*

[144] S.C.S., die 15 mart. 1596—*Fontes*, n. 2294.

[145] Benedictus XIV, const. *Impositi Nobis*, 27 febr. 1747, § 12—*Fontes*, n. 376.

[146] Donatus, *Rerum Regularium Praxis*, Tom. III, tr. III, qu. 10, n. 2; Benedictus XIV, *ibid.*, § 15; Piat, *Praelectiones*, II, p. 282, qu. 257.

[147] Cf. S.C.C., decr. 15 mart. 1596—*Fontes*, n. 2294.

[148] Const. *Impositi Nobis*, 27 febr. 1747, § 5—*Fontes*, n. 376.

[149] Conc. Trid. sess. XXIII, *de ref.*, c. 12.

cept and ratify the prudent judgment of the Provincial in a given case.[150]

Privileges of Regular Superiors in the matter of interstices had to be reckoned with in the regulations prohibiting the ordination of subjects without the observance of the usual intervals in the reception of the various Orders. Certain Regulars possessed privileges whereby they were exempt from the observance of the law regarding the interstices. In the case of the ordination of subjects of communities which possessed such a privilege no dispensation was necessary, since the privilege itself included a dispensation from the Holy See in this regard.[151]

In the case of institutes, however, which lacked such a privilege of exemption from the law of interstices, but which possessed privileges whereby the Superiors could dispense subjects from their observance, difficulties arose with the local Ordinaries. The Sacred Congregation of Bishops and Regulars, therefore, issued a compromise formula whereby the Regular Superior, usually the Provincial according to the particular law, should petition the local Ordinary to dispense from the interstices, in view of the fact that a dispensation from their observance had already been granted by the Provincial.[152]

Regulars enjoying the privilege of ordination outside of the canonical time could lawfully use such privileges, although no bishop could be obliged to ordain Regulars outside the proper time unless there was question of urgent necessity.[153] Moreover, the Sacred Congregation of the Council decreed that when ordination was conferred outside the regular time, it was to take place on holy days.[154] It was

[150] S.C. Ep. et Reg., *Ordinis Eremitarum Camaldulensium*, 13 iul. 1730—*Fontes*, n. 1847.

[151] Reiffenstuel, *Jus Canonicum Universum*, Lib. I, tit. XI, n. 157.

[152] S.C. Ep. et Reg., *Ordinis Eremitarum Camaldulensium*, 13 iul. 1730—*Fontes*, n. 1847.

[153] Benedictus XIV, const. *Impositi Nobis*, 27 febr. 1747, § 13—*Fontes*, n. 376.

[154] S.C.C., *Briocen.*, 15 ian. 1689—*Fontes*, n. 2908.

conceded, however, that even the suppressed holy days were days on which Sacred Orders could be conferred.

2) Present Law

With the clarification by the Code of the position of the Provincial as Ordinary and Major Superior of his subjects, the rights and duties commonly recognized as his in former times are now explicitly entrusted to him. Matters pertaining to the ordination of his subjects are reserved to his jurisdiction, so that the Local Superior has no rights over them at all, except in so far as he acts as a delegate of the Provincial. It is true that authors before the Code spoke of certain functions which the Local Superior *could* perform, but even then the particular law tended to reserve to the Provincial the questions which touched the ordination of his subjects.

If the Provincial is also a bishop, a case which is the exception, then in virtue of canon 959 he can confer all Orders on those for whom he can issue dimissorial letters. Ordinarily, however, religious are to be presented to the local Ordinary of the diocese wherein they reside, when it is time for their ordination. An exception to this rule is made in the event that the Order possesses a privilege, or that one of the comprehensively enumerated conditions so stated in canon 966, § 1, is verified.[155] The verification of these conditions can occur:

1) when the local Ordinary permits the candidates to be presented to some other bishop for their ordination;

[155] Benedict XIV (1740-1758) in his Constitution *Impositi Nobis* of February 27, 1747 (*Fontes*, n. 376), declared the necessity of a confirmation granted in *forma specifica* after the Council of Trent regarding the pre-Tridentine privileges which had accorded to religious the right of receiving ordination from any bishop. If the privilege which accorded that right was granted after the Council of Trent, then other Orders could not enjoy it in consequence of the general principle of the intercommunication of privileges.

2) when the religious and the local Ordinary are of different rites;
3) when the bishop is absent from the diocese;[156]
4) when the bishop is not to hold ordinations at the next time designated by law for ordinations;[157]
5) when the see is vacant and the administrator is not a bishop.

Cappello maintains, however, that the Provincial must in all probability send his subjects to the local Ordinary, even when the latter is about to confer Orders at the canonical season but in a remote section of the diocese, unless grave inconvenience be involved.[158]

The Code warns the Provincial not to transfer his subjects to a house in another diocese to avoid presenting them to the local Ordinary, and not to delay the issuing of the dimissorials until a time when one of the above-mentioned conditions will be verified.[159] In the event that one of these conditions is actually verified and that the Provincial is thereby entitled to send his subjects to another bishop for ordination, the pre-Code regulation which demanded an authentic certification of this fact is now demanded by the second paragraph of canon 966. The bishop may unjustly refuse either to ordain a subject, or to permit him to go to another bishop for ordination. In either event the only course open to the Provincial is recourse to the Holy See, but meanwhile the decision of the bishop is to be obeyed.[160]

156 Many (†1922) stated that authors agreed that this condition was verified if another bishop remained in charge of the diocese, or if the local Ordinary had brought in a bishop to the diocese to confer Orders in his place (*Praelectiones de Sacra Ordinatione* [Parisiis, 1905], n. 159 [herafter cited as *De Sacra Ordinatione*]).

157 These times are enumerated in canon 1006, § 2, as: the four Ember Saturdays; the Saturday before Passion Sunday; and Holy Saturday.

158 *Tractatus Canonico-Moralis de Sacramentis*, Vol. II, Pars, III, *De Sacra Ordinatione* (Taurinorum Augustae: Marietti, 1935), n. 344, 9 (hereafter cited as *De Sacra Ordinatione*).

159 Can. 967.

160 Many, *De Sacra Ordinatione*, n. 163.

Besides authorizing the subject's ordination, the purpose and character of the dimissorial letters of the Provincial, without which the local Ordinary cannot lawfully confer Orders on the former's subjects,[161] is to testify: 1) to the religious profession of the subject; 2) to the completion of the requisite studies; and 3) to the fulfillment of all other requirements of law, as well as to the possession of the requisite qualities for ordination.[162]

Responsibility for the fitness of the candidate rests with the Provincial, since the ordaining bishop has no need of testimonials in regard to it.[163] The bishop, however, is not relieved of all responsibility, since canon 973, § 3, requires him to ascertain with moral certitude the worthiness of those upon whom he confers Orders, and the Instruction of 1931 of the Sacred Congregation for Religious even gives liberty to the bishop to investigate the candidate's fitness both as to learning and as to moral qualities, if he deems it desirable.[164] In the absence of all positive doubt concerning the candidate's fitness after this investigation, the bishop is required to proceed to the ordination. If for some reason the subject is examined by the bishop and is found unworthy, the Provincial may not send such a subject to another bishop, since this factor is not listed in canon 966, §1, as a permissive condition. Rather, the Provincial may await either a successful examination by the subject before the same bishop, or he may legally seek redress with the Sacred Congregation of Religious.[165]

Since dimissorial letters are public documents, they must be issued by one who holds a public office. The issuance of them does not, however, involve the exercise of jurisdiction. They are valid, therefore, if issued by a Provincial

[161] Can. 964, § 2.

[162] Can. 995, § 1; S.C. de Religiosis, instr. 1 dec. 1931, § 12—*AAS*, XXIV (1932), 78.

[163] Cans. 995, § 2; 970.

[164] Instr., 1 dec. 1931, § 19—*AAS*, XXIV (1932), 81.

[165] Many, *De Sacra Ordinatione*, n. 163.

who is suspended, excommunicated or under interdict, provided that he has not been removed from office or deprived of his jurisdiction after a condemnatory or declaratory sentence.[166]

The Provincial or his successor can limit or revoke dimissorial letters, but they do not expire with the expiration of the jurisdiction of the one who issued them.[167] The Provincial is, of course, required to ascertain the worthiness of the candidate and his canonical fitness for Orders before he issues the dimissorials. Accordingly he may not present novices for promotion to tonsure or minor Orders before their temporary profession,[168] or religious in temporary vows for promotion to Sacred Orders.[169]

The Provincial is required to examine the candidates for Orders personally or through a delegate concerning the Order they are about to receive, and, if there is question of a Major Order, in certain points of Theology as well.[170] Only thus can he testify properly in his dimissorial letters concerning the completion by the candidate of the required studies.[171] Since the ordaining bishop may waive his right to examine the candidate, and may accept fully the testimonial of the Provincial, as he generally does, the Provincial's grave responsibility in this matter is particularly evident. This responsibility is further evident from the provisions of canon 970, which confer upon his the right to prohibit the ordination of subjects for any canonical cause. Should such a prohibition be put in effect, then the right of recourse to the General is retained by the subject, but meanwhile the decision of the Provincial must be observed (*recursus fit in devolutivo*). The canonical cause justifying

166 Cappello, *De Sacra Ordinatione*, n. 345, 2.

167 Can. 963.

168 Can. 567, § 2; S.C. Ep. et Reg., decr. *Auctis admodum*, 4 nov. 1892, n. 1—*Fontes*, n. 2020.

169 Can. 964, 3°, 4°.

170 Can. 996.

171 Cans. 995, § 1; 997, § 2.

this prohibition certainly includes the lack of any factors recounted in canon 974.[172]

Regarding the moral qualities required in the candidate and the judgment to be passed by the Provincial and other Superiors in this matter, reference should be made to the many documents of the Holy See to be found in the *Enchiridion Clericorum.*[173] Of particular importance in this respect is the Instruction of the Sacred Congregation of Religious of December 1, 1931, which must be religiously followed by the Provincial and other Superiors in the promotion of their subjects to Orders.[174]

In this connection, too, the exhortation of canon 972 must be emphasized, namely, the need for well-regulated minor seminaries, if they can possibly be provided, so that candidates may be formed and trained from their earliest years. The Provincial should not be deterred from this project by the thought of the difficulties involved or of the financial expenditures to be made, if it can be foreseen that the personnel of the province and its financial status can carry the burden without extraordinary hardship. Sacrifices made in this regard will be richly repaid.

The Provincial should insure that candidates for tonsure and minor Orders make a retreat of three full days at least, and that those who are to be elevated to Major Orders make a retreat of at least six full days.[175] The phrasing of the law exacts the minimum, and accordingly there rests with the Provincial a discretionary power to require a longer period

[172] The factors postulated in canon 974 are: 1) the previous reception of the Sacrament of Confirmation; 2) the endowment with moral qualities corresponding to the Order to be received; 3) the attainment of the canonical age; 4) the possession of the requisite knowledge; 5) the reception of the intermediate Orders; 6) the observance of the interstices; and 7) the holding of a canonical title.

[173] *Enchiridion Clericorum, Documenta Ecclesiae Sacrorum Alumnis Instituendis* Typis Polyglottis Vaticanis: MCMXXXVIII, venit apud Herder "S.A.L.E.R.").

[174] S.C. de Religiosis, instr. 1 dec. 1931—*AAS*, XXIV (1932), 74-81.

[175] Can. 1001, § 1.

for these retreats.[176] To him likewise is granted the judgment as to the necessity or feasibility of repeating the exercises, if for some reason the ordinations are postponed for a period less than a semester.[177]

He may also shorten the prescribed period of spiritual exercises to a minimum period of three days in the case of one who is promoted to the diaconate, if the candidate has received the subdiaconate after making the prescribed retreat within the same semester.[178] He is authorized to determine the place of the retreat, and should inform the ordaining bishop of the fulfillment of the requirements of the law by the candidates for Orders.[179] Finally, the Provincial is required to inform the pastor of the subject's place of Baptism regarding that subject's promotion to subdeaconship.[180]

6. *Sacred Places and Worship*

Closely allied to the rights and duties of the Provincial in relation to the Sacrament of the Blessed Eucharist are those which are treated in the Third Book of the Code as pertaining to sacred places and divine worship. These include matters related to the Blessed Sacrament, to churches and oratories, and to other sacred places and things.

Regulars who have obtained the permission of the local Ordinary as well as the *beneplacitum* of the Holy See to erect a new house in a diocese must obtain the permission of the local Ordinary before their church or oratory can be erected in a specific site.[181] Thus the right to construct an oratory or a church, which right is granted by canon 497, § 2, is limited in so far as the designation of the actual site of the oratory or the church must be approved by the local Ordinary. The latter cannot, however, preclude the right

[176] "Qui ad primam tonsuram et ordines minores promovendi sunt, spiritualibus exercitiis per tres saltem dies; qui vero ad ordines sacros, saltem per sex integros dies vacent; . . . "—can. 1001, § 1.

[177] Can. 1001, § 2.

[178] Can. 1001, § 1.

[179] Can. 1001, § § 3, 4.

[180] Can. 1011.

[181] Can. 1162, § 4.

of a clerical institute to erect either a church or an oratory.[182]

Canon 1157 states that no one, notwithstanding any privileges he may have, can consecrate or bless a sacred place without the permission of the Ordinary.[183] Through the unqualified use of the term "Ordinary" in this canon, the rights of the local Ordinary as well as those of the Provincial are equally protected.[184] Accordingly, the right to consecrate a church, an oratory or a sacred place pertains to the Ordinary of the place or to his delegate.[185]

Even in the event that the religious Ordinary is also a bishop, the permission of the local Ordinary will be necessary for him if he is lawfully to undertake the consecration of a sacred place pertaining to the community.[186]

On the other hand, the permission of the Provincial is required and, in itself, is sufficient for the solemn blessing of their own churches, in the event that he does not perform the blessing himself.[187] If the Order possesses further privileges, for instance, the privilege whereby a Local Superior can bless a sacred place, the rights of the Provincial are protected by this canon to the extent that the use of such privileges are subordinated to the consent of the Provincial, which can, however, be reasonably presumed.[188]

Certain privileges of Regulars, extant before the Code, have been left intact by the present law. Thus, if the local Ordinary is unwilling, or if beyond four months he delays performing the consecration, the blessing, or the laying of the corner-stone of churches or of oratories, the Provincial

[182] Larraona, "*Commentarium Codicis*"—*CpR*, V (1924), 427.

[183] "Non obstante quolibet privilegio, nemo potest locum sacrum consecrare vel benedicere sine Ordinarii consensu."

[184] Keene, *Religious Ordinaries and Canon 198*, p. 71; Vermeersch-Creusen, *Epitome*, II, n. 471; Coronata, *Institutiones*, II, p. 29, n. 726.

[185] Cans. 1155, § § 1, 2; 1157.

[186] Keene, *loc. cit.*; Beste, *Introductio*, p. 554.

[187] Can. 1156; Coronata, *Institutiones*, II, p. 29, n. 726; Keene, *loc. cit.*

[188] Coronata, *loc. cit.*

may invite any bishop in union with Rome, without obtaining the permission of the local Ordinary.[189]

The right to bless sacred places which belong to exempt religious, or to lay the corner-stone of their churches or oratories, is reserved by the Code to the Provincial or to the Major Superior. As in the case of other ordinary powers, the Provincial can delegate another to perform this duty.[190] The Provincial's right in these matters is traced historically to the privileges granted in the past to Regulars,[191] which privileges have now become recognized as ordinary rights in canons 1156 and 1163 of the Code.

Canon 1176, § 2, grants to the Provincial of Regulars the power to reconcile a consecrated church of his province when it has suffered violation, even though he is not a bishop. Moreover, in case of necessity, when the Provincial cannot be approached, it is lawful for the rector to do the same, although he is required to notify the Provincial later of his action.[192]

Authors agree that the Provincial is included in the term *Ordinary* as employed in canon 1192, § 1, with regard to the erection of semi-public oratories, and that his permission suffices for their erection in the houses of his province.[193] Moreover, his permission is required to reduce them to profane use.[194] The determination that the factor of necessity or of great usefulness requires more than one oratory in the religious house is left entirely to the judgment of the Provincial.[195]

189 Paulus III, const. *Licet debitum*, 18 oct. 1548, § 25—*Bull. Rom. Taur.*, VI, 394.

190 Cans. 1156; 1163.

191 Coelestinus V. const. *Etsi cunctos*, 27 sept. 1294—Potthast, *Regesta*, n. 23976; Julius II, const. *Dudùm ad sacrum*, 28 iul. 1506—*Bull. Rom. Taur.*, V., 426.

192 Can. 1176, § 3.

193 Vermeersch-Creusen, *Epitome*, II, n. 501; Blat, *Commentarium*, Lib. III, Partes 11-VI (2. ed., Romae: apud Institutum Pontificium Internationale "Angelicum," 1934), p. 62.

194 Can. 1192, § 3.

195 Cf. can. 1192, § 4; Vermeersch-Creusen, *Epitome*, II, n. 351.

Some hold that only in virtue of a privilege granted by Pope Gregory XIII (1721-1724) can the Provincial permit semi-public oratories to be established in the summer homes of his subjects.[196] However, it seems more in keeping with the Provincial's position as Ordinary, and with the norm of the law as enacted in canon 1192, § 4, to hold that these oratories can be erected by the Provincial for his subjects in virtue of an explicit right conceded in the Code. He can, in accordance with canon 1193, restrict the performance of certain services in all semi-public oratories for the establishment of which he has given permission, although such a restriction is not to be presumed. Hence, in the absence of his special limitation, all functions may be performed there, unless the rubrics or a special decree forbid certain functions.[197]

Even if it be objected that the Provincial is not contemplated by the law in its use of the term Ordinary in canon 1192, § 1, it is still true that he is entitled to establish semi-public oratories, even more than one in a given house, independently of the local Ordinary, in virtue of a papal privilege. Gregory XIII (1721-1724) granted it to the Major Superiors of the Jesuits. Other religious who enjoyed the prerogative of participating and sharing in the privileges accorded to the Jesuits obtained it as well.[198]

The Code grants certain rights to the Provincial with regard also to altars. Canon 1200, § 1, permits him or his delegate to *reconsecrate* a fixed altar in an exempt church or oratory, if the altar has lost its consecration in consequence

[196] Const. *Decet Romanum*, 3 maii 1575—cited by Augustinus a Virgine Maria, *Compendium Privilegiorum Omnium Religiosorum*, p. 156; Schaefer, *De Religiosis* p. 851, n. 464; Cappello, *Summa Iuris Canonici*, II, p. 319, n. 684.

[197] Keene, *Religious Ordinaries and Canon 198*, p. 81; Augustine, *Commentary*, VI, 75-76; Goyeneche, "Consultationes"—*CpR*, XII (1931), 444-446.

[198] Const. *Decet Romanum*, 3 maii, 1575—*loc. cit.*

of the separation of the table from the base.[199] With his permission the title of any portable altar which he has erected can be changed.[200]

For a just and reasonable cause in extraordinary cases he can permit by way of individual grant (*per modum actus*) the celebration of Mass outside the church or oratory, either in the exempt religious house or on its grounds, provided that the place be appropriate.[201]

Unless the community or the individual religious possesses a privilege for the celebration of Mass on a portable altar in any fitting place, the Provincial may not permit the celebration of Mass in places outside the monastery or its grounds. Recourse must in these cases be made to the local Ordinary in virtue of canon 822, § 4.[202]

Finally, the Provincial of an exempt clerical institute can designate and declare one altar in all the churches of the province to be privileged daily and perpetually, provided that the church does not already possess one such altar.[203]

Ordinarily the responsibility for the custody of the Blessed Sacrament, with its consequent obligations for the

[199] Pejška, *Ius Canonicum Religiosorum*, p. 256; Beste, *Introductio*, p. 579; Vermeersch-Creusen, *Epitome*, II, n. 507.

[200] Can. 1201, § 3; Blat, *De Locis Sacris et de Bonis Ecclesiae Temporalibus*, p. 78.

[201] Can. 822, § 4. In relation to the Provincial, this canon applies to those places within the monasteries or grounds which are subject to him. Particular privileges possessed by certain institutes for the celebration of Mass in places not under the jurisdiction of the Provincial must be examined if further rights are to be determined on given occasions.

[202] With regard to the faculty of the local Ordinary to permit the celebration of Mass outside a church or oratory in a private home (can. 822, § 4), the Pontifical Commission for the Interpretation of the Code, when asked in 1919 whether this faculty was to be interpreted restrictively, replied in the affirmative (*AAS*, XI [1919], 478). Beste states that the use of this faculty is not warranted for reasons solely of devotion, but that some additional reason of necessity or of utility is also required (*Introductio*, p. 490).

[203] Can. 916.

proper ornamentation of the altar or the repository, and for the custody of the tabernacle key[204] devolves upon the Local Superior as the head of the community.[205] The Provincial, however, must inquire into these details at the time of his visitation, and see to their proper fulfillment.[206]

With regard to the cult of the Blessed Sacrament, canon 1274, § 1, states that private exposition of the Blessed Sacrament can be held for any just reason and without the permission of the local Ordinary. With regard to the public exposition of the Blessed Sacrament, however, the same paragraph of this canon lists the days on which it can be held, and beyond which the permission of the local Ordinary is required, even in churches belonging to exempt religious.[207]

7. *The Approval of Preachers*

The office of preaching is committed primarily to the Holy Father for the whole Church, and to the bishops for their respective dioceses.[208] No one, therefore, is allowed to preach until he has obtained the canonical mission to do so from a legitimate authority to whom this duty is entrusted.[209]

[204] Cans. 609, § 1; 1268, § 4; S.C. de Sacramentis, instr. 26 maii 1938—*AAS*, XXX (1938), 198.

[205] Clancy, *The Local Superior*, p. 170.

[206] Cf. *supra*, p. 70.

[207] Wernz (*Ius Decretalium*, III, p. 560, nota 235) stated that the opinion of authors who asserted that Regulars could hold public exposition in their churches or oratories with the permission of their Ordinary alone, namely, the Provincial, could not be proved contrary to the prescriptions of the Council of Trent or the various decrees of the Holy See, and therefore did not lack probability. The Code has not changed the law on this point, and therefore O'Brien (*The Exemption of Religious*, p. 142), Vermeersch-Creusen (*Epitome*, II, n. 599), Wernz-Vidal (*De Rebus*, I, p. 544, nota 50) and Capobianco (*Privilegia et Facultates Ordinis Minorum*, n. 90) all claim as probable the right of the Provincial to permit public benediction of the Blessed Sacrament, *ianuis clausis*, in the churches and oratories of his province for his subjects alone.

[208] Can. 1327, § 1.

[209] Can. 1328.

Before one is commissioned for this ministry, however, it is necessary that he be approved by the proper eclesiastical authority. Particular law may, in the case of religious, establish specific requirements for the candidate, and determine which Superior is authorized to confer the necessary approbation. Generally, an initial approbation of this nature is sufficient to render a candidate eligible for faculties to preach, unless positive doubt arises later as to his fitness. After this initial approbation, in the case of religious, the permission of the Local Superior is all that is required for a subject who is to preach.[210] This rule exists for the sake of the good order and the proper observance in the religious house.

Before examining the law of the Code for religious with regard to the ministry of the word, the writer proposes to furnish a few historical notes which will serve to illustrate the Church's serious attitude in this matter.

A. Pre-Code Legislation

Legislation dealing with the hearing of confessions of the faithful by Regulars frequently touched upon the question of the approval of their preachers in a similar fashion, and accordingly analogous legislative provisions generally obtained in regard to the latter.[211]

In the early history of the Mendicants the Church's need for preachers to combat heresy was great. The IV General Council of the Lateran (1215) had decreed that bishops provide suitable men to exercise the office of preaching.[212] Bishops enlisted the aid of the friars, and pontiffs favored them with many privileges to preach anywhere, provided they were approved and designated by the Superior of their Order.[213]

[210] Can. 1339, § 2. [211] Cf. *supra*, pp. 187-198.

[212] C. 15, X, *de officio iudicis ordinarii*, I, 31; Schroeder, *Disciplinary Decrees*, p. 251.

[213] Gregorius IX, const., *Quoniam abundavit*, 21 apr. 1227—Potthast, *Regesta*, n. 7880; Clemens IV, const. *Quidem temere*, 20 iun. 1265—

The Council of Trent required Regular preachers, before they should preach, to be approved by their Superiors regarding their life, morals and knowledge.[214] Although the Council of Trent spoke of the examination required for the approbation of preachers, it did not specify which Superior was authorized to give the approbation. Particular law generally reserved the approval of confessors to the Provincial or a Major Superior.[215] Moreover, there is some reason to believe that even in the use of the word "Superiors" the Council of Trent intended to signify either the Provincial, or, the Superior designated by the particular law. Legislation previous to the Council had reserved the approval of preachers to the Provincial or the General.[216]

However, in view of the Constitution *"Superna maiestatis"* of Leo X (1513-1521), it can be argued that the approbation given by the Local Superior was sufficient at that time.[217] It seems, then, that the only satisfactory answer in this matter can be obtained from what was specified in the particular law, although the nature of the office of preaching seems to require the approval of the Provincial by reason of the analogy between his office and that of the local Ordinary who gave the approval to his priests.

Similarly, after the Council of Trent the Church continued to emphasize the necessity of approval on the part of the Superiors for religious preachers, but the actual determination of the Superior authorized to confer this approbation must be sought in the particular law.[218]

Potthast, *Regesta*, n. 19216; Martinus IV, const. *Ad fructus uberes*, 10 iun. 1282—Potthast, *Regesta*, n. 21821.

[214] Conc. Trident., sess. V, *de ref.*, c. 2; Schroeder, *Canons and Decrees*, p. 27.

[215] Cf. *supra*, p. 190.

[216] Cf. Bonifatius VIII, const. *Super cathedram*, 18 febr. 1300—c. 2, *de sepulturis*, III, 6, in Extravag. com.; Benedictus XI, const. *Inter cunctas*, 17 febr. 1304—c. 1, *de privilegiis*, V, 7, in Extravag. com.; Clemens V, const. *"Dudum"*, 6 maii 1312—c. 2, *de sepulturis*, III, 7, in Clem.

[217] 19 dec. 1516—*Fontes*, n. 71.

[218] The Provincials of the Carmelite and Franciscan Orders seem

Regulars were not, however, obliged to submit to an examination under the direction of the local Ordinary in order to enjoy the right to preach in their own churches.[219] For a reasonable cause, an individual preacher could be forbidden to preach thus, but all the preachers of a community could not be restricted in this manner.[220] On the other hand, the bishop was fully authorized to examine them if they were to preach in churches other than their own.[221]

B. Present Law

The exemption of religious is closely restricted by the Code in the matter of preaching. If Regulars wish to preach to the faithful, including nuns subject to them, the permission of the local Ordinary is necessary, except in the case of those included within the scope of canon 514, § 1.[222] If the sermon is to be preached to the subjects or residents in a house of Regulars,[223] the Local Superior can give the faculties to the preacher, unless the particular law restricts him in this right. In the event that the Local Superior confers the faculties, it seems that the initial approbation of the preacher by the proper Superior is presupposed, if that Superior is other than the Local Superior. If, however, the sermon is to be preached by a diocesan priest or a member of another Order, the same Superior can give the faculties, provided that the preacher has already been approved for such ministry by his own Ordinary or Superior.[224] From

---

to have been exclusively authorized to confer this approbation, and seem even to have received a privilege to appoint preachers in the contingency that the General, at any future date, should regard this right as reserved to himself.—Lezana, *Mare Magnum Ordinum Praedicatorum, Minorum, Eremitarum Sancti Augustini, Carmelitarum cum ipsorum Regula, Servitarum et iMnorum* (I Vol. in 2 partes, Venetiis, 1653), Pars I, p. 48, n. 14.

[219] Cf. S.C.C., *Senonen.*, 28 febr. 1654, ad 5—*Fontes*, n. 2734.

[220] S.C.C., *loc. cit.;* Piat, *Praelectiones*, II, p. 249, qu. 309.

[221] Conc. Trident., sess. V, *de ref.*, c. 2; Clemens X, const. *Superna*, 21 iun. 1670, § 3—*Fontes*, n. 246.

[222] Can. 1338, § 2. [223] Can. 514, § 1. [224] Can. 1338, § 1.

canon 1338, § 1, the need for an initial approbation for the office of preaching is evident. As in the question of the approval of Regular confessors, the Code is silent as to which Superior is competent to approve Regular preachers. It merely states that local Ordinaries and religious Superiors have a grave obligation in conscience to confer faculties for preaching only on those who have been approved upon an examination in the manner provided for prospective confessors according to canon 877, § 1. If the desired moral qualities and learning are lacking in the subject, Superiors are required to revoke the faculties granted for preaching, and in cases of positive doubt concerning his learning, they must resolve the doubt in favor of the subject only with positive arguments, inclusive of another examination, if necessary.[225]

Particular law should designate the proper Superior for the initial approbation. If particular law is silent on the point, it seems that the giving of this approbation should be reserved to the Provincial or his delegate, as it is reserved by law to the local Ordinary in regard to priests who wish to preach to the faithful who are his subjects.

Canon 1339, § 1, states that local Ordinaries should not without a grave reason deny faculties to a religious priest who has been presented by his Superior. The presentation mentioned in this canon seems to be within the competence of the Local Superior, unless the particular law states the contrary, since the Code has not specified a particular Superior, and furthermore seems to presuppose the previous approbation of the subject according to his own particular law so that he can lawfully be presented for diocesan faculties. Generally, however, faculties for preaching and for the hearing of confessions are granted simultaneously, and it does not appear from canon 874 that the presentation of a subject for diocesan faculties is reserved to the Provincial, to the exclusion of the Local Superior. If, however, a subject is to be presented for some parochial assignment or for a chaplaincy, the presentation should be made by the Pro-

[225] Can. 1340, § § 1, 2.

vincial as the proper Ordinary of the subject, unless the particular law has conferred the right of presentation upon the Local Superior.[226]

Since the office of preaching in a diocese is primarily entrusted to the bishop, the Provincial and his subjects, though exempt, are subject to episcopal regulations whenever they preach to the faithful. Moreover, the local Ordinary may lawfully impose limitations or conditions in connection with the faculties to be granted to Regular priests for preaching to seculars in his diocese.[227]

In accordance with canon 1345, the local Ordinary can require brief instructions of the catechism or explanations of the Gospel at all Masses attended by the faithful in the churches and public oratories of the diocese. Exempt religious in all probability are bound to observe these regulations when the faithful attend Sunday or Holy Day Mass in their semi-public oratories regularly in consequence of the fact that a public attendance at the Mass has not in any way been barred.

Although the exclusive jurisdiction of the local Ordinary extends to the granting of the faculties for preaching even to exempt nuns, under their privilege of exemption and subjection to the Provincial they cannot be forced to accept a preacher sent to them by the local Ordinary against their will.[228]

[226] In this latter case it seems that the Local Superior should indicate his right of presentation in the petition not only as a measure of courtesy, but also as a practical method of expediting the appointment.

[227] Cf. S.C.C., *Normae*, 28 iun. 1917, nn. 2,3—*AAS*, IX (1917), 329.

[228] O'Brien, *The Exemption of Religious in Church Law*, p. 218; Vermeersch-Creusen, *Epitome*, n. 673.

CHAPTER XII

THE COERCIVE POWER OF THE PROVINCIAL SUPERIOR

Coercive power is a necessary adjunct of the Provincial's office for the enforcement of law and order within the province of an exempt clerical institute. The historical development of the legislation concerning this point shows that it has always been recognized as an essential attribute of the Provincial's jurisdiction. Before undertaking a study of the Provincial's coercive rights established in the present law, the writer proposes a brief examination of the legislation previous to the Code for the sake of a fuller understanding of the Provincial's competence in regard to the use and application of penalties.

1. *The Existence of the Provincial's Coercive Power*

1. PRE-CODE LEGISLATION

Decretal law considered the office of a jurisdictional Superior useless unless it was vested with coercive rights, even to the extent of imposing ecclesiastical censures and penalties, within the scope of its jurisdiction.[1] Such authority was considered as not reserved to secular prelates alone but as also enjoyed by Regular prelates.[2] Moreover, local Ordinaries were obliged to sustain the censures imposed by the latter provided that they were in accord with the demands of justice to the subject.[3] In fact a similar penal jurisdiction was accorded to secular and religious prelates with regard to their subjects. This is clear from the teachings of St. Raymond of Pennafort (1175-1275), who held that the Regular prelate could even impose a major excommunication upon his subjects.[4]

[1] C. 28, 29, X, *de officio et potestate iudicis delegati,* I, 29.

[2] C. 10, X, *de maioritate et obedientia,* I, 33.

[3] C. 3, *de officio iudicis ordinarii,* I, 31.

[4] *Summa* (ed. nova, Veronae, 1744), lib. III, tit. XXIII, par. VII, p. 392.

In the early period of the history of the Mendicants it was clear that, generically at least, quasi-episcopal power comprehended coercive power, and that perhaps even Local Superiors possessed it, depending upon their particular law.[5] Particular law was clear on the point in relation to the Provincial. His duty was one of supervision over the Local Superiors with coercive rights for the accomplishment of his task.[6]

In the period after the Council of Trent, authors commonly agreed that the Provincial possessed coercive power, and many attributed the same to the Local Superior as well.[7] Frequently the powers of the various Regular prelates were not clearly distinguished, for the authors wrote of the coercive powers of Regular prelates in general.[8] It was recognized, however, that the Provincial could remove a subject from office for a just reason.[9] Under particular law, gross negligence in the performance of one's duties was specified as a cause for removal from office.[10]

The power of the Provincial in coercive matters extended both to temporal and to spiritual penalties. Thus, in virtue

[5] Cf. St. Raymond of Pennafort, *loc. cit.*

[6] According to the Carmelite Constitutions of the period, Provincials not only possessed the use of coercive power, but also had the competence and the obligation to deprive negligent Local Superiors of their office.—*Monumenta Carmelitana,* I 64-65.

[7] Suarez, *De Religione,* Lib. II, Cap. XIV, n. 4; St. Alphonsus, *Theologia Moralis* (ed. absolutissima, 9 vols., Vesontione, 1832), lib. VI, cap. I, n. 10; Passerinus, *Tractatus de Electione Canonica,* cap. XXVI, n. 4. Although these authors indicated that the Local Superior as well enjoyed full coercive rights, Donatus (*Rerum Regularium Praxis,* Tom. III, Pars II, tr. IX, qu. 12, nn. 1-2) denied the fullness of coercive power necessary for the Local Superior to inflict the more grave canonical penalties.

[8] Cf. Wernz, *Ius Decretalium,* III, p. 771, n. 691; Suarez, *loc. cit.;* Piat, *Praelectiones,* I, pp. 625-628, qq. 772-777.

[9] Clemens VII, const. *Pro statu religiosorum,—Bull. Carm.,* II, 24; Lezana, *Summa Quaestionum Regularium,* Vol. II, Pars II, cap. XIII, n. 56; Piat, *Praelectiones,* I, p. 628, qu. 778.

[10] Cf. e.g., *Monumenta Carmelitana,* I, 63.

of the authority conferred upon the bishop to forcefully detain delinquents when there existed reasonable fear that they might escape before judgment,[11] the right to make use of the penalty of incarceration was likewise conceded to the Provincial.[12] Reiffenstuel (1642-1703)[13] and Schmalzgrueber (1663-1735)[14] acknowledged a possibility for the penalty of flagellation, provided that it did not proceed to the point of bloodshed, or that it was not administered by a layman.[15] Expulsion was allowed in accordance with the constitutions of the institute, provided that the subject was not yet in sacred Orders.[16] The infliction of these penalties was permitted to the Provincial as a function of his coercive power. Whether or not this function belonged also to the Local Superior depended upon the particular law of the institute.

With regard to spiritual penalties, the Provincial with reference to his subjects possessed an authority which was, in general, coextensive with that of the bishop over his diocesan subjects.[17] Therefore he could inflict most of the spiritual penalties, including ecclesiastical censures, upon a subject,[18] although the right to impose a general interdict or suspension upon his chapter, as well as the right to impose a local interdict, was denied him.[19] For a grave reason he could also suspend his subjects *ex informata conscientia.*[20]

[11] Cf. c. 3, *de poenis*, V, 9, in VI°; Conc. Trident, sess. XXV, *de ref.*, c. 6.

[12] Piat, *Praelectiones*, I, p. 629, qu. 781.

[13] *Jus Canonicum Universum*, Lib. V, tit. XXXVII, n. 104.

[14] *Ius Ecclesiasticum Universum*, Lib. V, tit. XXXVII, n. 204.

[15] Cf. c. 24, X, *de sententia excommunicationis*, V, 39.

[16] Lezana, *Summa Quaestionum Regularium*, Lib. I, Pars I, cap. XXII, n. 25.

[17] Suarez, *De Religione*, Lib. II, Cap. IX, n. 4; Piat, *Praelectiones*, p. 626, qu. 775.

[18] Suarez, *loc. cit.*, Piat, *loc. cit.;* Bouix, *De Jure Regularium*, II, 439.

[19] Suarez, *ibid.*, nn. 5-6; Piat, *loc. cit.*

[20] S.C. Ep. et Reg., 2 mart. 1866—Bizzarri, *Collectanea*, p. 755; Wernz, *Ius Decretalium*, III, p. 771, n. 691; Ferraris, *Prompta Bibliotheca*, s.v. "approbatio", n. 20.

Finally, although the right to establish irregularities was reserved to the Holy Father, the Provincial could make an official declaration regarding the fact of an irregularity already incurred by a subject.[21]

2. Present Law

Coercive measures are employed in the government of the Church as a visible society. Accordingly they pertain to the external forum. Consequently it is only Superiors who hold power in the external forum who can employ these means.[22] Such measures remain without valid effect if they are employed by one who lacks the proper jurisdiction in the external forum, and accordingly would have to be regarded as implying disorderly force or violence, rather than orderly functions of government.

Canon 500, § 1, grants jurisdiction within the limits of the common and the particular law to all religious Superiors of clerical exempt communities. By reason of their exemption from the jurisdiction of the local Ordinary, the jurisdiction of such Superiors cannot reasonably be restricted to the internal forum, since they must provide both for the spiritual welfare of their subjects and for their external government as well. Necessarily, therefore, they must possess coercive power within the limits of the common and the particular law.

Since coercive power accompanies the possession of jurisdiction in the external forum, a Superior who possesses such jurisdiction can employ all, or some, of the coercive measures recognized by the Code as comprised within the limits of his office.[23]

The authority of a Superior to make laws and to impose precepts implies his right to attach penalties to the laws he

[21] Suarez, *ibid.*, n. 7; Piat, *loc. cit.* [22] Cappello, *De Censuris*, n. 10.

[23] Even a lawful Superior who lacks jurisdictional power can impose penances and penal remedies, but cannot impose canonical penalties, whether they be of a medicinal or a vindicative nature, or whether they be of a *latae* or a *ferendae sententiae* character.

enacts and to the precepts he gives by way of penal sanctions.[24] A Superior's power to enact a true law confers upon him not only the right to invoke a penal sanction for the sake of enforcing compliance with his own law or that of his predecessor, but also, in certain circumstances, the right to invoke similar sanctions with reference to the divine law, or to ecclesiastical law enacted by a higher authority in the Church, and, finally, the right to intensify the penalty already established in the law.[25] Penalties established by law may be inflicted or declared judicially, i.e., according to the strict norms of judicial procedure, or, in certain contingencies, by precept executed in writing, or in the presence of two witnesses.[26] The Superior who possesses legislative and judicial powers can establish penalties in law, and, within the limits of his competence, inflict or declare them judicially.[27]

1) *Judicial Coercive Powers*

Penalties are, as a general rule, to be inflicted or declared according to the norms of judicial procedure, unless the law provides otherwise,[28] since they are penal sanctions invoked against canonical delicts, which ordinarily are to be judged judicially. Offenses or transgressions against which the law does not invoke any specific penal sanction, or which are not comprised within the scope of canon 2222, § 1, by reason of their special gravity or accompanying grave scandal, cannot be punished judicially, since canon 1933, § 1, states that

[24] Can. 2220, § 1.

[25] Can. 2221.

[26] Cans. 1933, §§ 1, 4; 2225.

[27] Can. 2220, § 1.

[28] Can. 1933, § 1; Noval, "De Ratione Corrigendi et Puniendi sive in Judicio sive extra Jure Codicis J.C."—*JP*, II (1922), 204; Coronata, *Institutiones*, III, p. 376, n. 1452. The writer expresses his indebtedness to the entire article of Noval cited above, and appearing in three installments (*JP*, II [1922], 147-156; *ibid.*, III [1923], 37-40; 204-209), for the study and summary of the coercive rights of Superiors, an application of which has been made to the office of the Provincial. Hereafter reference to this article will be máde thus: "*De Ratione Corrigendi et Puniendi.*"

only delicts, i.e., grave, external, and morally imputable violations of a law or of a precept to which has been attached at least an indeterminate canonical sanction,[29] are to be punished in this way. Such transgressions, however, are not to go unpunished, but are to be punished extra-judicially by means of penal remedies, admonitions, rebuke, or precept, according to the norms of canons 2307-2311, if such a means as that of paternal correction proves insufficient for dealing adequately with the culprit.[30]

Judicial accusations can, in virtue of canon 1933, § 1, be brought against delicts which are public,[31] whether they resulted from the transgression of a law or from the violation of a particular precept.[32] It is essential, however, for the prospective judicial procedure in such cases:

1) that potential cognizance regarding the delict has not been removed from the judicial competence of the appropriate Superior through the legal agency of canonical prescription;[33]
2) that the delict has not been expiated or has not already been sufficiently punished in the civil courts;[34]
3) that the delict is certain, or at least solidly probable;[35]
4) that the delict can not be sufficiently atoned for and expiated through judicial correction and the imposition of appropriate penances;[36]
5) that the delict, if the imposition of a censure is involved, has been committed despite the proper canonical warnings, unless there be question of a notably grave and

[29] Can. 2195, § 1.

[30] Noval, "De Ratione Corrigendi et Puniendi"—*JP*, II (1922), 148.

[31] I.e., those delicts, the knowledge of which is divulged actually at present, or virtually, in so far as the knowledge will easily be divulged (can. 2197, § 1), so that neither the fact itself, nor the probable malice of the culprit will remain occult, after the judicial inquisition according to the norms of canons 1939-1946.

[32] Can. 2195, § § 1, 2.

[33] Can. 2233, § 1; 1703.

[34] Can. 1933, § 3.

[35] Cans. 1939; 1946; § 2, 3°.

[36] Cans. 1947; 1948; 1952.

scandalous delict with reference to which no warning is postulated, and[37]

6) that the delict can be punished judicially, either because there is no impediment in the way of the trial,[38] or because, in the judgment of the Superior, no grave harm will result for the common good through the trial.[39]

Finally, grave transgressions of a law or of a precept which involve a special gravity and notable scandal, regardless of the notorious or occult nature of the offense, can be punished by the Superior, who is also authorized to dispense with the previous canonical warning which normally is to be invoked as a threat of the prospective penalty.[40] Although the law here dispenses the Superior from the necessity of a previous canonical warning with the threat of a penalty for the prospective culprit, the Superior must nevertheless, in public cases, adhere to a judicial procedure in virtue of canon 1933, § 1, unless a canonical trial is impossible, or unless the case be such as is contemplated in paragraph 2 of canon 2222.[41]

2) *Extra-judicial Coercive Powers*

Through his coercive rights of a judicial nature the Su-

[37] Cans. 2233, § 2; 2222, § 1. [38] Cf. can. 2191, § 3.

[39] Can. 2233, § 4. Although this canon commits the judgment to the Superior merely with regard to the declaration of *latae sententiae* penalties, an analogous right is also attributed to him in questions involving the imposition of *ferendae sententiae* penalties when the law confers the right in facultative words. Such discretionary power, however, is sedulously to be distinguished from the option of preceeding judicially or extra-judicially, which by no means is conferred (Noval, "De Ratione Corrigendi et Puniendi"—*JP*, II (1922), 150-153).

[40] Can. 2222, § 1.

[41] Can. 2222, § 2: "Pariter idem legitimus Superior, licet probabile tantum sit delictum fuisse commissum aut delicti certe commissi poenalis actio praescripta sit, non solum ius, sed etiam officium habet non promovendi clericum de cuius idoneitate non constat, et, ad scandalum evitandum, prohibendi clerico exercitium sacri ministerii aut etiam eundem ab officio, ad normam iuris, amovendi; quae omnia in casu non habent rationem poenae."

perior safeguards the law of the Church and his Order by declaring or inflicting statutory penalties. The Church, however, desires to prevent the commission of delicts not only by means of the infliction of penalties on past offenders, but also by means of prevention with reference to prospective offenders. The Church prefers to correct the prospective delinquent before it is necessary to penalize him. Even after the commission of a statutory delict that is occult, the common good and the welfare of the individual should not be jeopardized by the revelation of the delict through a judicial trial. On the other hand, public delicts which in certain circumstances cannot be punished judicially should not go unpunished altogether. These three situations suggest the necessity of a procedure that is extra-judicial. The power to proceed thus is possessed by Superiors in exempt clerical communities of men, and therefore by the Provincial, as will be seen in the following section of this Chapter wherein the extent of his coercive rights will be determined.

An examination of canons 1933, § 1, and 2225 reveals that the Church has established two ordinary modes for the imposition or declaration of penalties, namely, by way of judicial sentence, and after the manner of a personal precept (*per modum praecepti*).[42] Thus canon 2225 states that if a penalty is declared or imposed by means of a judicial sentence, the norms prescribed by the canons with regard to the judicial sentence are to be followed.[43] From canon 1933, §

[42] The interpretations given to these two canons, 1933, § § 1, 4, and 2225, are many and varied. Esswein (*The Extrajudicial Coercive Powers of Ecclesiastical Superiors*, The Catholic University of America Canon Law Studies, no. 127 Washington, D.C.: The Catholic University of America Press, 1941, pp. 11-114) has considered these interpretations and correctly concludes, in the mind of the writer, that until an authentic decision is rendered, the view of Noval, as expressed in the article cited above and followed in this section, which considers canon 1933, § 4, to be modified and restricted by canon 2225, is the most tenable.

[43] "Si poena declaretur vel infligatur per sententiam iudicialem, serventur canonum praescripta circa sententiae iudicialis pronuntiationem, ..."

1, it follows that public delicts are to be tried judicially,[44] and therefore, through an application of canon 2225, that the norms of judicial procedure are to be followed. On the other hand, canon 1933, § 4, states that canonical penances, excommunication, suspension and interdict can be imposed *per modum praecepti.* From a consideration of canon 1933, § 4, in conjunction with the latter half of canon 2225, which states that a penalty, if imposed *per modum praecepti,* should ordinarily be imposed or declared in writing or before two witnesses, with an indication, except as provided in canon 2193, of the reasons for the penalty,[45] it follows, in the view of Noval, that if the penal measures listed in canon 1933, § 4, are established by way of precept, they are to be established in accordance with canon 2225, namely, *per modum praecepti,* either in writing or before two witnesses. Interpreting the phrase *"inflicta sit ad modum praecepti particularis"* of canon 2225 in the sense that these penalties are not only *inflicted* but also *constituted per modum praecepti,* Noval maintains that the list of penalties of canon 1933, § 4, is an exhaustive one, and may be applied *per modum praecepti* only when they are enacted as the result of a precept.[46]

Gravely culpable faults which may lead to more serious transgressions, as well as grave delicts consisting in the transgression of a particular precept, can therefore be punished extra-judicially *per modum praecepti.* The punish-

[44] "Delicta quae cadunt sub criminali iudicio sunt delicta publica."

[45] ". . . . si vero poena latae vel ferendae sententiae inflicta sit ad modum praecepti particularis, scripto aut coram duobus testibus ordinario declaretur vel irrogetur, indicatis poenae causis, salvo praescripto can. 2193."

[46] Esswein, *loc. cit.* Esswein states that this interpretation of Noval seems to be in harmony with the language and terminology used in the Code when it speaks of penalties. Furthermore, Roberti states ("Quaenam Poenae Applicari Possint per Modum Praecepti?"—*Apollinaris,* IV [1931] 296) that this is the strict interpretation. It is the one, therefore, that has the prior right and claim to practical application, since this is a question involving penal measures (can. 2219, § 1).

ment is effected in accordance with the procedure *per modum praecepti,* i.e., by means of the imposition or declaration of penances, penal remedies, censures, and interdicts or suspensions even as vindicative penalties, provided, of course, that an equitable proportion be observed between the delict and the gravity of the precept.[47]

Although delicts resulting from the violation of a precept thus imposed are ordinarily occult by nature, they can nevertheless be punished extra-judicially if they are public, since the legislator, in canon 1933, § § 1, 4, has established the two methods of procedure, not according as the delicts are public or occult by nature, but rather in line with the fact of their publicity or the fact that they imply the violation of a penal precept. Consequently a delict, though it be public, can nevertheless be punished extra-judicially if it involves the violation of a penal precept.[48]

Finally, with regard to the extra-judicial method of exercising coercive measures over subjects, it is to be noted that, although the list of penalties that may be imposed *per modum praecepti* according to canon 1933, § 4, is recounted exhaustively, this canon makes no distinction between penalties which are of a medicinal or a vindicative nature. Excommunication is always a medicinal penalty, that is, a censure,[49] but the other penalties enumerated can be envisaged either as vindicative or as medicinal, inasmuch as canon 1933, § 4, has not distinguished between these two possibilities. But only a grave, external delict which in its commission is accompanied with contumacy is to be punished with a censure.[50]

[47] The equitable proportion between the penalty and the transgression of the precept is required in the case of extra-judicial coercive measures since the Superior who imposes or declares the penalty punishes directly and in his own name the violation of his precept, and only indirectly the violation of the law which prompted the precept (Noval, "De Ratione Corrigendi et Puniendi"—*JP,* III [1923], 37).

[48] Noval, *"art. cit."*—*JP,* II (1922), 155-156.

[49] Can. 2255, § 2.

[50] Can. 2242, § 1.

Noval believes that for the infliction of a censure the mere external character of the delict is not sufficient in itself, but that the delict must be external with regard to the resultant harm or detriment, in the sense that it is perceived or felt by someone other than the culprit. Thus one who exists in a proximate occasion of committing a delict which is occult, and therefore potentially harmful to himself alone, can be admonished, rebuked, made the recipient of a penal precept, punished with penances, or put under interdict or suspension in their nature of vindicative penalties once he has violated a previously given precept, but he cannot be punished with a censure.[51]

Besides the ordinary extra-judicial procedure examined above, there are two extraordinary methods of procedure pertinent to the office of the Provincial. One of these, namely the suspension *ex informata conscientia,* will be examined in the immediately following section of this Chapter. The other is the extraordinary procedure delineated in canon 2222, § 1. It has been seen that in delicts which involve a special gravity or a notable scandal, the Superior may proceed judicially to impose an appropriate penalty. It can happen, however, that a judicial procedure remains impossible. In such cases, then, since the public good demands that the culprit be punished as soon as possible, the Superior need not issue a previous warning as a basis for eventual punishment in the event of new violation, but in accordance with the prescriptions of canon 24 for the warranted juridical enforcement of precepts he may impose a just penalty immediately, since in the contemplated case, the public order and the punishment of the culprit demand immediate action.[52]

2. *The Extent of the Provincial's Coercive Power*

In the actual determination of the Provincial's coercive powers the particular law of the community must be a pri-

[51] Noval, *"art. cit."—JP,* III (1923), 37.
[52] Noval, *"art. cit."—JP,* III (1923), 38-40.

mary consideration, since the only limitation of his jurisdiction in the Code is that which is establshed by the particular law and his subjection to the General.[53] Judicial power in the province is ordinarily reserved to the Provincial.[54] In view of this power he possesses certain rights with regard to the declaration or imposition of penalties.

Although there is nothing in the Code which denies him legislative power,[55] it seems impractical to consider his office as one actually vested with that power. In view of the fact that such constitutions as the writer could examine reflected no instance of an actual grant of legislative power in the past to the Provincial, his office will be considered as one actually restricted in the matter of law-making. Such a position is completely in harmony with the juridic traditions of seven centuries of particular law. Thus the Provincial cannot enact laws with penalties attached to them as penal sanctions, nor can he attach penalties in the manner of law as penal sanctions to already existing laws. In view then of the limited legislative power in the office of the Provincial, the extent of the Provincial's coercive rights will be somewhat less than those of the local Ordinary in this respect, since explicit legislative power is attributed to the latter in canon 335, § 1. On the other hand, the coercive rights of the Provincial should be more extensive than those of the Local Superior in view of the broader scope of his jurisdiction. Accordingly a summary of his powers seems indicated as a practical application of what has been considered in the previous section.

A. Judicial Coercive Powers

Since the Provincial ordinarily enjoys judicial power in the province,[56] he has the right to take judicial cognizance of the delicts of his subjects which are not excluded by law from his competence. His competence is restricted with regard to matters pertaining to the Holy Office,[57] such as

[53] Can. 501, § 1.
[54] Can. 1579, § 1.
[55] Cf. *supra*, p. 37.
[56] Can. 1579, § 1.
[57] Can. 501, § 2.

heresy, schism, apostasy from the Faith,[58] or crimes rendering one suspect of heresy,[59] and also in those matters which are reserved to the General's competence by the particular law of the institute.

Since public delicts alone constitute matter for a formal judicial procedure in criminal cases, it remains for the Provincial to determine the nature of the delict and whether the essential requisites as above indicated are present to warrant a judicial procedure. He must provide that the requisite judicial procedure is accurately observed in the punishment of public delicts which have resulted from the violation of some given penal law.

It may sometimes be necessary for the Provincial to investigate a report or a well-founded rumor to determine whether an allegedly guilty subject should be cited judicially.[60] The purpose of this special investigation will be to determine the truth of the alleged charges. If they appear to be true as a result of this special investigation, the subject should be summoned. If the latter admits his guilt, the Provincial may decide to substitute a stern judicial rebuke (*correptio iudicialis*) for the judicial trial,[61] provided that the law permits such a measure in the case in question.[62]

Similarly, he may judge at any moment before the conclusion of a trial that the alternative method of dealing with the subject is more salutary, and thus may abandon the judicial process, provided again that the law permits him to make use of the stern judicial rebuke.[63] With regard to the rights of the Provincial in connection with the judicial punishment of delicts it is to be noted that they are exclusively his in virtue of the judicial competence attributed to him over the province. Particular law may, however, confer judicial competence upon the Local Superior, in

[58] Can. 2314, § 2.

[59] Can. 2316.

[60] Cans. 1939-1946.

[61] Cans. 1947-1953.

[62] Cf. can. 1948. This canon enumerates the cases in which a judicial rebuke does not suffice.

[63] Can. 1950.

which case these rights would be enjoyed by him within the limits of the competence conferred by the particular law.

B. Extra-judicial Coercive Powers

Since Local Superiors of exempt clerical communities are prelates and enjoy ecclesiastical jurisdiction as well as dominative power over their subjects,[64] the Provincial and the Local Superior enjoy certain coercive rights in a cumulative manner, whereas others are exclusively within the competence of the Provincial as Ordinary of the province. In the following enumeration of the coercive rights of the Provincial, it will be indicated which coercive rights are also enjoyed by the Local Superior, so that the coercive authority of the Provincial can be seen in its proper position in the jurisdictional hierarchy of the clerical exempt community.[65]

1) *Penal Remedies*

The Provincial, in view of his position as Ordinary, has the duty to deter delinquent subjects from further transgressions and culpable conduct, since the Church desires not only the punishment of the delinquent but also the prevention of delicts as well. To this end he can employ the penal remedies mentioned in canon 2306, namely, admonitions, rebukes (*correptio*), precepts, or surveillance (*vigilantia*), i.e., the appointment of some prudent subject to watch over a delinquent with a view to the prevention of further transgressions, or as an additional penal sanction against offenses of especial gravity.[66]

[64] Clancy, *The Local Superior*, pp. 30-36.

[65] The writer cites for his authority in the following enumeration of the coercive rights of the Provincial, Noval, "De Ratione Corrigendi et Puniendi"—*JP*, III (1923), 206-210.

[66] Ayrinhac-Lydon imply that the four penal remedies mentioned in canon 2306 represent perhaps an exhaustive list (*Penal Legislation in the New Code of Canon Law* [revised edition, New York: Benziger, 1936] pp. 135-136. But Vermeersch-Creusen (*Epitome*, III, n. 501) maintain that the listing need not be regarded as a comprehensive one.

Since the canons which treat of the penal remedies, i.e., canons 2306-2311, make repeated mention of the term *Ordinary,*[67] and only once use the term *Superior* in a context which implies the concept of an Ordinary,[68] it is safe to infer that the use of the coercive measures known as penal remedies, as also the employment of canonical penances,[69] is restricted to the Provincial or other Major Superiors, to the exclusion of the Local Superior.[70]

An admonition is given by the Provincial when a subject is in the proximate occasion of committing some offense, or when there exists a well-founded suspicion that an offense has been committed. Rebuke may be employed when scandal or serious disorder has arisen as a result of the delinquent's action, and it differs from an admonition in as much as it is administered when scandal or disorder has arisen.[71] The rebuke, however, is still a corrective measure, and therefore it should contain no threat of punishment, for the accompaniment of such a threat would make it partake of the nature of a precept.[72]

These measures, i.e., admonition and rebuke, may be administered publicly or secretly by the Provincial. Since his position in the province is not only that of an Ordinary, but also that of a pastor, his paternal solicitude will sometimes prompt a secret administration of them as a paternal means of correction. A record should be preserved, however, if

[67] Cf. cans. 2307; 2308; 2309, § 3; 2311.

[68] Can. 2309, § 6.

[69] Cans. 2312; 2313.

[70] Noval, *De Processibus,* I, n. 758, 4. Noval states, however, that even though the Local Superior cannot make use of the canonical precept in its nature of a penal remedy, he can nevertheless impose a precept which involves a certain command or prohibition to which may be attached a certain penalty which follows from the precept as something accessory to it (*ibid.*, n. 761; Clancy, *The Local Superior*, p. 193, note 77).

[71] Esswein, *The Extrajudicial Coercive Powers of Superiors*, p. 103.

[72] Esswein, *op. cit.*, p. 104; Coronata, *Institutiones*, IV, p. 278, n. 1841.

they are administered in secret. The precise words or document need not be kept, provided that a notation is preserved to indicate that the admonition or rebuke was administered secretly, and, if more than once, a notation of the number of times.[73]

Although moral certitude or even a sound probability will justify the administration of these measures secretly, canon 2309, § 3, states that a public rebuke can be administered only to a guilty party who has confessed the fault extrajudicially, or who has been convicted of it upon the word of two trustworthy witnesses who for just reasons will not appear against the culprit in a judicial process.[74] The public rebuke should, moreover, be made in the presence of two witnesses, or before a notary constituted by the Provincial,[75] or by registered mail which calls for a receipt acknowledging the fact of its reception.[76] In this way the gravity of the admonition or rebuke is further impressed upon the subject, and at the same time there will thus be provided a record which will furnish proof of obstinacy, and clear the way for further canonical penance or penalties.[77]

With regard to the administration of these measures, it is left to the judgment of the Provincial to determine the manner in which they are to be administered as well as to determine whether they shall be repeated one or more times.[78]

[73] Can. 2309, § 5; Esswein, *loc. cit.*; Noval, "De Ratione Corrigendi et Puniendi"—*JP*, III (1923), 206.

[74] Noval, *ibid.*, p. 207.

[75] Can. 503.

[76] Cans. 2309, § 2; 2143; Esswein, *loc. cit.*

[77] Esswein, *loc. cit.*; Cappello, *De Censuris*, n. 34, 5°; Noval, *ibid.*, p. 206.

[78] Can. 2309, § 6. In the event that a *ferendae sententiae* censure threatened in the law is to be inflicted, one admonition is sufficient, although under the old law three admonitions were required with an interval of two days, or at least one peremptory decree (Coronata, *Institutiones*, IV, p. 128, n. 1724). Esswein states that the law may contain a general threat of punishment, but the punishment is inflicted only in particular cases by the Superior. With regard to the

When admonition and rebuke have proved ineffective for the eliminating of serious faults or dangerous occasions, or when the Superior foresees that they will be disregarded, he may immediately proceed to the issuance of the canonical precept, which is a command enjoining the delinquent to do, or to refrain from doing, certain acts under pain of a clearly determined punishment. The canonical precept differs from the admonition and rebuke in that it contains an explicit threat of a penalty.

The Provincial can be guided by canons 24 and 2225 in the imposition of the precept in order to insure its continued duration. The precept, therefore, should be drawn up in writing, with mention of the preceptor's name, the name of the subject, the precept itself, and the penalty. If the penalty is to be a vindicative one, the duration of time for which it is imposed must be stated. The subject is to be cited in order that he may hear the injunction. Unless he has a defense to justify himself, the command of the Provincial, the cause of the precept, and the threatened penalty are to be read to him when he appears in the presence of two canonically qualified witnesses.[79] A record of the transaction is then to be signed and preserved in the archives by the Provincial.[80]

Instead of the oral announcement, the intimation of the precept may be made by means of a decree of the Provincial which will incorporate mention of the import of the precept and of the other details enumerated above, and also will bear the signature of the Provincial and of his notary, along with a notation of the place, day, month and year of the precept's

---

necessity of the canonical warning for the valid infliction of such a censure, he maintains that in view of canon 11 it is safe to hold that because of the *dubium iuris* this warning need not be regarded as a condition for the valid and effective infliction of the censure (*op. cit.* p. 105).

[79] Cans. 1756-1758.

[80] Ayrinhac-Lydon, *Penal Legislation in the New Code of Canon Law,* 137-139; Esswein, *op. cit.,* pp. 106-107.

issuance.[81] Adherence to either of these methods will effect a continued duration for the precept. For this reason, then, these two methods are the ordinary methods of procedure, although canon 2225 does not require a strict adherence to either form as a condition for validity.[82]

When a penal precept has been fortified by the Provincial in such a manner that its violation entails a *latae sententiae* penalty, then this penalty takes effect immediately with the violation of the precept, and no further admonition is required.[83] In view of a response of the Pontifical Commission for the Interpretation of the Code, the Provincial may proceed immediately to the infliction of a *ferendae sententiae* penalty when the precept which threatened this penalty has been violated.[84] However, if the delinqùent recedes from his contumacy before the *ferendae sententiae* censure has been imposed, he may no longer be penalized with the censure, whose purpose would have been that of punishing the contumacy of the delinquent, but the Provincial may nevertheless impose a vindicative penalty.[85]

Surveillance or vigilance, the last of the penal remedies enumerated in canon 2306, is dealt with in canon 2311, which states that if the gravity of the case demands it, and especially if the party in question is in danger of falling again into the same fault, the Ordinary may place him under observation or surveillance. Through this means the Provincial is empowered to provide in an exceptional manner against the further transgressions of a subject, or to increase the punishment of a subject whose grave transgressions warrant additional punishment.

[81] Esswein, *loc. cit.*

[82] Coronata, *Institutiones*, IV, p. 107, n. 1711; Cappello, *De Censuris*, n. 32; Esswein, *op. cit.*, p. 108.

[83] Can. 2242, § 2.

[84] PCI, 14 iul. 1922—*AAS*, XIV (1922), 330.

[85] Esswein, *op. cit.*, p. 108. If the Provincial nevertheless imposes a censure, the presumption is that the subject is still contumacious, and hence the censure must be regarded as effective in the external forum.

2) *Canonical Penances*

Besides the employment of the penal remedies as considered above, the Provincial, as Ordinary,[86] can make use of canonical penances as preventive measures against the occurrence of canonical delicts. Canonical penances are not to be confused with the practices of mortification of religious or with the penances imposed by the confessor in the tribunal of penance. Rather, they are works imposed by the Church in the external forum as a reparation for scandal given or for the restoration of the social order after it has been disturbed by delinquencies.[87]

They may be imposed as a substitute for a canonical penalty, so that the delinquent may escape severer penalties or be dispensed from penalties already incurred. They may be solemn or ordinary, public or private, according as the Provincial deems prudent. A guiding principle in the imposition of these and of other coercive measures within the competence of the Superior is that public penances may not be imposed for occult delinquencies.[88] In the moderated impostion of these penances the Provincial should attend more closely to the penitent's contrition than to the objective gravity and seriousness of the offense, and at the same time take due account of the condition and character of the person as well as of the various factors which attended the commission of the delict.[89]

Canon 2313 lists some of the principal penances that may be imposed. These are: the recitation of specified prayers; the making of pious pilgrimages or the performance of other works of piety; the observance of a special fast; the giving of alms for pious purposes; the entering upon a re-

[86] As was noted with regard to penal remedies, the almost exclusive use of the term *Ordinary* in the canons pertaining to penal remedies and canonical penances indicates that they are measures exclusively within the competence of the Provincial or Major Superior.

[87] Ayrinhac-Lydon, *Penal Legislation in the New Code of Canon Law,* p. 140.

[88] Can. 2312, § 2; Ayrinhac-Lydon, *loc. cit.*

[89] Can. 2312, § 3.

treat for some days in a religious house or pious institution. The second paragraph of canon 2313 confers on the Provincial the right to add penances to the penal remedies of admonition and rebuke according as he considers such measures prudent.

Finally, with regard to these measures as well as canonical penances, it is to be noted that, though their imposition is exclusively within the coercive rights of the Provincial and the scope of canon 1933, § 4, they are not strictly canonical penalties, but rather preventive measures, or in some cases substitutes for them, as is indicated in canon 2216, wherein the canonical penalties are distinguished from canonical penances and penal remedies.

3) *Penalties within the Provincial's extra-judicial competence*

Canon 1933, § 4, states that penal remedies, penances, excommunication, suspension and interdict may be inflicted by way of precept provided the offense is certain.[90] The preceptive application of such coercive measures, however, is limited to those cases which are expressly mentioned in canon 1933, § 4, and such measures can be applied only when they are enacted as a result of a precept.[91] Accordingly the ordinary extra-judicial competence of the Provincial is limited to the penalties enumerated in canon 1933, § 4, as being within his competence, and they can be applied only when in their nature of potential penalties they have been constituted *per modum praecepti*.

The penal remedies and canonical penances as mentioned in canon 1933, § 4, are within the Provincial's competence

[90] Cf. Esswein, *The Extrajudicial Coercive Powers of Ecclesiastical Superiors*, pp. 11-114, for a discussion of the various interpretations given to this canon and the conclusion that the restrictive view of Noval, adhered to in this section by the writer, is the most tenable.

[91] Noval, "De Ratione Corrigendi et Puniendi"—*JP*, II (1922), 155-156; Esswein, *loc. cit.;* Coronata, *Institutiones*, p. 378, n. 1453. Since this is the strict interpretation, it is, according to canon 2219, § 1, to be preferred.

as Ordinary. In keeping with the aim of this work, which is to differentiate the powers of the Provincial from those of the Local Superior, it is now proper to distinguish briefly which rights the Provincial possesses exclusively, and which rights he possesses cumulatively with the Local Superior.

Canon 2220, § 1, makes no distinction as to the type of penalty or as to the Superior capable of inflicting the penalty, provided, of course, that the Superior enjoys jurisdiction and that his preceptive power has not been restricted by the particular law. Comparing canons 2220, § 1, and 1933, § 4, one will note first of all that the superiority of the Provincial's competence is derivable from canon 1579, § 1. Ordinarily the Local Superior lacks judicial power, and therefore his employment of coercive measures *per modum praecepti* must in all of its attending phases remain of an extra-judicial character, whereas the Provincial may, when he has administered the penal precept in accordance with the conditions indicated in canons 24 and 2225, proceed in a judicial way to enforce compliance with it.

Secondly, the superiority of the Provincial's extra-judicial competence has already been noted with regard to canonical penances and penal remedies, the infliction of which is excluded from the authority of the Local Superior.

Thirdly, the Provincial, as Ordinary, enjoys exclusive competence in the province with regard to inflicting a suspension *ex informata conscientia,* since the inflicting of this penalty is reserved by the Code to Ordinaries.[92] He may inflict this extraordinary penalty whenever the delict of a subject is certain, but a judicial procedure is neither possible nor expedient. The suspension may be total or partial, but this should be clearly indicated.[93] If it is inflicted as a censure, the cause must be clearly stated to the subject; if it is inflicted as a vindicative penalty, the duration must be indicated.[94]

The inflicting of a suspension *ex informata conscientia* clearly connotes an extraordinary mode of procedure. This

[92] Can. 2186. [93] Can. 2186, §1. [94] Can. 2189, 2°.

method cannot be used lightly by the Provincial.[95] It is within the Provincial's competence, however, to decide when the inconvenience of the judicial process is sufficiently grave to justify the employment of this extraordinary remedy, but the inconvenience must bear a proper proportion to the suspension itself.[96] Canon 2191, § 3, offers examples of possible cases involving a sufficient reason for having recourse to the use of this remedy.

A detailed analysis of the suspension *ex informata conscientia* is not within the scope of this work. Yet it should be noted that the Provincial cannot inflict it licitly, or even validly, merely in consequence of private knowledge which does not allow of substantiation by proof that will bear a completely objective examination. Thus the secret, extra-judicial and extra-sacramental confession of the guilty party is not sufficient, since in the face of a denial of the confession, the Provincial lacks proof for the admissibility of his action.[97]

The suspension is truly a penalty, and can be imposed only for a delict. As a penalty it can be either medicinal or vindicative, but in case of doubt the legal presumption rests on the side of its medicinal character.[98] The determination of its nature, however, depends upon the Provincial. If he deems it better not to state the cause of the suspension, then he can inflict this suspension solely in the nature of a vindicative penalty, since otherwise the cause must be stated.[99]

It is to be inflicted by means of a written document bearing the proper date, expressly stating that the penalty is imposed as a suspension *ex informata conscientia,* and indicating its duration and scope.[100] Canon 2188, 2°, moreover,

[95] Cf. Murphy, *Suspension* EX INFORMATA CONSCIENTIA, The Catholic University of America Canon Law Studies, n. 76 (Washington, D.C.: The Catholic University of America, 1932), pp. 53-59.

[96] Bouix, *Tractatus de Judiciis Ecclesiasticis* (2 vols., Parisiis: 1862), II, 345.

[97] Murphy, *Suspension* EX INFORMATA CONSCIENTIA, pp. 87-90.

[98] Can. 2255, § 2. [99] Can. 2188, 2°. [100] Can. 2188, 1° - 3°.

warns the Ordinary to obstain from ever inflicting a perpetual suspension as a vindicative penalty. Authors agree that, when this suspension is inflicted as a vindicative penalty, its duration should not exceed six months.

Since the Provincial can apply extra-judicially only such penalties as are occasioned in consequence of the violation of a command or a prohibition which he or his predecessor has established *per modum praecepti,* neither he nor the Local Superior can impose a precept which threatens a *latae* or *ferendae sententiae* penalty in a matter already commanded or forbidden under penalty in the law itself.[101] *Latae sententiae* penalties threatened in the law itself take effect as soon as the law is transgressed,[102] but in some cases the public observance of the penalty may rightfully be deferred until the penalty has been declared as incurred.[103] If the penalties are threatened as *ferendae sententiae* penalties by the law itself, then the person concerned must be warned canonically and given time to repent.

In virtue of the exclusive judicial competence ordinarily enjoyed by the Provincial throughout the province,[104] he alone enjoys the power to inflict or apply these penalties as established in the law. Furthermore, in relation to the Local Superior, he has exclusive competence for issuing the canonical warning mentioned in canon 2307, which warning seems to be identical with that required in canon 2233, § 2, wherein it is stated that no censure is to be inflicted without a previous canonical warning.[105]

[101] In virtue of canon 2220, § 1, any Superior who enjoys the exercise of the power of jurisdiction can impose precepts, and therefore attach canonical penalties to them, unless this right has been restricted by the particular law. Therefore the Local Superior enjoys the power to inflict penalties *per modum praecepti* in so far as this right is not restricted by the common and the particular law.

[102] Cans. 2217, § 1, 2°; 2223, § 4.

[103] Cans. 2232, § 1 and 2223, § 4. Cf. also Clancy, *The Local Superior*, pp. 194-195.

[104] Can. 1579, § 1.

[105] Although the Local Superior is not competent to administer the

A final discussion among the authors should here be noted. The discussion deals with the character of the precepts issued by the Provincial or any other Superior when these precepts at the same time threaten a penalty in the event of their violation. If *latae sententiae* censures are threatened, then it seems that the absolution from these censures should not be considered as reserved unless that fact is explicitly established in the precept.[106] On the other hand, censures which are contracted in consequence of the violation of a penal precept are inflicted or imposed *ab homine*, and thus appear to be reserved under all circumstances.[107] The divergency between these two statements in the law has occasioned a *dubium iuris*. As a consequence, it seems safe to state that the incurred *latae sententiae* penalty which results from the violation of a particular precept is not reserved unless the Provincial or the Superior has, in connection with the issuing of the penal precept, specified expressly that upon being incurred, the threatened *latae sententiae* penalty is reserved to him for its absolution.[108]

By way of summarizing the extra-judicial coercive powers of the Provincial in exempt clerical religious institutes, one may state that the Provincial can:[109]

---

canonical warning thus required, he is nevertheless competent, in view of the response of the Pontifical Commission for the Interpretation of the Code (PCI, 14 iul. 1922—*AAS*, XIV [1922], 530), to issue a precept in connection with which he threatens a *ferendae sententiae* penalty which is to be inflicted in the event that the precept is violated. In such an instance there is no need of a new warning before the threatened penalty can be inflicted, provided, of course, that the violation of the penal precept is duly established by conclusive proof.

106 Can. 2245, § 4.

107 Cans. 2245, § 2; 2217, § 1, 3°.

108 Moriarty, *The Extraordinary Absolution from Censures*, The Catholic University of America Canon Law Studies, n. 113 (Washington, D. C.: The Catholic University of America, 1938), p. 196; Clancy, *The Local Superior*, p. 196.

109 Cf. Clancy, *The Local Superior*, pp. 196-197, for a parallel list of the extrajudicial coercive rights enjoyed by the Local Superior in exempt clerical religious communities.

(1) inflict (*infligere, applicare*) penal remedies and canonical penances for the prevention and punishment of transgressions;

(2) constitute or enact (*statuere*) *per modum praecepti* whatever canonical penalties the law allows to be invoked against the violation of an imposed precept;

(3) apply (*infligere, applicare*) the penalties which he has constituted, either by declaring that a *latae sententiae* penalty has been incurred, or by inflicting extra-judicially a *ferendae sententiae* penalty previously threatened in the precept in the event of its violation;

(4) apply the penalties similarly constituted by his predecessor, if they were constituted by means of a legitimate document or before two witnesses in accordance with the rule stated in canons 24 and 2225;

(5) punish with some just penalty any delict committed by one of his subjects, even though the law does not invoke any penalty, or even though the Superior in issuing his precept did not threaten any penalty, provided that the transgression gave rise to serious scandal or evinced a special heinousness or gravity; and

(6) inflict a suspension *ex informata conscientia.*

In relation to his own subjects the Local Superior enjoys the powers of the Provincial as enumerated above in nn. (2), (3), (4), and (5). The Provincial, however, in addition to the powers just enumerated, enjoys rights which derive from his judicial power. In virtue of these he can inflict whatever penalties require infliction by means of judicial process. Accordingly he can inflict *ferendae sententiae* penalties and declare *latae sententiae* penalties, even when these are constituted in the law. But he cannot establish by precept either *latae* or *ferendae sententiae* penalties for delicts which are already punishable in law, even if in the law the penalty be explicitly reserved to Ordinaries.[110]

[110] Esswein, *The Extrajudicial Coercive Powers of Superiors*, p. 128.

CONCLUSIONS

The following conclusions are offered as justified by the present study:

1. The office of the Provincial is an institute originating almost with the rise of the Mendicant Orders of the thirteenth century as an instrument of centralized government within a religious institute.

2. The quasi-episcopal power conceded to the Provincial and other Regular prelates was essentially jurisdiction like that of a bishop. Its purpose was to enable clerical exempt Superiors to fill the rôle of proper pastors over their subjects lest the papal grants of exemption from the jurisdiction of the local Ordinaries redound to the spiritual detriment of the religious.

3. Although no distinction between the quasi-episcopal powers of the Superiors constituting the Regular hierarchy of government was indicated in the common law, the power of the Provincial was soon regarded as analogous to that of a local Ordinary, rather than to that of a Local Superior, whose office was considered a minor one in relation to that of the Provincial.

4. Despite the fact that the Code has clarified the Provincial's position as that of a Major Superior with the rank of an Ordinary, one must always consult the particular law of the Order for determining the powers of a Provincial in a particular Order, since many of the canons make broad allowances for the prescriptions of the particular law.

5. The following principles will be helpful in determining the spheres of jurisdictional competence of the Provincial and the Local Superior when the particular law is silent and the Code speaks generically of Superiors:

a) when the nature of the case indicates the exclusive competence of the Provincial or some other Major Superior, the Minor Local Superior cannot interfere;

b) matters exceeding the bounds of local interest and concern are, as major issues, reserved by their very nature to the Provincial, unless their gravity and universal importance to the Order at large reserves them to the Superior General;

c) when one Superior has begun lawfully to act in a particular case, the jurisdiction of other Superiors who were equally competent is inoperative, unless sufficiently important circumstances or reasons justify the intervention of a higher Superior;

d) a just reason or cause will permit the higher Superior to suspend or restrict the exercise of the rights of the subordinate Superior, provided that these rights are not placed by law, privilege, or custom within the exclusive competence of the subordinate; but such intervention cannot be adopted as a customary practice or policy by the higher Superior.

6. Legislative competence is not incompatible with the office of the Provincial. In view, however, of the pre-Code jurisprudence and the silence of the Code, its actual possession by the Provincial depends entirely upon the concession of such power by the particular law of the institute.

7. The Provincial enjoys certain dispensatory powers over the general laws of the Church and over the particular laws of the Order, but not over the essential elements of the religious life.

8. As the executive head of the province, the Provincial has grave obligations to promote personally the regular observance of the province and the common good of the Order.

9. Matters pertaining to the reception and dismissal of postulants and novices, to their training, to their profession, and to their transfer within the province clearly exceed the bounds of the authority of the Local Superior, and are thus within the exclusive competence of the Provincial or of any other Superior designated by the particular law.

10. The permission of the Provincial, according to the norms of the particular law, is required in all matters of extraordinary temporal administration in the province. Furthermore, the Provincial has the obligation to supervise the administration and government of the houses of his province according to the norms of the particular law.

11. Matters pertaining to the ordination of subjects, to their initial approval as confessors and preachers, or to their presentation for diocesan offices or duties are matters for the Provincial's judgment, unless the particular law specifies otherwise. With regard to these questions, the pre-Code analogy between the jurisdictional offices of the Provincial and of the local Ordinary is especially evident.

12. The pre-Code privilege to dispense a subject from the disqualification for office in an Order in view of the subject's status of illegitimacy is unrevoked and the Provincial with his advisers may still grant this dispensation, unless the particular law has reserved the privilege to the General.

13. The coercive jurisdiction of the Provincial is more extensive than that of the Local Superior in the following points:

(a) it is more inclusive in that it extends to all the members of the province, whereas that of the Local Superior is confined to the subjects under his jurisdiction;

(b) in virtue of his judicial power the Provincial can inflict whatever penalties require a judicial procedure for their infliction; and

(c) the Provincial, as Ordinary, can employ penal remedies, canonical penances, and the extraordinary penal measure, namely, the suspension *ex informata conscientia.*

However, his jurisdiction in these matters, like that of the Local Superior, is limited to the application or infliction of the penalties listed in canon 1933, § 4, when by precept he has threatened their infliction or application in the event that the precept has later been violated. Furthermore, the Provincial cannot by precept establish or constitute any penalties for delicts which already are punished in law with reserved penalties, for in principle the law is disinclined to all duplication of penal jeopardy.

BIBLIOGRAPHY

SOURCES

Acta Apostolicae Sedis, Commentarium Officiale, Romae, 1909–.

Acta Sanctae Sedis, 41 vols., Romae, 1865-1908.

Augustinus a Virgine Maria, *Compendium Privilegiorum Omnium Religionum*, Lugdumi, 1661.

Bullarium Carmelitanum, 4 vols., Vols. I-II, ed. a E. Monsignano, 1715-1718; Vols. III-IV, ed. I. A. Ximenez, 1768, Romae.

Bullarium Ordinis Eremitarum S. Augustini, ed. L. Empoli, Romae, 1628.

Bullarium Ordinis FF. Praedicatorum, ed. a T. Ripoll, recognitum a A. Bremond, 8 vols., Romae, 1729-1740.

Bullarum Diplomatum et Privilegiorum Sanctorum Romanorum Pontificum Taurinensis Editio, 24 vols. et Appendix, Augustae Taurinorum, 1857-1872.

Bullarii Romani Continuatio Summorum Pontificum, 19 vols. in 20, Prati, 1835-1857.

Canones et Decreta Sacrosancti Oecumenici Concilii Tridentini, editio novissima ad fidem optimorum exemplarium castigate impressa, XIX Reimpressio Stereotypa, Taurini, 1913.

Codex Iuris Canonici Pii X Pontificis Maximi iussu digestus Benedicti XV auctoritate promulgatus, Romae: Typis Polyglottis Vaticanis, 1917.

Codicis Iuris Canonici Fontes cura Emi Petri Card. Gasparri editi, 9 vols., Romae (postea Civitate Vaticana): Typis Polyglottis Vaticanis, 1923-1939. (Vols. VII-IX cura et studio Emi Iustiniani Card. Serédi.)

Collectanea in Usum Secretariae Sacrae Congregationis Episcoporum et Regularium, cura A. Bizzarri Archiepiscopi Philippensis Secretarii edita, Romae, 1885.

Constitutiones Ordinis Fratrum Beatissimae Virginis Mariae de Monte Carmelo iussu Revmi P. Eliae Magennis Prioris Generalis in Lucem Editae praemissa Regula S. Alberti, Romae: Typis Polyglottis Vaticanis, MCMXXX.

Corpus Iuris Canonici, editio Lipsiensis secunda post Aemilii Ludovici Richteri curas ad librorum manu scriptorum et editionis Romanae fidem recognovit et adnotatione critica instruxit Aemilius Friedberg, Lipsiae, 1879-1881.

Decreta Authentica Congregationis Sacrorum Rituum, 6 vols., Romae, 1898-1927.

Enchiridion Clericorum, Documenta Ecclesiae Sacrorum Alumnis Instituendis, Typis Polyglottis Vaticanis: venit apud Herder, S.A.L.E.R., MCMXXXVIII.

Jaffé, Philippus, *Regesta Pontificum Romanorum ab condita Ecclesia ad annum post Christum natum MCXCVIII*, 2. ed., correctam et auctam auspiciis Gulielmi Wattenbach curaverunt S. Loewenfeld, F. Kaltenbrunner, P. Ewald, 2 vols. in 1, Lipsiae, 1885-1888.

Mansi, J. D., *Sacrorum Conciliorum Nova et Amplissima Collectio*, 53 vols. in 60, Parisiis, Arnhem, Lipsiae, 1901-1927.

Monumenta Historica Carmelitana, Vol. I, Continens Antiquas Ordinis Constitutiones, ed. a Benedicto Zimmerman, Lirinae, 1907.

Normae secundum quas S. Congr. Episcoporum et Regularium procedere solet in Approbandis Novis Institutis Votorum Simplicium, Romae, Typis S. C. de Propoganda Fidei, 1901.

Potthast, Augustus, *Regesta Pontificum Romanorum, inde ab A. post Christum natum MCXCVIII ad A. MCCCIV*, 2 vols., Berolini, 1874-1875.

Schroeder, Henry, J., *Canons and Decrees of the Council of Trent*, Original text with English Translation, St. Louis: Herder, 1941.

———, ———, *Disciplinary Decrees of the General Councils*, Text, Translation, and Commentary, St. Louis: Herder, 1937.

Reference Works

Acta Congressus Iuridici Internationalis, 5 vols., Romae: Apud Custodiam Librariam, Pont. Instituti Utriusque Iuris, 1935-1937.

Alphonsus Liguori, St., *Theologia Moralis*, ed. absolutissima, 9 vols., Vesontione, 1832.

Appeltern, V., *Compendium Praelectionum Iuris Regularis*, editio altera aucta et emendata, Parisiis, 1913.

Augustine, Charles, *A Commentary on the New Code of Canon Law*, 8 vols., Vol. II, 4. ed., 1923; Vol. III, 5. ed., 1938; Vol. IV, 2. ed., 1921; Vol. VI, 2. ed., 1923; Vol. VIII, 1922, St. Louis: Herder.

Ayrinhac, H. A.—Lydon, P. J., *Penal Legislation in the New Code of Canon Law*, revised edition, New York: Benziger, 1936.

Bachofen, Augustinus, *Compendium Juris Regularium*, New York, 1903.

Balzer, Ralph, *The Computation of Time in a Canonical Novitiate*, The Catholic University of America Canon Law Studies, n. 212, Washington, D. C.: The Catholic University of America Press, 1945.

Berutti, Christophorus, *Institutiones Iuris Canonici*, 6 vols. in 7, Vol. III, *De Religiosis*, Taurini-Romae: Marietti, 1936.

Beste, Udalricus, *Introductio in Codicem*, editio altera, Collegeville, Minn.: St. John's Abbey Press, 1944.

Bonaventura, St., *Doctoris Seraphici S. Bonaventurae Opera Omnia*, 11 vols., prope Florentiam, ad Claras Aquas (Quarrachi), 1882-1902; Vol. VIII, ed. Aloysii Lauer, 1898.

Biederlack, J.—Führich, M., *De Religiosis*, Oeniponte: Rauch, 1919.

Blat, Albertus, *Commentarium Textus Codicis Iuris Canonici*, 5 vols. in 6, Romae: Lib. II, *De Personis*, 2. ed., 1921; Lib. III, *De Rebus*, Pars I, 1920; Partes II-VI, 1923, 2. ed., 1934; Lib. IV, *De Processibus*, 1927; Lib. V, *De Delictis et Poenis*, 1924.

Bouix, Dominicus, *Tractatus de Jure Regularium*, 3. ed., 2 vols., Parisiis, 1883.

———, ———, *Tractatus de Judiciis Ecclesiasticis*, 3. ed., 2 vols., Parisiis, 1883.

Bouscaren, T. Lincoln, *The Canon Law Digest*, 2 vols., and Supplement, 1941, Milwaukee: Bruce Publishing Co., 1923-1941.

Capobianco, Pacificus, *Privilegia et Facultates Ordinis Fratrum Minorum*, Salerno: 1946.

Cappello, Felix, *Tractatus Canonico-Moralis de Sacramentis*, 3 vols. in 6; Vol. I, 4. ed., *De Sacramentis in Genere*, 1945; Vol. II, Pars, I, 4. ed., *De Poenitentia*, 1944; Vol. II, Pars III, *De Sacra Ordinatione*, 1935; Vol. III, editio altera emendata et aucta, *De Extrema Unctione*, 1942; Vol. III, Pars I-II, 4. ed., *De Matrimonio*, 1939.

———, ———, *Tractatus Canonico-Moralis de Censuris iuxta Codicem Iuris Canonici*, 3. ed. recognita et emendata, Taurinorum Augustae: Marietti, 1933.

———, ———, *Summa Iuris Canonici in Usum Scholarum Concinnata*, 3 vols., Romae: apud Aedes Universitatis Gregorianaė, Vols., I et II, 3. ed., 1938-1939.

———, ———, *Summa Iuris Publici Ecclesiastici*, editio altera, Romae, 1928.

Chelodi, Ioannes, *Ius de Personis iuxta Codicem Iuris Canonici*, ed. altera a Sac. Ernesto Bertagnolli recognita et aucta, Tridenti: Libr. Edit. Tridentum, 1927.

Clancy, Patrick, *The Local Religious Superior*, The Catholic University of America Canon Law Studies, n. 175, Washington, D.C.: The Catholic University of America Press, 1943.

Coronata, Matthaeus Conte a, *Institutiones Iuris Canonici ad Usum Utriusque Cleri et Scholarum*, 5 vols., Taurini: Marietti, 1936-1945; Vol. I, ed. altera et emendata, 1939; Vol. III, ed. altera aucta et emendata, 1941; Vol. IV, ed. altera et emendata, 1945.

Creusen, J., *Réligieux et Réligieuses d'après le Droit Ecclésiastique* 3. ed., Paris: Beauchesne, 1924.

Creusen, J., *Religious Men and Women in the Code*, translated by

Edward Garesché, 4, Eng. ed. by Adam Ellis, Milwaukee: Bruce Publishing Co., 1942.

Davis, H., *Moral and Pastoral Theology,* 4 vols., New York. Sheed and Ward, Inc., 1935.

Doheny, William J., *Practical Problems in Church Finance,* Milwaukee: Bruce Publishing Co., 1941.

Donatus, Hyacinthus, *Rerum Regularium Quadripartita Praxis Resolutoria,* 4 vols., Neapoli, 1652-1661.

Esswein, Anthony A., *The Extrajudicial Coercive Powers of Ecclesiastical Superiors,* The Catholic University of America Canon Law Studies, n. 127, Washington, D. C.: The Catholic University of America Press, 1941.

Fanfani, Ludovicus, *De Iure Parochorum ad Normam Codicis Iuris Canonici,* Taurini-Romae: Marietti, 1925.

———, *De Iure Religiosorum ad Normam Codicis Iuris Canonici,* 2. ed., Taurini-Romae: Marietti, 1925.

Ferraris, Lucius, *Prompta Bibliotheca Canonica, Iuridica, Moralis, Theologica, necnon Ascetica, Polemica, Rubricistica, Historica,* 11 vols., Venetiis, 1782-1794.

Goyeneche, Servus, *Iuris Canonici Summa Principia de Religiosis,* Roma: Tip. Pol. "Cuore di Maria", 1938.

Hefele, Carolus,—Leclercq, Henricus, *Histoire des Conciles,* 10 vols. in 19, Paris: Letouzey et Ané, 1907-1938.

Holzapfel, H., *Manuale Historiae Ordinis Fratrum Minorum,* Friburgi Brisgoviae, 1909.

Keene, Michael, *Religious Ordinaries and Canon 198,* The Catholic University of America Canon Law Studies, n. 135, Washington, D. C.: The Catholic University of America Press, 1942.

Lega, Michael, *Praelectiones in Textum Iuris Canonici, De Iudiciis Ecclesiasticis,* 4 vols., Romae, 1896-1901.

Lezana, Johannes Baptista, *Mare Magnum Ordinum Praedicatorum, Minorum, Eremitarum Sancti Augustini, Carmelitarum cum ipsorum Regula, Servitarum et Minorum,* 1 vol. in 2 partes, Venetiis, 1653.

———, *Summa Quaestionum Regularium seu de Casibus Conscientiae ad Personas Religiosas utriusque Sexus valde Spectantibus,* 2 vols. in 4 partes, Venetiis, MDCLIV.

McCormick, Robert, *Confessors of Religious,* The Catholic University of America Canon Law Studies, n. 33, Washington, D. C.: The Catholic University of America, 1926.

McManus, James, *The Administration of Temporal Goods in Religious Institutes,* The Catholic University of America Canon Law Studies, n. 109, Washington, D. C.: The Catholic University of America, 1937.

Many, S., *Praelectiones de Sacra Ordinatione*, Parisiis, 1905.

Maroto, Philippus, *Institutiones Iuris Canonici ad Normam Novi Codicis*, 2 vols., Romae-Barcinone-Matriti, 1919; Vol. I, 3. ed., 1921.

Michiels, Gommarus, *Normae Generales Iuris Canonici*, 2 vols., Lublin, Polonia: Universitas Catholica, 1932.

———, ———, *Principia Generalia de Personis in Ecclesia*, Lublin, Polonia: Universitas Catholica, 1932.

Molitor, Raphael, *Religiosi Iuris Capita Selecta*, Ratisbonae, Romae, Neo-Eboraci et Cincinnati: Pustet, 1909.

Moriarty, Francis, *The Extraordinary Absolution from Censures*, The Catholic University of America Canon Law Studies, n. 113, Washington, D. C.: The Catholic University of America, 1938.

Murphy, Edwin, *Suspension* EX INFORMATA CONSCIENTIA, The Catholic University of America Canon Law Studies, n. 76, Washington, D. C.: The Catholic University of America, 1932.

Noldin, H.,—Schönegger, A., *De Censuris*, 31. ed., Oeniponte: Rauch, 1936.

Noval, Josephus, *Commentarium Codicis Iuris Canonici*, lib. IV, *De Processibus*, 2 vols., Pars I, De Iudiciis, 1920; Pars II, *De Causis Beatificationis Servorum Dei et Canonizationis Beatorum*, 1932; Pars IV, *De Modo Procedendi in Nonnullis Expediendis Negotiis vel Sanctionibus Poenalibus Applicandis*, 1932, Augustae Taurinorum-Romae, Marietti.

O'Brien, Joseph D., *The Exemption of Religious in Canon Law*, Milwaukee: Bruce Publishing Co., 1943.

Oesterle, Gerardus, *Praelectiones Iuris Canonici*, Vol. I, Romae: apud Collegium S. Anselmi, 1931.

Ojetti, Benedictus, *Commentarium in Codicem Iuris Canonici*, 4 vols., Romae: apud Aedes Universitatis Gregorianae, 1927-1931.

Ottaviani, Alaphridus, *Compendium Iuris Publici Ecclesiastici ad Usum Auditorum S. Theologiae*, Romae: Typis Polyglottis Vaticanis, 1936.

———, *Institutiones Iuris Publici Ecclesiastici*, 2 vols., Romae: apud Aedes Facultatis Iuridicae ad S. Apollinaris, 1925.

Passerinus, Petrus Maria de Sextula, *De Hominum Statibus et Officiis*, ed. nova, 3 vols., Lucae, 1732.

———, *Tractatus de Electione Canonica*, ed. post Romanam prima in Germania, Coloniae Agrippinae, 1694.

Pejška, Josephus, *Ius Canonicum Religiosorum*, 3. ed., Friburgi Brisgoviae: Herder, 1927.

Piatus Montensis, *Praelectiones Iuris Regularis*, 3. ed., 2 vols., Tornaci, 1906.

Prümmer, Dominicus, *Manuale Iuris Ecclesiasticae*, Tom. II, *Ius Regularium Speciale*, Friburgi Brisgoviae, 1907.

———, *Manuale Iuris Canonici in Usum Scholarum*, 6. ed., Friburgi-Brisgoviae: Herder, 1938.

Raymundus de Pennafort, St., *Summa*, ed. nova, Veronae, 1744.

Reiffenstuel, Anacletus, *Jus Canonicum Universum*, 5 vols. in 7, Parisiis, 1864-1870.

Reilly, Thomas F., *Visitation of Religious*, The Catholic University of America Canon Law Studies, n. 112, Washington, D.C.: The Catholic University of America Press, 1942.

Riesner, Albert Joseph, *Apostates and Fugitives from Religious Institutes*, The Catholic University of America Canon Law Studies, n. 168, Washington, D. C.: The Catholic University of America Press, 1942.

Rodericus, Emmanuel, *Nova Collectio et Compilatio Privilegiorum Apostolicorum Regularium Mendicantium et non Mendicantium praesertim in quibus ipsae Religiones Communicant*, editio ultima, Antverpiae, 1623.

Schaaf, Valentine, *The Cloister*, The Catholic University of America Canon Law Studies, n. 13, Washington, D.C.: The Catholic University of America, 1921.

Schaefer, Timotheus, *De Religiosis ad Normam Codicis Iuris Canonici*, 3. ed., Romae: S.A.L.E.R., 1940.

Schmalzgrueber, Franciscus, *Ius Ecclesiasticum Universum*, 5 vols. in 12, Romae, 1843-1845.

Shuhler, Ralph, *Privileges of Regulars to Absolve and Dispense*, The Catholic University of America Canon Law Studies, n. 186, Washington, D.C.: The Catholic University of America Press, 1943.

Smith, Mariner, *The Penal Law for Religious*, The Catholic University of America Canon Law Studies, n. 98, Washington, D.C.: The Catholic University of America, 1935.

Suarez, Franciscus, *Opera Omnia*, ed. nova, 28 vols., Tom. I-IV a D. M. André; Tom. V-XXVI a Carolo Berton, Parisiis, 1856-1878.

Thomas Aquinas, St., *Doctoris Angelici Opera Omnia iussu impensaque Leonis XIII, P. M. edita*, Romae, 1882- —; *Summa Theologica*, Romae, 1888-1906.

Van Etten, Gregorius, *Compendium Privilegiorum Regularium Praecipue Ordinis Eremitarum S. Augustini*, Romae, 1900.

Van Hove, A., *Commentarium Lovaniense in Codicem Iuris Canonici*, Vol. I, Tom. II, *De Legibus Ecclesiasticis*, Mechliniae-Romae: Dessain, 1930; Vol. I, Tom. I, *Prolegomena*, Mechliniae-Romae; Dessain, 1928.

Verhoeven, Marianus, *De Praxi a Parochis Observanda in Celebratione Missae pro Populo,* Hasseleti, 1849.

Vermeersch, A.,-Creusen, J., *Epitome Iuris Canonici cum Commentariis ad Scholas et ad Usum Privatum,* 5. ed., 3 vols., Mechliniae-Romae: Dessain, 1933-1936.

Vermeersch, A., *De Religiosis Institutis et Personis Tractatus Canonico-Moralis ad Recentissimas Leges Exactus,* 2 vols., Romae et Ratisbonae: 1902.

———, —., *Theologiae Moralis Principia, Responsa, Consilia,* 4 vols., Romae: 1922-1924.

Vromant, G., *De Bonis Ecclesiae temporalibus,* Louvain, 1934.

Wernz, Franciscus X., *Ius Decretalium ad usum Praelectionum in Scholis Textus Canonici sive Iuris Decretalium,* 2. ed., 6 vols. in 7, Romae-Prati, 1906-1913.

Wernz, F. -Vidal, Petrus, *Ius Canonicum ad Codicis Normam Exactum,* 7 toms, in 8 vols., Romae: apud Aedes Universitatis Gregorianae, 1923-1938; Tom. II, *De Personis,* 2. ed., 1928; Tom. III, *De Religiosis,* 1933; Tom. IV, Pars I-II, *De Rebus,* 1934-1935.

Articles

Canuto, A., "De regimine domus studiorum in religione clericali exempta ad normam can. 588,"—*Apollinaris,* IX (1936), 19-39.

Denifle, H., "Die Constitutionen des Predigerordens in der Redaction Raimonds von Peñafort",—*Archiv für Literatur und Kirchengeschichte des Mittelalters,* V (1889), 530-564.

Frison, B., "Ex-Seminarian and Novice: A Clarification,"—*The Jurist,* VI (1946), 416-418.

Goyeneche, S., "Consultationes",—II (1921), 263-272; III (1922), 53-58; 217-219; 263-272; IV (1923), 47-52; 120-122; VI (1925), 203-208; VII (1926), 37-42; 249-254; 455-456; IX (1928), 427; XII (1931), 130-133; 443-449.

Hannan, J., "Ex-Seminarian and Novice,"—*The Jurist,* II (1942), 380-382.

Heston, E., "Stable Capital in Temporal Administration,"—*The Jurist,* II (1942), 120-133.

Hilling, N., "Uber den Gebrauch des Ausdrucks *iurisdictio* im kanonischen Recht während der ersten Hälfte des Mittelalters,"—*AKKR,* CXVIII (1938), 165-170.

Jombart, E., "Subordination dans l'Exercice de l'Autorité,"—*Révue des Communautés Réligieuses,* XI (1935), 69-74.

Larraona, A., "Commentarium Codicis,"—*CpR,* II (1921), 134-139; 341; III (1922), 133-138; V (1924), 417-436; VII (1926), 239-248; 296-300; VIII (1927), 166-176; XIII (1932), 184-195; XIV (1933), 169-182.

———, —, "Consultationes,"—I (1920), 365-374; II (1921), 181-186; 218-220; 296; 340-342.

———, —, "Responsa Minora,"—II (1921), 114-115.

———, —, "De Potestate Dominativa Publica in Iure Canonico,"—*Acta Congressus Iuridici Internationalis*, IV, 145-180.

Maroto, P., "Annotationes,"—*CpRM*, XVI (1936), 218-231.

Noval, J., "De Ratione Corrigendi et Puniendi sive in Judicio sive extra Jure Codicis J. C.,"—*JP*, II (1922), 147-156; III (1923), 36-40; 204-210.

Piontek, C., "Choir Duty and Conventual Mass in Religious Communities"—*The Homiletic and Pastoral Review*, XLIII (1943), 602-608.

———, —, "An Application of the Principles"—*The Homiletic and Pastoral Review*, XLIII (1943), 925-931.

Roberti, F., "Quaenam poenae applicari possint per modum praecepti," —*Apollinaris*, IV (1931), 294-300.

Toso, A., "De Conceptu Legis,"—*JP*, IV (1924), 34.

Van de Kerckhove, M., "De Notione Jurisdictionis in Jure Romano,"—*JP*, XVI (1936), 49-65.

———, —, "De Notione Jurisdictionis apud Decretistas et Priores Decretalistas"—*JP*, XVIII (1938), 10-14.

Voltas, P., "Consultationes,"—*CpR*, II (1921), 218-225.

———, —, "De Reservatione Episcopali quoad Regulares,"—*CpR*, III (1922), 69-77.

Vermeersch, A., "Dissertationes et Quaesita,"—*Periodica*, X (1921), (36).

———, —, "Annotationes,"—*Periodica*, XI (1922), 28.

———, —, "Annotationes,"—*Periodica*, XII (1923), 156.

Periodicals

Analecta Iuris Pontificii, Romae: 1855-1869: Parisiis: 1872-1891.

Apollinaris, Romae, 1928- —.

Archiv für katholisches Kirchenrecht, Innsbruck, 1857-1861; Mainz, 1862- —.

Commentarium pro Religiosis, Romae, 1920- —;ab anno 1935: *Commentarium pro Religiosis et Missionariis*.

Homiletic and Pastoral Review, The, New York, 1900- —.

Jurist, The, Washington, D. C., 1941- —.

Jus Pontificium, Romae, 1921- —.

Nouvelle Révue Théologique, Paris, 1869- —.

Periodica de Re Canonica et Morali utili praesertim Religiosis et Missionariis, Brugis, 1905- —; ab anno 1927; *Periodica de Re Canonica, Morali, Liturgica*.

Révue des Communautés Réligieuses, Enghien, Belgique, 1925- —.

Abbreviations

AAS— *Acta Apostolicae Sedis.*
AKKR— *Archiv für katholisches Kirchenrecht.*
ASS— *Acta Sanctae Sedis.*
Bull. Carm.— *Bullarium Carmelitanum.*
Bull. Praed.— *Bullarium Ordinis FF. Praedicatorum.*
Bull. Rom. Taur.— *Bullarum Diplomatum et Privilegiorum Romanorum Taurinensis Editio.*
CpR— *Commentarium pro Religiosis.*
CpRM— *Commentarium pro Religiosis et Missionariis.*
Constitutiones O. Carm.— *Constitutiones Ordinis Fratrum Beatissimae Virginis de Monte Carmelo.*
Fontes— *Codicis Iuris Canonici Fontes* cura .... Gasparri editi.
Hefele— *Histoire des Conciles.*
JP— *Jus Pontificium.*
Mansi— *Sacrorum Conciliorum Nova et Amplissima Collectio.*
PCI—Pontificia Commissio ad Codicis Canones authentice interpretandos.
Periodica— *Periodica de Re Canonica et Morali utili praesertim Religiosis et Missionariis.*
Regesta— Potthast, *Regesta Pontificum Romanorum.*
S. C. C.— Sacra Congregatio Concilii.
S. C. de Prop. Fide— Sacra Congregatio de Propaganda Fide.
S. C. Ep. et Reg.— Sacra Congregatio Episcoporum et Regularium.
S. C. S. Off.— Sacra Congregatio Sancti Officii.
S. R. C.— Sacrorum Rituum Congregatio.
S. C. de Rel.— Sacra Congregatio de Religiosis.

ALPHABETICAL INDEX

Absence,
  from Provincial residence, 62.
Accusation,
  judicial, 237.
Acquisition,
  of temporal goods, 163.
Administration,
  of temporal goods,
    acts of extraordinary, 167, 170, 175;
    acts of ordinary, 167, 172;
    of individual houses, 169, 171;
    of the province, 172;
    penalties for violations in, 180;
    permission of General in, 173;
    permission of Provincial in, 170.
Admonition,
  canonical,
    censures and, 237, 247 note 78;
    dismissal and, 162;
    penal remedy, 245.
Alienation,
  definition of, 168;
  liciety of, 173;
  Provincial and, 173, 175;
  sanctions for violations of, 180;
  validity of, 173.
Alms,
  solicitation of, 165.
Altar,
  of Blessed Sacrament, 226;
  outside of sacred place, 225;
  privileged, 225;
  reconsecration of, 224.
Annuities, 174.
Anticipation,
  of renewal of vows, 101.
Apostate religious, 155.
Appointment,
  of Provincial, 28.
Approval,
  of confessors, 137, 187, 193, cf. Confessor, Preacher.
Assistance,
  to diocesan clergy, 137;
    Local Superior and, 138;
    necessity of, 138.
Attestation of freedom,
  before profession, 98.
Authority,
  precepts and, 37;
  Provincial and,
    dominative power, 16;
    jurisdictional power, 15;
  society and, 10.

Baptism,
  sponsor at, 182.
Beatification,
  process of, 60.
Benediction of Blessed Sacrament, 226.
Bequests, 164.
Bishop,
  coercive power of, 203 note 97;
  exemption from authority of, 4;
  proper, for ordination, 216;
  role in,
    appointment of,
      confessors of religious, 197;
      parochial vicars, 142;
      preachers, 229;
      religious pastor, 142;
    permission for investments, 177;
    solicitation of alms, 166.
Blessed Sacrament,
  Benediction of, 226;
  custody of, 225;
  visits to, 226.

Blessing,
of altars, 222;
of sacred places, 222;
of sacred vessels, 80.
Bonds,
issuance of, 174.
Books,
censorship and prohibition of, 135;
dispensation for prohibited, 49.

Candidate for Provincialate,
obligation to accept office, 29;
qualities of, 25.
Canonical Penances, 250.
Canonization,
process of, 60.
Capital,
alienation of, 173, 175;
investment of, 175;
stable and unstable, 168.
Care of souls,
assistance to diocese in, 137.
Cases,
moral and liturgical, 107.
Celebret, 184.
Censorship of books, 135.
Censures,
latae sententiae, 203;
privileges of Regulars and, 203 note 97;
reserved, 198, 201, 202.
Chaplain,
jurisdiction for confessions and, 80;
of exempt nuns, 80.
Chapter,
general,
dominative power of, 14;
legislative authority of, 34.
Choir obligations,
Conventual Mass and, 131, 133.
Churches of religious, 140.
Cloister,
absence from, 117;
change of limits of, 122;
custody of, 117;
external works and, 118;
life outside of, 119;
limits of, 115;
penalties for violation of, 121.
Coercive power,
existence of, 232;
extent of, 235;
judicial rights and, 236;
measures of,
judicial, 236;
extrajudicial, 238;
modes of use of, 239;
of Provincial,
extent of, 242;
extrajudicial rights of, 245;
judicial rights of, 243;
of Provincial and Local Superior, 252;
penalties within Provincial's authority, 252;
purposes of, 238;
summary of Provincial's rights, 256;
suspension, 253.
Common life,
necessity of, 103;
notion of, 112;
penalties for violation of, 113.
Communion,
frequent, 127.
Confession,
nuns and, 196;
religious and, 195, 197;
weekly, 126;
seculars and, 197.
Confessor,
approbation of and licit action of, 194;
approval of, 187, 193;
irregularities and, 210;
nuns and, 196;
ordinary, 195;

privileges of Regular, 201.
Confirmation,
sponsors at, 182.
Constitutions,
authority of Provincial and, 6;
limitation of authority in, 16;
period of postulancy in, 84;
Superiors and, 20.
Constitutions,
Carmelite,
approval of confessors, 189 note 31;
censures, 55;
delegation of jurisdiction, 195 note 58;
dispensation from illegitimacy, 17;
removal of Local Superiors, 233 note 6;
temporal goods, 166 note 20;
visitation, 72.
Controversies,
judicial,
between house and subject, 58;
between houses of province, 57;
between subjects in province, 57;
between two provinces, 58.
Conventual Mass,
obligation of, 131
Cooperatores vicarii, 144.
Corner-stone, 223.
Council,
advisory body, 76, 90;
authority of, 74;
convocation of, 76;
deliberation in common and, 75;
dubium iuris on action of, 76, 89;
declaration of dismissal, 158;
erection of parish and, 141;
investment, 176;
legitimacy of status and, 211 note 127;
necessity and purpose of, 74;
Provincial as *praeses* of, 76;
role in,
admission of candidates, 83;
admission of novices, 88, 89;
admission to profession, 95.
Councillor,
associate judge as, 59;
failure to vote, 77;
qualities of, 74;
requisites for, 74.
Custom,
limiting competence, 17.
Debts and obligations,
responsibility for, 177.
Declaration of freedom,
before solemn profession, 98;
before temporary profession, 98.
Decree,
dismissal by, 159;
of Holy See, 64.
Definitor, cf. Council.
Delicts,
public, 237;
mode of penalizing, 239.
Denuntiation,
during visitation, 71, 72.
Departure of religious,
lawful, 152;
unlawful, 155.
(cf. Dismissal, Exclaustration, Secularization).
Dimissorial letter, 218.
Dismissal,
by decree, 159;
ipso facto effective, 157;
judicial process in, 161;
novices and, 93;
religious in solemn vows and, 161;

religious in temporary vows
and, 160.
Dispensation,
act of jurisdiction, 42;
Provincial Superior and,
from general law, 43;
from particular law, 49;
from vows and oaths, 51.
Disposition,
of temporal goods, 98;
transfer of religious and, 150.
Document of profession, 99.
Dominative power,
definition of, 14;
extension of, 15;
jurisdiction and, 15;
Provincial and, 14;
source of, 14.
Dowry,
investment of, 79.
Dubium iuris on reserved penalty,
255.

Election,
of Superioress of Nuns, 81.
Erection,
of chapel,
approval of site, 221;
blessing of, 222;
of house, 221;
of parish, 141;
of semi-public oratories, 223.
Examination,
approval of confessors and,
194;
approval of preachers and, 230;
before Orders, 219;
junior clergy and, 107;
Orders and, 219.
Exclaustration,
indult of, 153.
Executive power of Provincial,
canonical visitation, 66;
council, cf. Council;
enforcement of decrees, 64;
nature of, 61, cf. Provincial;
Nuns, 78;
obligation of residency, 61;
obligation to prayer, 73;
personal obligations, 65, 72.
Executor of pious bequest,
permission of Provincial and,
165.
Exemption,
episcopal censures and, 203
note 97;
privilege of, 3.
Exercises of piety, 125.
Extreme Unction,
administration of, 183.

Familiares,
confession and, 194.
Fast,
dispensation from,
Church fast and, 47;
Eucharistic fast and, 186.
Franc,
gold, 173 note 37.
Fuga, 155, 157.
Fugitive religious, 155, 156, 157.

Habit,
reception of, 91;
wearing of, 127;
excusing cause and, 50.
Hierarchy of Regular Superiors,
and dispensatory power over
vows and oaths, 52;
dominative power of, 15;
Major Superior and, 7;
Minor Superior and, 7;
quasi-episcopal power of, 18.
Holy Eucharist, 183.
Holy Orders,
role of Provincial,
bishop's refusal to confer
and, 217;
examinations of ordinands
and, 219;
general duties and, 216;

issuing dimissorials and, 218;
judging qualities of subject, 220;
prohibiting promotion to, 219;
regard to retreat for, 220;
regard to time, 217 note 157.

Illegitimacy,
dispensation from, 211.

Images,
alienation of, 174.

Inheritance, 164.

Investments, 175; cf. Administration.

Irregularity,
and illegitimacy, 211;
ex delicto occulto, 210;
privileges of Regulars over, 210.

Judicial power,
limitation of Provincial's, 243;
notion of, 54;
role of Provincial,
in appointment of offices, 59;
in judging, 57, 243;
in trials, 59, 236.

Jurisdiction,
competence of Regular Prelates, 20;
concept of, 10;
delegation of,
for hearing confessions, 193;
for preaching, 229;
distinction from dominative power, 15;
divisions of, 12;
functions of, 14;
historical evolution of term, 11;
limitation of, 15, 20;
modified by constitutions, 21;
modified by principles of law, 23;
novices as subjects of, 94;
nuns as subjects of, 78.
(cf. Executive, Judicial, Legislative, Provincial Superior).

Law,
precept and, 38.

Legislative power,
dispensatory power and,
over general laws of church, 43, 45;
over particular law, 49, 50;
over vows and oaths, 51, 52.
general chapter and, 34;
General Superior in Carmelite Order and, 34;
imposition of canonical penalties and, 252;
of Provincial Superior, 33, 35;
precepts of Provincial and, 37;
to individuals, 39;
to groups, 40.

Legitimacy of birth,
bishop and, 26;
legitimation and, 27;
Provincial and, 26.

Letters,
dimissorial, 218;
testimonial, 94;
for transfer, 149 note 12.

Letter-writing, 122.

Liturgical,
cases, solutions of, 107;
laws, observance of, 109.

Mass,
attendance at, 126, 131, 133;
conventual, 131, 133;
pro provincia, 73;
stipends, 185.

Matrimony, 183.

Meditation, 125.

Mendicant Orders,
administration of, 2;
canonical visitation in, 67;
elements, essential, 1;

exemption, 3;
four commonly known, 3;
hierarchy of prelates in, 6;
jurisdiction for preaching and, 229;
penalties of Local Ordinaries and, 203, note 97;
Poverty in, 2;
solicitation of alms by, 165;
Superiors of, 18.

Notary,
constitution of, 20, 59.

Novices,
admission of, 87;
dismissal of, 93;
penalties for admitting unworthy, 91;
Provincial's authority over, 89, 94;
reception of habit and, 91;
right to profession of, 94;
subjects of Provincial, 94;
testimonial letters and, 94.

Novice Master,
absence from novitiate, 93;
obligation of, 92;
socius of, 91;
training of novices by, 91;
transfer of novices and, 93.

Novitiate,
admission to, 87, 90;
validity of, 89.

Nuns,
Provincial,
as superior of, 78;
role in,
account of temporal administration, 79;
appointment of chaplain, 80;
blessing of sacred utensils, 80;
disposition of goods, 79;
election of Superior, 81;
exploration of will, 80;
supervision of cloister, 80;
jurisdiction,
for confessions, 80;
for preaching, 80.

Oath,
before judicial trials, 59;
before solemn vows, 98;
dispensation from, 51.

Observance,
religious,
choral obligations and, 128;
cloister and, 114;
common life and, 112;
pious practices of, 125;
religious habit and, 127;
Rule and, 122;
vows and, 111.

Obligations,
responsibility for, 177.

Office,
divine,
choir obligations and, 128;
dispensation from, 130;
privileges in recitation of, 131.

Oratories,
semi-public, 223;
summer homes and, 224.

Ordinance,
character of, 42;
of Provincial, 38, 41;

Ordinary,
Local,
and cloister, 121;
the term,
Provincial and, 19, 45;
qualified use of, 8;
unqualified use of, 8.

Ordinary administration, 167; cf. Administration.

Ordination, cf. Holy Orders.

Parish,
assistants and, 142;
erection of, 141;
religious, 140.
Parochial work,
care of souls and, 136;
cooperatores and, 144.
Pastor,
religious,
habitualis, 142;
presentation to Local Ordinary of, 143;
removal of, 143;
Superior and, 144.
Penal remedies, 245.
Penalties,
established by Local Ordinary, 203 note 97;
modes of inflicting, 239;
per modum praecepti, 240;
principle for declaration of, 236;
purposes of, 238;
reserved penalty and *dubium iuris*, 255;
within competence of Provincial, 251.
(cf. Coercive power)
Penance,
canonical, 250;
weekly reception of Sacrament of, 126.
Perfection,
evangelical, 82;
state of life of, 109.
Periodicals,
articles for, 135;
publication of, 135.
Piety,
exercises of, 125.
Pious foundations,
acceptance of, 164.
Places,
sacred, 221;
blessing of, 222;
consecration of, 222;
privileges in regard to, 222;
reconciliation of, 223;
worship and, 221.
Postulancy,
admission to, 83, 85;
duration of, 84;
law of, 83;
necessity of, 84;
notion of, 83;
prorogation of, 83;
purpose of, 83.
Postulants,
admission of, 83;
age of, 86;
dismissal of, 86;
subjects of Provincial and, 86.
Prayer,
canonical penance and, 250;
Provincial's obligation to province and, 73.
Preacher,
approval of, 226, 229;
religious subject and, 229.
Precept,
definition of, 37;
distinction between law and, 38;
groups and, 40;
individuals and, 39;
Provincial and, 37.
Precious objects,
alienation of, 174.
Prelate,
Regular,
Code and, 3;
dominative power and, 6;
essential laws and, 49;
exemption and, 3;
hierarchy of, 6;
judicial power and, 54;
jurisdiction and, 5;
Penance and, 189.

Priest,
student, 104;
junior clergy, 107.
Privilege,
exemption and quasi-episcopal power as, 18;
limiting jurisdictional competence, 17.
Process,
in dismissal of religious, 161.
Procurator,
provincial, 172;
incompatible offices and, 169;
responsibility of, 169 note 29.
Profession,
religious,
anticipation of, 101;
attestation of freedom and, 98;
disposition of goods and, 98;
duration of temporary, 99, 100;
notion of, 95, 96;
prorogation of, 99.
Prohibition of books, 135.
Prorogation,
postulancy and, 83;
religious profession and, 99.

Quasi-episcopal power, 4-9, 18;
extent of, 19.

Rebuke,
as penal remedy, 245.
Reception of habit, 91.
Reconciliation of violated church, 223.
Reduction of pious bequest, 164.
Religious,
departure of, 146, 151;
norms of law and, 152;
unlawful, 155.
(cf. Dismissal)
Remedies,
penal, 245.
Reservation,
of censures, 198;
of sins, 198, 204.
Residence,
law of,
alms gathering and, 166;
application of, 62;
confinement and, 118;
negligence in, 63;
novices and, 93;
Provincial and, 62;
reasons for absence of, 62;
religious and, 117.
Retreat,
yearly,
duration of, 125;
Orders and, 220;
Provincial and, 125.
Rite of profession, 98.
Rosary,
daily recitation of, 125.

Sacraments,
Provincial and, 182.
Sacred Places,
blessing of, 222;
consecration of, 222;
privileges in regard to, 222;
reconciliation, 223;
worship and, 221.
Secularization,
indult of, 154.
Seminaries,
impossibility to establish, 105;
internal government, 103, note 93;
major, 103;
minor, 220;
perfect *common life* in, 103;
Spiritual Director in, 106;
studies in, 102.
Society,
church, as a, 10;
definition of, 10.

Souls,
care of, 136.
Spiritual Director,
students and, 106.
Sponsor,
Baptism and, 182;
Confirmation and, 182.
Statutes,
Provincial and, 38.
Students,
particular exemptions of,
program of studies of, 102;
sacerdotes simplices, 104, 139;
seminaries for, 102;
studies in secular schools, 108.
Summer homes,
oratories and, 224.
Superior,
General (supreme).
Code of Canon Law and, 21;
dispensatory power of, 52;
judicial power of, 57, 58;
preceptive power of, 111;
residence of, 62;
role in,
admission to profession, 97;
dismissal of religious, 160;
enforcing residence, 63;
relation to Provincial, 22, 49;
safeguarding *common life*, 64;
visitation, 69;
welfare of Order, 22;
major,
as Ordinary, 8, 45;
canonical visitation of, 66,69;
council of, 74;
competence of, 22;
dispensatory power of, 47;
extent of power, 19;
principles of law and, 23;
Provincial as, 45;
role in,
admission of novices, 88;
admission to postulancy, 85;
prorogation of postulancy, 83;
religious profession, 95, 97;
wearing the habit and, 50;
Provincial,
alms gathering and, 165;
books, publication of, 135;
candidate for, 25;
canonical visitation by, cf. Visitation;
choral obligations and, 134;
cloister and, 114;
coercive power of, 232, 256;
constitutions and, 6;
conventual Mass and, 131;
council of, cf. Council;
cura animarum and, 136, 138;
decrees of Holy See and, 64;
dispensatory power and,
Romani Pontificis, 43;
fast days, 47;
general laws, 43, 45;
irregularities, 48, 206;
laws of institute, 49;
occult cases, 49;
particular laws, 49, 50;
prohibition of books, 49;
rights in constitutions, 50;
urgent cases, 45;
vows and oaths, 46, 51;
executive power and,
absence from province, 62;
parishes, 140;
program of studies, 102;
publications, 135;
sacred places, 221;
temporal goods, 163;
irregularities, 206;
judicial power and,
controversies between subjects, 57;

controversies between houses, 58;
controversies between provinces, 58;
designation of notary, 59;
designation of officials, 59;
limitation by Code, 59;
Holy Office, 60;
ordinary power, 58;
jurisdiction and,
constitutions, 17;
delegation for confessions, 193;
determination of, 23;
exclusive cases of, 15;
existence of, 15;
General Superior, 22;
Local Superior, 24;
legislative power, 33-35;
Novice Master and, 91;
Nuns, 78;
obligations of,
personal, 65, 72;
prayer for subjects, 32, 73;
office,
acceptance of, 29;
appointment to, 28;
candidate for, 25;
early history of, 3;
obligations of, 31;
purpose of, 62;
qualities for, 25;
term of, 28;
Ordinary for religious, 19;
parish of religious, 140-142;
penal remedies, 245;
preceptive power and,
common precepts, 40;
individual precepts, 39;
penalties, 238;
statutes, 38;
prelate, 3;
provincial procurator, 172;
religious observance, 109, 122;
reserved censures, 194;
role in,
admission of candidates, 82;
admission of novices, 85, 88, 90;
admission of postulants, 83;
admission to profession, 95;
approval of confessors, 187, 193;
approval of preachers, 226, 229;
departure of religious, 152;
dismissal of novices, 93;
dismissal of religious, 160, 161;
transfer of religious, 146;
Sacraments and, 182;
sacred places and, 221;
seminary, 102, 220;
suspension *ex informata conscientia*, 252;
temporal goods, cf. Administration.
Local,
absence of pastor, 143;
alms gathering, 165;
assistance to clergy, 138
celebret, 184;
choral obligations, 134;
coercive power, 193
council, 74;
decrees of Holy See, 64;
dispensatory power, 46;
vows and oaths, 52;
exercises of piety, 126;
investment, 177;
judicial power, 57;
limitation of authority, 23;
Mass obligations, 185;
obligations of clerics, 124;
Penance, 193;
postulants, 85;
preceptive power, 111;

relationship to Provincial, 19, 23;
residence of, 61, 64;
subjects and residence, 118;
visitation, 70.
Surveillance,
penal remedy, 245.
Suspension,
duration of, 254;
ex informata conscientia, 252;
manner of inflicting, 253;
medicinal or vindicative measure, 253.

Temporal goods,
acquisition of, 163;
administration of, 167;
alienation of, 168;
disposition before profession and, 98;
individual houses and, 167, 169, 171;
investment of, 175;
province and, 172.
Testimonial letters,
novices and, 94;
transfer of religious and, 149 note 12.
Transfer of religious,
before ordination, 147;
Local Superior and, 149;
new institute and, 148;
seniority and, 26;
Trials,
assistance of religious at, 60.
Trusteeship, 164.
Urgent cases,
dispensation in, 45.
Vessels,
sacred,
blessing of, 80.
Vestments,
blessing of, 80.
Viaticum, 186 note 15.
Vicarii,
adiutores, 144;
cooperatores, 144.
Vigilance,
penal remedies and, 245;
Superior and,
against business ventures, 165;
over Mass stipends, 165, 185.
Violated church,
reconciliation of, 223.
Visitation,
canonical,
avoidance of defamation and, 69;
decrees derived from, 71;
general character of, 72;
government of monastery during, 68;
judicial procedure in, 69;
matter of, 70;
purpose of, 68;
role of Provincial, 67, 69;
ordinary procedure, 71;
rights and duties, 69.
Vows,
anticipation of renewal of, 101;
observance of, 111.

Worship,
approval of site for chapel and, 221;
privileges in regard to, 222;
reconciliation of sacred place, 223;
sacred places and, 221.
Worthiness,
personal,
of Provincial, 28.

BIOGRAPHICAL NOTE

Romaeus W. O'Brien, O. Carm., was born on September 15, 1916, in Chicago, Illinois. After completing his elementary education at St. Thomas the Apostle parochial school, he attended the Carmelite Preparatory Seminary at Niagara Falls, Ontario, Canada. He entered the novitiate of the Order of Carmelites at Niagara Falls, where he made his religious profession on August 15, 1935. At the completion of his college and theological training at the Catholic University of America and Whitefriars Hall, the Carmelite House of Theology, he was ordained to the priesthood at the National Shrine of the Little Flower in Chicago, on May 23, 1942. In June of 1944 he received the degree of Master of Arts at the Catholic University of America. In the fall of the same year he entered the School of Canon Law at the Catholic University of America, and received the degree of Bachelor of Canon Law in June, 1945, and the Licentiate of Canon Law in June, 1946.

CANON LAW STUDIES*

1. FRERIKS, REV. CELESTINE A., C.PP.S., J.C.D., Religious Congregations in Their External Relations, 121 pp., 1916.
2. GALLIHER, REV. DANIEL M., O.P., J.C.D., Canonical Elections, 117 pp., 1917.
3. BORKOWSKI, REV. AURELIUS, L., O.F.M., J.C.D., De Confraternitatibus Ecclesiasticis, 136 pp., 1918.
4. CASTILLO, REV. CAYO, J.C.D., Disertacion Historico-Canonica sobre la Potestad del Cabildo en Sede Vacante o Impedida del Vicario Capitular, 99 pp., 1919 (1918).
5. KUBELBECK, REV. WILLIAM J., S.T.B., J.C.D., The Sacred Penitentiaria and Its Relation to Faculties of Ordinaries and Priests, 129 pp., 1918.
6. PETROVITS, REV. JOSEPH, J.C., S.T.D., J.C.D., The New Church Law on Matrimony, X-461 pp., 1919.
7. HICKEY, REV. JOHN J., S.T.B., J.C.D., Irregularities and Simple Impediments in the New Code of Canon Law, 100 pp., 1920.
8. KLEKOTKA, REV. PETER J., S.T.B., J.C.D., Diocesan Consultors, 179 pp., 1920.
9. WANENMACHER, REV. FRANCIS, J.C.D., The Evidence in Ecclesiastical Procedure Affecting the Marriage Bond, 1920 (Printed 1935).
10. GOLDEN, REV. HENRY FRANCIS, J.C.D., Parochial Benefices in the New Code, IV-119 pp., 1921 (Printed 1925).
11. KOUDELKA, REV. CHARLES J., J.C.D., Pastors, Their Rights and Duties According to the New Code of Canon Law, 211 pp., 1921.
12. MELO, REV. ANTONIUS, O.F.M., J.C.D., De Exemptione Regularium, X-188 pp., 1921.
13. SCHAAF, REV. VALENTINE THEODORE, O.F.M., S.T.B., J.C.D., The Cloister, X-180 pp., 1921.
14. BURKE, REV. THOMAS JOSEPH, S.T.D., J.C.D., Competence in Ecclesiastical Tribunals, IV-117 pp., 1922.
15. LEECH, REV. GEORGE LEO, J.C.D., A Comparative Study of the Constitution "Apostolicae Sedis" and the "Codex Juris Canonici," 179 pp., 1922.
16. MOTRY, REV. HUBERT LOUIS, S.T.D., J.C.D., Diocesan Faculties According to the Code of Canon Law, II-167 pp., 1922.
17. MURPHY, REV. GEORGE LAWRENCE, J.C.D., Delinquencies and Penalties in the Administration and the Reception of the Sacraments, IV-121 pp., 1923.

* From nn. 1-100 only n. 25 is still obtainable. From n. 101 onward all numbers are available except the following: 101-114, also 116, 118, 120 and 122.

18. O'REILLY, REV. JOHN ANTHONY, S.T.B., J.C.D., Ecclesiastical Sepulture in the New Code of Canon Law, II-129 pp., 1923.

19. MICHALICKA, REV. WENCESLAS CYRILL, O.S.B., J.C.D., Judicial Procedure in Dismissal of Clerical Exempt Religious, 107 pp., 1923.

20. DARGIN, REV. EDWARD VINCENT, S.T.B., J.C.D., Reserved Cases According to the Code of Canon Law, II-167 pp., 1922.

21. GODFREY, REV. JOHN A., S.T.B., J.C.D., The Right of Patronage According to the Code of Canon Law, 153 pp., 1924.

22. HAGEDORN, REV. FRANCIS EDWARD, J.C.D., General Legislation on Indulgences, II-154 pp., 1924.

23. KING, REV. JAMES IGNATIUS, J.C.D., The Administration of the Sacraments to Dying Non-Catholics, V-141 pp., 1924.

24. WINSLOW, REV. FRANCIS JOSEPH, O.F.M., J.C.D., Vicars and Prefects Apostolic, IV-149 pp., 1924.

25. CORREA, REV. JOSE SERVELION, S.T.L., J.C.D., La Potestad Legislativa de la Iglesia Catolica, IV-127 pp., 1925.

26. DUGAN, REV. HENRY FRANCIS, A.M., J.C.D., The Judiciary Department of the Diocesan Curia, 87 pp., 1925.

27. KELLER, REV. CHARLES FREDERICK, S.T.B., J.C.D., Mass Stipends, 167 pp., 1925.

28. PASCHANG, REV. JOHN LINUS, J.C.D., The Sacramentals According to the Code of Canon Law, 129 pp., 1925.

29. PIONTEK, REV. CYRILLUS, O.F.M., S.T.B., J.C.D., De Indulto Exclaustrationis necnon Saecularizationis, XIII-289 pp., 1925.

30. KEARNEY, REV. RICHARD JOSEPH, S.T.B., J.C.D., Sponsors at Baptism According to the Code of Canon Law, IV-127 pp., 1925.

31. BARTLETT, REV. CHESTER JOSEPH, A.M., LL.B., J.C.D., The Tenure of Parochial Property in the United States of America, V-108 pp., 1926.

32. KILKER, REV. ADRIAN JEROME, J.C.D., Extreme Unction, V-425 pp., 1926.

33. MCCORMICK, REV. ROBERT EMMETT, J.C.D., Confessors of Religious, VIII-266 pp., 1926.

34. MILLER, REV. NEWTON THOMAS, J.C.D., Founded Masses According to the Code of Canon Law, VII-93 pp., 1926.

35. ROELKER, REV. EDWARD G., S.T.D., J.C.D., Principles of Privilege According to the Code of Canon Law, XI-166 pp., 1926.

36. BAKALARCZYK, REV. RICHARDUS, M.I.C., J.U.D., De Novitiatu, VIII-208 pp., 1927.

37. PIZZUTI, REV. LAWRENCE, O.F.M., J.U.L., De Parochis Religiosis, 1927. (Not Printed.)

38. BLILEY, REV. NICHOLAS MARTIN, O.S.B., J.C.D., Altars According to the Code of Canon Law, XIX-132 pp., 1927.

39. BROWN, MR. BRENDAN FRANCIS, A.B., LL.M., J.U.D., The Canonical Juristic Personality with Special Reference to its Status in the United States of America, V-212 pp., 1927.
40. CAVANAUGH, REV. WILLIAM THOMAS, C.P., J.U.D., The Reservation of the Blessed Sacrament, VIII-101 pp., 1927.
41. DOHENY, REV. WILLIAM J., C.S.C., A.B., J.U.D., Church Property: Modes of Acquisition, X-118 pp., 1927.
42. FELDHAUS, REV. ALOYSIUS H., C.PP.S., J.C.D., Oratories, IX-141 pp., 1927.
43. KELLY, REV. JAMES PATRICK, A.B., J.C.D., The Jurisdiction of the Simple Confessor, X-208 pp., 1927.
44. NEUBERGER, REV. NICHOLAS J., J.C.D., Canon 6 or the Relation of the Codex Juris Canonici to the Preceding Legislation, V-95 pp., 1927.
45. O'KEEFE, REV. GERALD MICHAEL, J.C.D., Matrimonial Dispensations, Powers of Bishops, Priests, and Confessors, VIII-232 pp., 1927.
46. QUIGLEY, REV. JOSEPH A. M., A.B., J.C.D., Condemned Societies, 139 pp., 1927.
47. ZAPLOTNIK, REV. JOHANNES LEO, J.C.D., De Vicariis Foraneis, X-142 pp., 1927.
48. DUSKIE, REV. JOHN ALOYSIUS, A.B., J.C.D., The Canonical Status of the Orientals in the United States, VIII-196 pp., 1928.
49. HYLAND, REV. FRANCIS EDWARD, J.C.D., Excommunication, Its Nature, Historical Development and Effects, VII-181 pp., 1928.
50. REINMANN, REV. GERALD JOSEPH, O.M.C., J.C.D., The Third Order Secular of Saint Francis, 201 pp., 1928.
51. SCHENK, REV. FRANCIS J., J.C.D., The Matrimonial Impediments of Mixed Religion and Disparity of Cult, XVI-318 pp., 1929.
52. COADY, REV. JOHN JOSEPH, S.T.D., J.U.D., A.M., The Appointment of Pastors, VIII-150 pp., 1929.
53. KAY, REV. THOMAS HENRY, J.C.D., Competence in Matrimonial Procedure, VIII-164 pp., 1929.
54. TURNER, REV. SIDNEY JOSEPH, C.P., J.U.D., The Vow of Poverty, XLIX-217 pp., 1929.
55. KEARNEY, REV. RAYMOND A., A.B., S.T.D., J.C.D., The Principles of Delegation, VII-149 pp., 1929.
56. CONRAN, REV. EDWARD JAMES, A.B., J.C.D., The Interdict, V-163 pp., 1930.
57. O'NEILL, REV. WILLIAM H., J.C.D., Papal Rescripts of Favor, VII-218 pp., 1930.
58. BASTNAGEL, REV. CLEMENT VINCENT, J.U.D., The Appointment of Parochial Adjutants and Assistants, XV-257 pp., 1930.
59. FERRY, REV. WILLIAM A., A.B., J.C.D., Stole Fees, V-136 pp., 1930.

60. COSTELLO, REV. JOHN MICHAEL, A.B., J.C.D., Domicile and Quasi-Domicile, VII-201 pp., 1930.
61. KREMPER, REV. MICHAEL NICHOLAS, A.B., S.T.B., J.C.D., Church Support in the United States, VI-136 pp., 1930.
62. ANGULO, REV. LUIS, C.M., J.C.D., Legislation de la Iglesia sobre la intension en la application de la Santa Misa, VII-104 pp., 1931.
63. FREY, REV. WOLFGANG NORBERT, O.S.B., A.B., J.C.D., The Act of Religious Profession, VIII-174 pp., 1931.
64. ROBERTS, REV. JAMES BRENDAN, A.B., J.C.D., The Banns of Marriage, XIV-140 pp., 1931.
65. RYDER, REV. RAYMOND ALOYSIUS, A.B., J.C.D., Simony, IX-151 pp., 1931.
66. CAMPAGNA, REV. ANGELO, PH.D., J.U.D., Il Vicario Generale del Vescovo, VII-205 pp., 1931.
67. COX, REV. JOSEPH GODFREY, A.B., J.C.D., The Administration of Seminaries, VI-124 pp., 1931.
68. GREGORY, REV. DONALD J., J.U.D., The Pauline Privilege, XV-165 pp., 1931.
69. DONOHUE, REV. JOHN F., J.C.D., The Impediment of Crime, VII-110 pp., 1931.
70. DOOLEY, REV. EUGENE A., O.M.I., J.C.D., Church Law on Sacred Relics, IX-143 pp., 1931.
71. ORTH, REV. CLEMENT RAYMOND, O.M.C., J.C.D., The Approbation of Religious Institutes, 171 pp., 1931.
72. PERNICONE, REV. JOSEPH M., A.B., J.C.D., The Ecclesiastical Prohibition of Books, XII-267 pp., 1932.
73. CLINTON, REV. CONNELL, A.B., J.C.D., The Paschal Precept, IX-108 pp., 1932.
74. DONNELLY, REV. FRANCIS B., A.M., S.T.L., J.C.D., The Diocesan Synod, VIII-125 pp., 1932.
75. TORRENTE, REV. CAMILO, C.M.F., J.C.D., Las Procesiones Sagradas, V-145 pp., 1932.
76. MURPHY, REV. EDWIN J., C.PP.S., J.C.D., Suspension *Ex Informata Conscientia*, XI-122 pp., 1932.
77. MACKENZIE, REV. ERIC F., A.M., S.T.L., J.C.D., The Delict of Heresy in its Commission, Penalization, Absolution, VII-124 pp., 1932.
78. LYONS, REV. AVITUS T., S.T.B., J.C.D., The Collegiate Tribunal of First Instance, XI-147 pp., 1932.
79. CONNOLLY, REV. THOMAS A., J.C.D., Appeals, XI-195 pp., 1932.
80. SANGMEISTER, REV. JOSEPH V., A.B., J.C.D., Force and Fear as Precluding Matrimonial Consent, V-211 pp., 1932.
81. JAEGER, REV. LEO A., J.C.D., The Administration of Vacant and

Quasi-Vacant Episcopal Sees in the United States, IX-229 pp., 1932.

82. Rimlinger, Rev. Herbert T., J.C.D., Error Invalidating Matrimonial Consent, VII-79 pp., 1932.
83. Barrett, Rev. John D. M., S.S., J.C.D., A Comparative Study of the Councils of Baltimore and the Code of Canon Law, X-223 pp., 1932.
84. Carberry, Rev. John J., Ph.D., S.T.D., J.C.D., The Juridical Form of Marriage, X-177 pp., 1934.
85. Dolan, Rev. John L., A.B., J.C.D., The Defensor Vinculi, XII-157 pp., 1934.
86. Hannan, Rev. Jerome D., A.M., S.T.D., LL.B., J.C.D., The Canon Law of Wills, IX-517 pp., 1934.
87. Lemieux, Rev. Delise A., A.M., J.C.D., The Sentence in Ecclesiastical Procedure, IX-131 pp., 1934.
88. O'Rourke, Rev. James J., A.B., J.C.D., Parish Registers, VII-109 pp., 1934.
89. Timlin, Rev. Bartholomew, O.F.M., A.M., J.C.D., Conditional Matrimonial Consent, X-381 pp., 1934.
90. Wahl, Rev. Francis X., A.B., J.C.D., The Matrimonial Impediments of Consanguinity and Affinity, VI-125 pp., 1934.
91. White, Rev. Robert J., A.B., LL.B., S.T.B., J.C.D., Canonical Ante-Nuptial Promises and the Civil Law, VI-152 pp., 1934.
92. Herrera, Rev. Antonio Parra, O.C.D., J.C.D., Legislacion Ecclesiastica sobra el Ayuno y la Abstinencia, XI-191 pp., 1935.
93. Kennedy, Rev. Edwin J., J.C.D., The Special Matrimonial Process in Cases of Evident Nullity, X-165 pp., 1935.
94. Manning, Rev. John J., A.B., J.C.D., Presumption of Law in Matrimonial Procedure, XI-111 pp., 1935.
95. Moeder, Rev. John M., J.C.D., The Proper Bishop for Ordination and Dimissorial Letters, VII-135 pp., 1935.
96. O'Mara, Rev. William A., A.B., J.C.D., Canonical Causes for Matrimonial Dispensations, IX-155 pp., 1935.
97. Reilly, Rev. Peter, J.C.D., Residence of Pastors, IX-81 pp., 1935.
98. Smith, Rev. Mariner T., O.P., S.T.Lr., J.C.D., The Penal Law for Religious, VIII-169 pp., 1935.
99. Whalen, Rev. Donald W., A.M., J.C.D., The Value of Testimonial Evidence in Matrimonial Procedure, XIII-297 pp., 1935.
100. Cleary, Rev. Joseph F., J.C.D., Canonical Limitations on the Alienation of Church Property, VIII-141 pp., 1936.
101. Glynn, Rev. John C., J.C.D., The Promoter of Justice, XX-337 pp., 1936.
102. Brennan, Rev. James H., S.S., M.A., S.T.B., J.C.D., The Simple Convalidation of Marriage, VI-135 pp., 1937.

103. BRUNINI, REV. JOSEPH BERNARD, J.C.D., The Clerical Obligations of Canons 139 and 142, X-121 pp., 1937.
104. CONNOR, REV. MAURICE, A.B., J.C.D., The Administrative Removal of Pastors, VIII-159 pp., 1937.
105. GUILFOYLE, REV. MERLIN JOSEPH, J.C.D., Custom, XI-144 pp., 1937.
106. HUGHES, REV. JAMES AUSTIN, A.B., A.M., J.C.D., Witnesses in Criminal Trials of Clerics, IX-140 pp., 1937.
107. JANSEN, REV. RAYMOND J., A.B., S.T.L., J.C.D., Canonical Provisions for Catechetical Instruction, VII-153 pp., 1937.
108. KEALY, REV. JOHN JAMES, A.B., J.C.D., The Introductory Libellus in Church Court Procedure, XI-121 pp., 1937.
109. MCMANUS, REV. JAMES EDWARD, C.SS.R., J.C.D., The Administration of Temporal Goods in Religious Institutes, XVI-196 pp., 1937.
110. MORIARITY, REV. EUGENE JAMES, J.C.D., Oaths in Ecclesiastical Courts, X-115 pp., 1937.
111. RAINER, REV. ELIGIUS GEORGE, C.SS.R., J.C.D., Suspension of Clerics, XVII-249 pp., 1937.
112. REILLY, REV. THOMAS F., C.SS.R., J.C.D., Visitation of Religious, VI-195 pp., 1938.
113. MORIARITY, REV. FRANCIS E., C.SS.R., J.C.D., The Extraordinary Absolution from Censures, XV-334 pp., 1938.
114. CONNOLLY, REV. NICHOLAS P., J.C.D., The Canonical Erection of Parishes, X-132 pp., 1938.
115. DONOVAN, REV. JAMES JOSEPH, J.C.D., The Pastor's Obligation in Prenuptial Investigation, XII-322 pp., 1938.
116. HARRIGAN, REV. ROBERT J., M.A., S.T.B., J.C.D., The Radical Sanation of Invalid Marriages, VIII-208 pp., 1938.
117. BOFFA, REV. CONRAD HUMBERT, J.C.D., Canonical Provisions for Catholic Schools, VII-211 pp., 1939.
118. PARSONS, REV. ANSCAR JOHN, O.M.Cap., J.C.D., Canonical Elections, XII-236 pp., 1939.
119. REILLY, REV. EDWARD MICHAEL, A.B., J.C.D., The General Norms of Dispensation, XII-156 pp., 1939.
120. RYAN, REV. GERALD ALOYSIUS, A.B., J.C.D., Principles of Episcopal Jurisdiction, XII-172 pp., 1939.
121. BURTON, REV. FRANCIS JAMES, C.S.C., A.B., J.C.D., A Commentary on Canon 1125, X-222 pp., 1940.
122. MIASKIEWICZ, REV. FRANCIS SIGISMUND, J.C.D., Supplied Jurisdiction According to Canon 209, XII-340 pp., 1940.
123. RICE, REV. PATRICK WILLIAM, A.B., J.C.D., Proof of Death in Prenuptial Investigation, VIII-156 pp., 1940.

124. ANGLIN, REV. THOMAS FRANCIS, M.S., J.C.D., The Eucharistic Fast, VIII-183 pp., 1941.
125. COLEMAN, REV. JOHN JEROME, J.C.D., The Minister of Confirmation, VI-153 pp., 1941.
126. DOWNS, REV. JOHN EMMANUEL, A.B., J.C.D., The Concept of Clerical Immunity, XI-163 pp., 1941.
127. ESSWEIN, REV. ANTHONY ALBERT, J.C.D., Extrajudicial Penal Powers of Ecclesiastical Superiors, X-144 pp., 1941.
128. FARRELL, REV. BENJAMIN FRANCIS, M.A., S.T.L., J.C.D., The Rights and Duties of the Local Ordinary Regarding Congregations of Women Religious of Pontifical Approval, V-195 pp., 1941.
129. FEENEY, REV. THOMAS JOHN, A.B., S.T.L., J.C.D., Restitutio in Integrum, VI-169 pp., 1941.
130. FINDLAY, REV. STEPHEN WILLIAM, O.S.B., A.B., J.C.D., Canonical Norms Governing the Deposition and Degradation of Clerics, XVII-279 pp., 1941.
131. GOODWINE, REV. JOHN, A.B., S.T.L., J.C.D., The Right of the Church to Acquire Property, VIII-119 pp., 1941.
132. HESTON, REV. EDWARD LOUIS, C.S.C., Ph.D., S.T.D., J.C.D., The Alienation of Church Property in the United States, XII-222 pp., 1941.
133. HOGAN, REV. JAMES JOHN, A.B., S.T.L., J.C.D., Judicial Advocates and Procurators, XIII-200 pp., 1941.
134. KEALY, REV. THOMAS M., A.B., Litt.B., J.C.D., Dowry of Women Religious, IX-152 pp., 1941.
135. KEENE, REV. MICHAEL JAMES, O.S.B., J.C.D., Religious Ordinaries and Canon 198, V-164 pp., 1942.
136. KERIN, REV. CHARLES A., S.S., M.A., S.T.B., J.C.D., The Privation of Christian Burial, XVI-279 pp., 1941.
137. LOUIS, REV. WILLIAM FRANCIS, M.A., J.C.D., Diocesan Archives, X-101 pp., 1941.
138. MCDEVITT, REV. GILBERT JOSEPH, A.B., J.C.D., Legitimacy and Legitimation, X-247 pp., 1941.
139. MCDONOUGH, REV. THOMAS JOSEPH, A.B., J.C.D., Apostolic Administrators, X-217 pp., 1941.
140. MEIER, REV. CARL ANTHONY, A.B., J.C.D., Penal Administrative Procedure Against Negligent Pastors, XI-240 pp., 1941.
141. SCHMIDT, REV. JOHN ROGG, A.B., J.C.D., The Principles of Authentic Interpretation in Canon 17 of the Code of Canon Law, XII-331 pp., 1941.
142. SLAFKOSKY, REV. ANDREW LEONARD, A.B., J.C.D., The Canonical Episcopal Visitations of the Diocese, X-197 pp., 1941.

143. SWOBODA, REV. INNOCENT ROBERT, O.F.M., J.C.D., Ignorance in Relation to the Imputability of Delicts, IX-271 pp., 1941.
144. DUBÉ, REV. ARTHUR JOSEPH, A.B., J.C.D., The General Principles for the Reckoning of Time in Canon Law, VIII-299 pp., 1941.
145. MCBRIDE, REV. JAMES T., A.B., J.C.D., Incardination and Excardination of Seculars, XX-585 pp., 1941.
146. KRÓL, REV. JOHN T., J.C.D., The Defendant in Ecclesiastical Trials, XII-207 pp., 1942.
147. COMYNS, REV. JOSEPH J., C.SS.R., A.B., J.C.D., Papal and Episcopal Administration of Church Property, XIV-155 pp., 1942.
148. BARRY, REV. GARRETT FRANCIS, O.M.I., J.C.D., Violation of the Cloister, XII-260 pp., 1942.
149. BOLDUC, REV. GATIEN, C.S.V., A.B., S.T.L., J.C.D., Les Études dans les Réligions Cléricales, VIII-155 pp., 1942.
150. BOYLE, REV. DAVID JOHN, M.A., J.C.D., The Juridic Effects of Moral Certitude on Pre-Nuptial Guarantees, XII-188 pp., 1942.
151. CANAVAN, REV. WALTER JOSEPH, M.A., Litt.D., J.C.D., The Profession of Faith, XII-143 pp., 1942.
152. DESROCHERS, REV. BRUNO, A.B., Ph.L., S.T.B., J.C.D., Le Premier Concile Plénier de Québec et le Code de Droit Canonique, XIV-186 pp., 1942.
153. DILLON, REV. ROBERT EDWARD, A.B., J.C.D., Common Law Marriage, X-148 pp., 1942.
154. DODWELL, REV. EDWARD JOHN, Ph.D., S.T.B., J.C.D., The Time and Place for the Celebration of Marriage, X-156 pp., 1942.
155. DONNELLAN, REV. THOMAS ANDREW, A.B., J.C.D., The Obligation of the Missa pro Populo, VII-131 pp., 1942.
156. ELTZ, REV. LOUIS ANTHONY, A.B., J.C.D., Cooperation in Crime, XII-208 pp., 1942.
157. GASS, REV. SYLVESTER FRANCIS, M.A., J.C.D., Ecclesiastical Pensions, XI-206 pp., 1942.
158. GUINIVEN, REV. JOHN JOSEPH, C.SS.R., J.C.D., The Precept of Hearing Mass, XIV-188 pp., 1942.
159. GULCYNSKI, REV. JOHN THEOPHILUS, J.C.D., The Desecration and Violation of Churches, X-126 pp., 1942.
160. HAMMILL, REV. JOHN LEO, M.A., J.C.D., The Obligations of the Traveler According to Canon 14, VIII-204 pp., 1942.
161. HAYDT, REV. JOHN JOSEPH, A.B., J.C.D., Reserved Benefices, XI-148 pp., 1942.
162. HUSER, REV. ROGER JOHN, O.F.M., A.B., J.C.D., The Crime of Abortion in Canon Law, XII-187 pp., 1942.
163. KEARNEY, REV. FRANCIS PATRICK, A.B., S.T.L., J.C.D., The Principles of Canon 1127, X-162 pp., 1942.

164. LINAHEN, REV. LEO JAMES, S.T.L., J.C.D., De Absolutione Complicis In Peccato Turpi, 114 pp., 1942.

165. MCCLOSKEY, REV. JOSEPH ALOYSIUS, A.B., J.C.D., The Subject of Ecclesiastical Law According to Canon 12, XVII-246 pp., 1942.

166. O'NEILL, REV. FRANCIS JOSEPH, C.SS.R., J.C.D., The Dismissal of Religious in Temporary Vows, XIII-220 pp., 1942.

167. PRINCE, REV. JOHN EDWARD, A.B., S.T.B., J.C.D., The Diocesan Chancellor, X-136 pp., 1942.

168. RIESNER, REV. ALBERT JOSEPH, C.SS.R., J.C.D., Apostates and Fugitives from Religious Institutes, IX-168 pp., 1942.

169. STENGER, REV. JOSEPH BERNARD, J.C.D., The Mortgaging of Church Property, 186 pp., 1942.

170. WALDRON, REV. JOSEPH FRANCIS, A.B., J.C.D., The Minister of Baptism, XII-197 pp., 1942.

17. WILLETT, REV. ROBERT ALBERT, J.C.D., The Probative Value of Documents in Ecclesiastical Trials, X-124 pp., 1942.

172. WOEBER, REV. EDWARD MARTIN, M.A., J.C.D., The Interpellations, XII-161 pp., 1942.

173. BENKO, REV. MATTHEW ALOYSIUS, O.S.B., M.A., J.C.D., The Abbot *Nullius*, XVI-148 pp., 1943.

174. CHRIST, REV. JOSEPH JAMES, M.A., S.T.L., J.C.D., Dispensation from Vindicative Penalties, XIII-285 pp., 1943.

175. CLANCY, REV. PATRICK M. J., O.P., A.B., S.T.Lr., J.C.D., The Local Religious Superior, X-229 pp., 1943.

176. CLARKE, REV. THOMAS JAMES, J.C.D., Parish Societies, XII-147 pp., 1943.

177. CONNOLLY, REV. JOHN PATRICK, S.T.L., J.C.D., Synodal Examiners, and Parish Priest Consultors, X-223 pp., 1943.

178. DRUMM, REV. WILLIAM MARTIN, A.B., J.C.D., Hospital Chaplains, XII-175 pp., 1943.

179. FLANAGAN, REV. BERNARD JOSEPH, A.B., S.T.L., J.C.D., The Canonical Erection of Religious Houses, X-147 pp., 1943.

180. KELLEHER, REV. STEPHEN JOSEPH, A.B., S.T.B., J.C.D., Discussions with Non-Catholics: Canonical Legislation, X-93 pp., 1943.

181. LEWIS, REV. GORDIAN, C.P., J.C.D., Chapters in Religious Institutes, XII-169 pp., 1943.

182. MARX, REV. ADOLPH, J.C.D., The Declaration of Nullity of Marriages Contracted Outside the Church, X-151 pp., 1943.

183. MATULENAS, REV. RAYMOND ANTHONY, O.S.B., A.B., J.C.D., Communication, a Source of Privileges, XII-225 pp., 1943.

184. O'LEARY, REV. CHARLES GERARD, C.SS.R., J.C.D., Religious Dismissed After Perpetual Profession, X-213 pp., 1943.

185. POWER, REV. CORNELIUS MICHAEL, J.C.D., The Blessing of Cemeteries, XII-231 pp., 1943.

186. SHUHLER, REV. RALPH VINCENT, O.S.A., J.C.D., Privileges of Regulars to Absolve and Dispense, XII-195 pp., 1943.

187. ZIOLKOWSKI, REV. THADDEUS STANISLAUS, A.B., J.C.D., The Consecration and Blessing of Churches, XII-151 pp., 1943.

188. HENEGHAN, REV. JOHN JOSEPH, S.T.D., J.C.D., The Marriages of Unworthy Catholics: Canons 1065 and 1066, XVI-213 pp., 1944.

189. CARROLL, REV. COLEMAN FRANCIS, M.A., S.T.L., J.C.L., Charitable Institutions.

190. CIESLUK, REV. JOSEPH EDWARD, PH.B., S.T.L., J.C.D., National Parishes in the United States, VI-178 pp., 1944.

191. COBURN, REV. VINCENT PAUL, A.B., J.C.D., Marriages of Conscience, XII-172 pp., 1944.

192. CONNORS, REV. CHARLES PAUL, C.S.SP., A.B., J.C.D., Extra-Judicial Procurators in the Code of Canon Law, X-94 pp., 1944.

193. COYLE, REV. PAUL RAYMOND, A.B., J.C.D., Judicial Exceptions, IX-142 pp., 1944.

194. FAIR, REV. BARTHOLOMEW FRANCIS, A.B., S.T.L., J.C.D., The Impediment of Abduction, XII-122 pp., 1944.

195. GALLAGHER, REV. THOMAS RAPHAEL, O.P., A.B., S.T.LR., J.C.D., The Examination of the Qualities of the Ordinand, X-166 pp., 1944.

196. GANNON, REV. JOHN MARK, S.T.L., J.C.D., The Interstices Required for the Promotion to Orders, VII-100 pp., 1944.

197. GOLDSMITH, REV. J. WILLIAM, B.C.S., S.T.L., J.C.D., The Competence of Church and State Over Marriage—Disputed Points, X-128 pp., 1944.

198. GOODWINE, REV. JOSEPH GERARD, A.B., S.T.B., J.C.D., The Reception of Converts, XIV-326 pp., 1944.

199. KOWALSKI, REV. ROMUALD EUGENE, O.F.M., A.B., J.C.D., Sustenance of Religious Houses of Regulars, X-174 pp., 1944.

200. MCCOY, REV. ALAN EDWARD, O.F.M., J.C.D., Force and Fear in Relation to Delictual Imputability and Penal Responsibility, XII-160 pp., 1944.

201. MCDEVITT, REV. VINCENT JOHN, PH.B., S.T.L., J.C.L., Perjury.

202. MARTIN, REV. THOMAS OWEN, PH.D., S.T.D., J.C.D., Adverse Possession, Prescription and Limitation of Actions: The Canonical "Praescriptio," XX-208 pp., 1944.

203. MIKLOSOVIC, REV. PAUL JOHN, A.B., J.C.L., Attempted Marriages and Their Consequent Juridic Effects.

204. MUNDY, REV. THOMAS MAURICE, A.B., S.T.L., J.C.D., The Union of Parishes, X-164 pp., 1944.

205. O'Dea, Rev. John Coyle, A.B., J.C.D., The Matrimonial Impediment of Nonage, VIII-126 pp., 1944.
206. Olalia, Rev. Alexander Ayson, S.T.L., J.C.D., A Comparative Study of the Christian Constitution of States and the Constitution of the Philippine Commonwealth, XII-136 pp., 1944.
207. Poisson, Rev. Pierre Marie, C.S.C., A.B., Ph.L., J.C.L., Droits Patrimoniaux des Maisons et des Eglises Réligieuses.
208. Stadalnikas, Rev. Casimir Joseph, M.I.C., J.C.D., Reservation of Censures, X-141 pp., 1944.
209. Sullivan, Rev. Eugene Henry, S.T.L., J.C.D., Proof of the Reception of the Sacraments, X-165 pp., 1944.
210. Vaughan, Rev. William Edward, J.C.D., Constitutions for Diocesan Courts, X-210 pp., 1944.
211. Paro, Rev. Gino, S.T.D., J.C.L., The Right of Apostolic Delegation.
212. Balzer, Rev. Ralph Francis, C.P., J.C.D., The Computation of Time in a Canonical Novitiate, X-227 pp., 1945.
213. Dougherty, Rev. John Whelan, A.B., S.T.L., J.C.D., De Inquisitione Speciali, XII-195 pp., 1945.
214. Dziob, Rev. Michael Walter, J.C.D., The Sacred Congregation for the Oriental Church, XII-181 pp., 1945.
215. Eidenschink, Rev. John Albert, O.S.B., B.A., J.C.D., The Election of Bishops in the Letters of Pope Gregory the Great, VII-200 pp., 1945.
216. Gill, Rev. Nicholas, C.P., J.C.D., The Spiritual Prefect in Clerical Religious Houses of Study, X-140 pp., 1945.
217. Hynes, Rev. Harry Gerard, S.T.L., J.C.D., The Privileges of Cardinals, XII-183 pp., 1945.
218. McDevitt, Rev. Gerald Vincent, S.T.L., J.C.D., The Renunciation of an Ecclesiastical Office, XIV-179 pp., 1945.
219. Manning, Rev. Joseph Leroy, J.C.D., The Free Conferral of Offices, VIII-116 pp., 1945.
220. Meyer, Rev. Louis G., O.S.B., A.B., S.T.B., J.C.D., Alms-gathering by Religious, XII-163 pp., 1945.
221. O'Donnell, Rev. Cletus Francis, M.A., J.C.D., The Marriage of Minors, XII-268 pp., 1945.
222. Prunskis, Rev. Joseph, J.C.D., Comparative Law, Ecclesiastical and Civil, in Lithuanian Concordat, X-161 pp., 1945.
223. Sweeney, Rev. Francis Patrick, C.SS.R., J.C.D., The Reduction of Clerics to the Lay State, X-199 pp., 1945.
224. Vogelpohl, Rev. Henry John, J.C.D., The Simple Impediments to Holy Orders, XVI-190 pp., 1945.
225. Brockhaus, Rev. Thomas Aquinas, O.S.B., J.C.D., Religious who are known as *Conversi*, X-127 pp., 1945.

226. GRIESE, REV. N. ORVILLE, S.T.D., J.C.D., The Marriage Contract and the Procreation of Offspring, XVI-224 pp., 1946.
227. BOUDREAUX, REV. WARREN LOUIS, J.C.L., The *"ab acatholicis nati"* of Canon 1099, § 2.
228. BOWE, REV. THOMAS JOSEPH, A.B., J.C.D., Religious Superioresses, VIII-216 pp., 1946.
229. DIEDERICHS, REV. MICHAEL FERDINAND, S.C.J., J.C.D., The Jurisdiction of the Latin Ordinaries over their Oriental Subjects, XIV-153 pp., 1946.
230. DINGMAN, REV. MAURICE JOHN, A.B., S.T.L., J.C.L., The Plaintiff in Contentious Trials.
231. FRISON, REV. BASIL, C.M.F., M.MUS., J.C.D., The Retroactivity of Law, X-221 pp., 1946.
232. GALVIN, REV. WILLIAM ANTHONY, M.A., J.C.D., The Administrative Transfer of Pastors, XII-288 pp., 1946.
233. GORACY, REV. JOSEPH C., J.C.L., The Diriment Matrimonial Impediment of Major Orders.
234. HALE, REV. JOSEPH FRANCIS, M.A., S.T.L., J.C.L., The Pastor of Burial.
235. HENRY, REV. JOSEPH ARTHUR, A.B., J.C.D., The Mass and Holy Communion: Inter-Ritual Law, XII-138 pp., 1946.
236. LINENBERGER, REV. HERBERT, C.PP.S., J.C.L., The False Denunciation of an Innocent Confessor.
237. LOWRY, REV. JAMES MARTIN, A.B., J.C.D., Dispensation from Private Vows, XII-266 pp., 1946.
238. LYNCH, REV. GEORGE EDWARD, A.B., S.T.L., J.C.D., Coadjutors and Auxiliaries of Bishops, X-107 pp., 1947.
239. LYNCH, REV. TIMOTHY, M.S.SS.T., J.C.D., Contracts between Bishops and Religious Congregations, XIV-232 pp., 1946.
240. MCCLUNN, REV. JUSTIN DAVID, A.B., S.T.L., J.C.D., Administrative Recourse, VII-142 pp., 1946.
241. LOHMULLER, REV. MARTIN NICHOLAS, A.B., J.C.D., The Promulgation of Law, XII-140 pp., 1947.
242. MCGRATH, REV. JAMES, A.B., J.C.D., The Privilege of the Canon, XII-156 pp., 1946.
243. MARBACH, REV. JOSEPH FRANCIS, A.B., J.C.D., Marriage Legislation for the Catholics of the Oriental Rites in the United States and Canada, XIV-314 pp., 1946.
244. SHIMKUS, REV. BERNARD ALOYSIUS, A.B., J.C.L., The Determination and Transfer of Rite.
245. SMITH, REV. VINCENT MICHAEL, A.B., S.T.L., J.C.L., Ignorance Affecting Matrimonial Consent.
246. WACHTRLE, REV. PAUL ANTHONY, A.B., J.C.L., The Baptism of the Children of Non-Catholics.

247. CROTTY, REV. MATTHEW M., J.C.L., The Recipient of First Holy Communion.

248. EAGLETON, REV. GEORGE, J.C.L., The Quinquennial Faculties: Formula IV.

249. GIBBONS, REV. MARION L., C.M., J.C.L., Domicile of the Wife Unlawfully Separated from her Husband.

250. KELLY, REV. BERNARD M., J.C.L., The Functions Reserved to Pastors.

251. KILCULLEN, REV. THOMAS J., J.C.D., The Collegiate Moral Person as Party Litigant.

252. LAFONTAINE, REV. GERMAIN J., W.F., J.C.L., Rélations canoniques entre le missionaire et ses supérieurs.

253. LANE, LORAS T., J.C.L., Matrimonial Procedure in Ordinary Court of Second Instance.

254. LOVER, REV. JAMES F., J.C.L., The Novice Master.

255. MCNICHOLAS, REV. TIMOTHY J., J.C.L., The *Septime Manus* Witness.

256. MAROSITZ, REV. JOSEPH J., M.S.C., J.C.L., Obligations and Privileges of Religious Promoted to the Episcopal and Cardinalitial Dignities.

257. MURPHY, REV FRANCIS J., J.C.L., Legislative Powers of the Provincial Council.

258. O'BRIEN, REV. ROMAEUS W., O.Carm., J.C.L., M.A., The Provincial Superior in Religious Orders of Men.

259. PFALLER, REV. BENEDICT, O.S.B., J.C.L., The *ipso facto* Effected Dismissal of Religious.

260. POPEK, REV. ALPHONSE S., J.C.L., The Rights and Obligations of Metropolitans.

261. RISTUCCIA, REV. BERNARD J., C.M., J.C.L., Quasi-religious.

262. SONNTAG, REV. NATHANIEL L., O.F.M., J.C.L., Censorship of Special Classes of Books.

263. STADLER, REV. JOSEPH N., J.C.L., Frequent Holy Communion.

264. SZAL, REV. IGNATIUS J., J.C.L., The Communication of Catholics with Schismatics.

265. WAGNER, REV. URBAN S., O.F.M., Conv., J.C.D., Parochial Substitue Vicars and Supplying Priests.

www.ingramcontent.com/pod-product-compliance
Lightning Source LLC
LaVergne TN
LVHW050256080826
844660LV00012B/646